Spousal Violence among World Christians

Also Available from Bloomsbury

Figurations and Sensations of the Unseen in Judaism, Christianity and Islam, edited by Birgit Meyer and Terje Stordalen
Christian Tourist Attractions, Mythmaking, and Identity Formation, edited by Erin Roberts and Jennifer Eyl
Lesbian, Gay, Bisexual and Transgender Christians, Bronwyn Fielder and Douglas Ezzy

Spousal Violence among World Christians

Silent Scandal

Elizabeth Koepping

BLOOMSBURY ACADEMIC
LONDON • NEW YORK • OXFORD • NEW DELHI • SYDNEY

BLOOMSBURY ACADEMIC
Bloomsbury Publishing Plc
50 Bedford Square, London, WC1B 3DP, UK
1385 Broadway, New York, NY 10018, USA
29 Earlsfort Terrace, Dublin 2, Ireland

BLOOMSBURY, BLOOMSBURY ACADEMIC and the Diana logo
are trademarks of Bloomsbury Publishing Plc

First published in Great Britain 2021
This paperback edition published 2022

Copyright © Elizabeth Koepping, 2021

Elizabeth Koepping has asserted her right under the Copyright, Designs
and Patents Act, 1988, to be identified as Author of this work.

For legal purposes the Acknowledgements on p. viii constitute
an extension of this copyright page.

All rights reserved. No part of this publication may be reproduced or
transmitted in any form or by any means, electronic or mechanical, including
photocopying, recording, or any information storage or retrieval system,
without prior permission in writing from the publishers.

Bloomsbury Publishing Plc does not have any control over, or responsibility for,
any third-party websites referred to or in this book. All internet addresses given
in this book were correct at the time of going to press. The author and publisher
regret any inconvenience caused if addresses have changed or sites have
ceased to exist, but can accept no responsibility for any such changes.

A catalogue record for this book is available from the British Library.

Library of Congress Control Number: 2020940528

ISBN: HB: 978-1-3500-8055-3
PB: 978-1-3501-8419-0
ePDF: 978-1-3500-8056-0
eBook: 978-1-3500-8057-7

Typeset by Integra Software Services Pvt. Ltd.

To find out more about our authors and books visit www.bloomsbury.com
and sign up for our newsletters

'The Glory of God is a Human Being Fully Alive'
(Irenaeus 180 CE)
*This book is for all those who as a result of marital
violence are not fully alive.
May the silent speak.*

Contents

Acknowledgements   viii

Part 1   The problem

1   'The glory of God is a human being fully alive'   3
2   Legal and sociological approaches to marital violence   23
3   The disciplining of wives in church history   41

Part 2   Views from the field

4   Church leaders as abusing husbands   63
5   Ordained, professed and appointed church workers: Mixed views   85
6   Laywomen and the church: What they think, receive and want   111

Part 3   Threads to a conclusion

7   Is the glory of the church really a human being fully alive?   137
Addendum: More of the same: Marital violence in Buddhism and Islam   157

Bibliography   167
Index   175

Acknowledgements

Teachers are always indebted to their students. Realizing several Christian postgraduates in the Divinity School in Edinburgh did not see the relevance of domestic violence to current issues in theology, one pointing out that 'where I come from no one bothers about that', I decided to use my training in anthropology and theology to pursue the issue in Christian contexts worldwide. Thanks to them, and others formerly at the Centre for World Christianity at the University of Edinburgh, for their interest and to former Divinity students for on-site support in several countries discussed here: Kim Keong Min, Ayra Inderyas, Angel Wang, Joan Meade, Maggie Gitau, Pearly Walter, Rosemary Amenga-Etego, Chingno Mung, Mele Niumeitolu and others were invaluable.

Various colleagues linked to the University of Edinburgh School of Divinity were helpful during both research and writing, especially Cecelia Clegg, Paul Foster, Nick Wyatt and the late Larry Hurtado. Irim Sarwar proofread and Carolyn Mason and Eliza Getman were great discussants. Particular thanks to Fauzia Viqar, and Elizabeth Harris for reading the sections on Islam and Buddhism with great care, to Jun Guichun for translations, and to Tony Gittins for long-term faith in the project. Primary thanks go to all willing to discuss spousal violence: the faces, voices and silences of certain abused and unsupported women stay in my mind, as do the cool voices of certain colluding men and especially women, keeping away from their abused sisters 'as if we've got measles', as more than one such abused woman said. My thanks also go to members of Christ Church, Edinburgh; The English Church, Heidelberg; and the Chipping Norton Deanery, Oxfordshire, before whom I have preached and through whom I understand more.

Research on which this book draws was supported by various donors, principally the Carnegie Trust for Scotland, the Hayter Fund of The University of Edinburgh, The University of Edinburgh and The German Research Foundation (DFG). Shortly before he died, my late husband Peter encouraged me to write the book proposal. Finally, thanks to my new husband Brian Ford who has negotiated my total involvement in thinking through and writing this text with exemplary patience, and to Lalle in London and Shanmathi in Pondicherry for their publishing midwifery.

Part one

The problem

1

'The glory of God is a human being fully alive'

It is a contention of this book that *no* human whose body and mind are intentionally and continually damaged by their marital partner *can* be fully alive, nor live as confident and fruitful a life as their circumstances would otherwise allow. Worldwide, it is women who bear the main burden of such abuse at the hands of their husbands. This is evident not only in current literature but also in the research in the sixteen countries between Trinidad and Tonga via Africa, Europe, Asia and Australia on which this book is based. Yet both men *and* women collude through silence, whether the silence of the knowing observer or the silence of the complicit institution. Such silence by faith communities supports both abuser and silent bystander, but not the survivor.

Why are the lives of wives less likely to be lived fully, imaging and reflecting God, than that of husbands? Irenaeus wrote 1800 years ago, yet too many lives are still constricted by physical, emotional and other forms of violence, each of which reduces the survivor's capacity to be fully alive. Physical attacks against husbands certainly do occur, but not as part of a socially acceptable campaign of control and *never* with the tacit or open support of religious leaders. Families also experience other forms of violence: parents or step-parents against children, adult children against co-dwelling parents, mothers against daughters-in-law were all mentioned during this research. Yet the focus remains physical violence against wives, commonly backed by varying degrees of spiritual abuse (Oakley and Humphreys 2019). This is partly because survivors found punching, kicking and attempted killing easier to talk of than other forms of abuse, and partly because the evidence is less easy for colluders to wriggle around. Cohabiting women suffer similar abuse, which some religious leaders feel morally able to dismiss. However, as *no* tradition accepts uncontrolled violence aimed at wives by husbands, no priest, imam, rabbi or monk of integrity can ignore wife-abuse.

While not discounting the immediate and long-term effects of violence against husbands and the debilitating shame they may face, this book therefore focuses on attacks by husbands against their wives and the collusion in this by religious authorities and individuals across the world. A handful of vignettes illustrate varied elements: a demanding but fruitful two-day workshop in Pakistan for eighty-five female and male church workers; a lively meeting in Kenya with sixty vocal peasant women with varied views; a long lunch with five German Roman Catholic women, all of whom initially denied knowing any abused women yet each eventually bringing to mind just such a close family member; young Myanmar female and male church workers realizing they too were complicit in silencing women as well as the poor; a group of Tongan men insisting they could beat their wives as Jesus beat the money changers – he didn't, and they're not Jesus, but trivialities like that are as nothing when validating abuse. There was the chat on a London train platform with two Californian men who insisted there was no spousal violence in America though 'a lot' in the UAE where they worked. 'Yes,' they replied to my mentioning such violence in Kentucky (Websdale, 1998), 'there's a lot of that in Kentucky, but *they're* strange': the devout Scottish divorcee, dutifully alone for over forty years after her violent marriage ended; the gutsy Trinidadian mother who asked her abusing son to hit her as 'I too am a wife'; and the Kiribati pastor who apologized to the parents of his two abused daughters-in-law, vowing to protect their daughters in future as if they were his own. So much violence, supported by too much silence.

In recent decades, many legal systems and countries have increasingly prohibited marital violence, with varying success, discussed in Chapter 2. Some regions stress the social and family disruption caused, others the affront to the human rights of each person. Although not the first text on the rights of the individual, the 1948 United Nations Declaration on Human Rights, and subsequent Conventions, supports the view that each person has value. Yet, or because of that last point, the contribution of *religion* to ending violence against wives is mixed, whether among widely spread Hindu, Buddhist, Jewish, Daoist, Christian, Muslim, Sikh or more localized traditions.

In the largest tradition, Christianity, high-level deliberations and well-planned programmes of the last forty years *may* trickle down to regional and local levels, but they might not. Despite sporadic, even heroic, efforts by the few who acknowledge and speak against physical, psychological and emotional abuse in faith contexts, there has been no coherent and *effective* faith-based opposition to marital violence in this or any other world religion. Such shortfall is unsurprising. All faith traditions interact and are entangled with each context, and usually fail to see the mote in their own contextually embedded eye. Religious practice, irrespective of oral or written tradition as well as of apparently universal religious institutions, occurs at local level. Roman Catholics in Paderborn, Lima,

Lagos and Broome carry the same label, but not necessarily the same reason for and view of practice, the same holding for Muslims in Riyadh, Fez and rural Borneo or indeed Buddhists in Kalimantan, New York or Kathmandu.

However, tacit or overt support for wife-abuse by faith traditions, their leaders, congregations and followers is and will increasingly be challenged. As a theologian has bluntly noted, and this includes all major traditions: 'Premodern religious androcentrism is incompatible with the secular 20th century concept of universal human rights for both sexes' (Børresen, 2010:259). Faith traditions may not applaud husbands who hit wives willy-nilly, yet their texts are easily misused. This risk can be mitigated, the biblical scholar Fowl suggests, by reading Scripture 'over against oneself' (1991:42), maintaining a lively suspicion of a too-ready enthusiasm for a particular tag. Failure to read self-critically supports the culturally biased intentions of *any* reader, *any*where, even if this opposes fundamental faith themes such as peace, justice, mercy, kindness or love, never mind the near-universal: 'Do unto others as you would have them do unto you.'

Buddha, for example, taught, respected and ordained both male and female disciples, yet abused Buddhist women may be encouraged to accept their plight as just desserts for wrongdoing in a previous life. As the Buddhist Khuankaew points out, 'Just as Christian women are often taught to bear their cross, Buddhist women are taught to accept their karma' (2007:180). Chapter Four verse 34 of the Qur'an seems to allow a Muslim husband in certain circumstances to beat, tap or leave his wife, following a set sequence of action: yet it may not, as the Addendum makes clear in discussing crucial Buddhist and Muslim texts.

There is no parallel exegesis of Christian texts in this book, because how texts are taught, ignored and used by leaders and followers is embedded in individual and community views. Consequently, actual discussants' understanding and use of texts they have absorbed are the central interest, rather than exegetical analysis by theologians and biblical scholars, vital though that can be. The question here is: how do people, both those living out their formal training in theology and scripture, and those living out their understanding in life-skills and faith, *use* the Bible, *use* a theology, to support or oppose a husband who hits and otherwise abuses his wife?

Let me make a crucial point here. Neither users of nor listeners to a text, irrespective of faithfulness, are necessarily oppressed, wise, nasty, stupid, gullible or hypocritical. Christian women and men who *accept* that Eve's taking of the apple in Eden mandates a husband's rule over them (Genesis 2–3), or that given a husband's family headship (Ephesians 5.23), wifely obedience (Ephesians 5.22) is due, are not misguided fatalists, even if the outworking of these texts may be illegitimately used to 'validate' violence. That is what their background, experience, teaching and milieu tell them and that is how they manage their lives. Christian women and men who *reject* marital violence, using Genesis 1.27 'God made man and woman in God's image,' or Ephesians 5.21 'Husbands and wives live in mutual submission one with another', or 'Husbands do not be harsh to your wives [...] so that nothing may hinder your prayers' (1 Peter 3.7), are by the same token neither automatically wise nor feminist, manipulative nor virtuous. That is what their background, experience, teaching and milieu tell them and that is how they manage their lives. Threads weaving through discussants' use of texts are drawn together in Chapter 7.

Verses can impact behaviour in the sense of not only explaining it – 'He hit me because he is "head of the house" and I spoke out of turn' – but also changing it. Take one verse relevant for Christians, Muslims and Jews: 'God made man and woman in God's image' (Genesis 1.27), of which Goodman wrote, 'deliberately harming another person desecrates God's name' (2003:58). Taught in a confirmation lesson in northern England in 2017, this verse led one older candidate to leave her husband. As she said to her surprised female priest two days after her confirmation: 'My husband has hit me for the 43 years of our marriage. Now I know I'm made in God's image and equal to my husband: I'm off.'

Such an assertion of self may evoke the spectre of feminism lurking behind any discussion of marital violence, illustrated in a recent Christian discussion on Eve. The author notes that because of the expulsion of Adam and Eve from Eden, partners will battle for supremacy, in a

> familiar struggle played out in the ideological conflict between male tyranny (a horrible feature of some cultures and religions) and militant feminism. It doesn't just happen in the political arena; it is expressed in battles and tensions in countless households. (Paine, 2014:140)

The ordained writer's moral equivalence between 'male tyranny' over wives and an unexplained 'militant feminism' exemplifies the illogicality endemic in this area. Male household tyranny, Paine seems to imply, is a feature neither of his religious tradition, Christian, nor of his country, Britain, a view readily disputed by abused Christian British wives. Such buck-passing is the key for *all* people, of no faith and of any faith, to ignore the issue for a quiet conscience and an easy life. That this contributes to violence against actual women is as easily dismissed as their pain, and others' shame, is trivialized.

Irrespective of brand, actual Christians working for or worshipping in local churches and too many seminaries have, with the odd exception, ignored wife-abuse, or at best responded to it in terms of 'being kind to the weak and troubled'. This may help individual abused women find a roof. However, if it enables implicit and explicit support for marital violence to continue unchallenged, such tinkering at the edges is theologically and morally barren. Churches benefit from the topic being 'unsuitable for a pleasant chat by nice people'. Leaders of churches can and do say that because no Bible verse opposed the beating or otherwise abusing of wives *in those words*, it is not a subject for sermons. Religiously oriented survivors of abuse, just as others, may prefer to 'forget' it, the better to get through the day. Abused people commonly internalize blame, accepting their tormentor's scathing views and their own part in 'causing' the violence. However, a faith survivor may add a salvific slant, believing *her* 'supposed sin' counts against her, rather than the actual sin of the white-washed assailant counting against *him*. This assumption is underwritten by much church teaching past and present.

Both Christian women in general and victims and survivors in particular talk about it far less than might be imagined. (Both 'victim' and 'survivor' are used in this book: if the abused woman *feels* herself a victim, at that point she *is* one. She may eventually feel herself a survivor, after or during the period in which violence is an ever-present possibility. However, using only survivor to stress female agency is unacceptable.) To give an example of silence from this research, a female hospital counsellor who had arranged a talk for me in a South Indian Christian city hospital asked the nurses the next day how they had found it. She reported:

> They wanted to hear more about it. I asked why they hadn't said much when questions began. They said, 'We didn't know what to say because we'd never heard anything like that before and we were shocked.' Most came from small villages, where 'no one ever talks about such things'.

She attributed silence to the nurses' rural background. Yet just two days later in that same large city, she attended a small evening meeting of high-caste female church friends to discuss the issue. As we departed, she commented to full agreement from the other women: 'We've known each other for years, but we've never talked about this before. We always talk with a certain reserve, and we're very careful not to go over boundaries.'

Nor is it a richer world-poorer world split. A group of women in Scotland had that same response: 'Keep quiet, keep any problems under wraps, get by.' Villagers in northern England did speak up, albeit rather late in the day:

> As the widow followed the coffin of her late husband out of the church, the congregation began to applaud, tentatively at first and then with increasing

conviction. The widow having survived forty-six years of an abusive marriage in quiet submission, villagers were expressing their solidarity with her. Her closest friend described the event as the village 'telling her that they stood by her all those years, that they *knew* and that they *saw* it all, and that they'd cared all along.'

By 'seeing', the speaker meant *understand* rather than *see* the violence, the 'privacy of the family' enabling silence to be the cowardly choice for observers as well as the rational choice for abused women who fear further retaliation and lack family and church support.

Much the same ignoring or silencing of the issue applies to other faith traditions. Individual pastors, imams, rabbis and priests *do* quietly oppose marital violence, *do* say the right thing, *do* offer real support, as do the laity. Yet faith circles rarely mention it in teaching or preaching and then usually as a potential pastoral problem or irritation, yet another sign of human failure due to Adam and Eve, the rebellious nature of women, failings in a previous life or the failure of feminist-influenced wives to refrain from that rebellion which merits chastisement. Overall, the issue seems at best an optional single-lecture add-on in the already lowly esteemed practical theology training of religious leaders. Yet it is *there*, where church leaders are trained, where survivors' voices should be heard, and *there* where sloppy Bible-reading and sin-supporting theology should be challenged.

But it is not just faith traditions which sidle around the issue. An anthropology volume on domestic violence planned in the mid-1980s and first published in 1992 (Counts, Brown and Campbell) noted that some anthropologists failed to contribute a chapter lest they 'expose the dark side of a culture': others felt that publishing on it might preclude their gaining entry to continue research or that writing about it meant imposing a political agenda from outside. One man felt domestic violence should not be examined 'lest it encourage women to protest traditional gender roles and destabilise family life' (1999:xviii).

The impact of violence within a marital relationship is not restricted to wives and mothers: children suffer too.

> It is very painful for children to watch their dad beating their mother. I [female] used to plead with dad to stop. His behaviour discouraged me from marriage. I love him very much, but what he used to do to my mum keeps haunting me (Kenya).

> On bad nights, she'd bring her kids to her father's house to sleep or to my [male] porch so they were safe. The abuse was so bad she had to leave lest she died.

The second daughter killed herself when she was twenty. There were many scars on the children (Trinidad).

The school children (aged nine) don't say much when I [female] teach the ten commandments until we get to marriage and adultery. Then they talk about the fighting and hitting between their parents, most saying they should split rather than fight (Germany).

The son of a man who hit both his wife and his children said: 'I didn't go to church on Father's Day for years because I just couldn't face the memories of his violence.' Replication by imitation may affect the sons of an abuser, both those who abuse *their* wives and those who are crippled by the fear that they might: 'My father hit my mother. I was so afraid I'd hit my wife that in a dispute I was paralysed, backing off.' Some hold off or do not marry at all, explaining, 'I'm too scared to marry in case I also hit my wife.' Others avoid such unappealing options in a mutually happy married life.

Such anxiety that a marriage of people with direct or indirect experience of abuse would be negatively affected by an inability to negotiate a full and balanced relationship came up again and again. Anxiety also affects daughters who marry late in the hope of avoiding an abuser or, marrying early to avoid home violence, are chosen by men who pick out vulnerable women. These are *not* women who *want* to be beaten. To daughters of violence, such men may represent normality, the intermittent sweetness of their abusive father being part of the cycle of violence. With no peaceful family to return to, their future can be bleak and lonely.

Children may deal with their faith tradition's tacit support for violence by leaving the church themselves, as a German woman explained:

My stepfather hit my mum a lot back in St Lucia. The pastor said 'pray, persevere, be patient and God will deal with it.' I decided at fourteen not to have anything to do with the church if that's what they said and I haven't until today.

That advice could have come from *any* continent, *any* country. The voices of those damaged by church collusion are lost wherever angry or damaged people turn their back on the church. Yet their voices should be heard and their departure taken as a wake-up call to the institution, which more readily blames them. The effect the marital violence of an ordained father has on the life and faith of the children remains to be seen: snippets gleaned during this research suggest it is not positive.

The research process

This book includes material from historians and theologians, especially but not only in Chapter 3. However, the primary witnesses are people encountered in the research, who are not identified beyond gender and, if relevant, country and denomination. Lay and ordained, of varied and variable faith, they talked about their opposition to, experience of and at times support for the physical control of wives by husbands in marriage, all knowing my background and commitment to writing this book to which all willingly contributed.

Discussions generally took place in houses, universities and seminaries, churches, house prayer groups, informal gatherings, women's shelters and individuals reached through multiple church or secular contacts. These involved lay and ordained people in largely Christian communities against a background of Buddhist, Christian, Hindu, Indigenous or Muslim tradition in Europe (England, Scotland and Germany), Africa (Ghana and Kenya), Asia (Pakistan, India, Myanmar, Malaysia, Taiwan and Korea), Australasia (Australia and Tonga), North America (United States) and the Caribbean (Trinidad and the Antilles). Denominations included African Initiated Churches, Anglican, Assemblies of God, Baptist, Lutheran, Mar Thoma, Methodist and Methodist Zion, Pentecostal, Presbyterian, Roman Catholic, Salvation Army, Syrian Orthodox and True Jesus.

It is important to make clear that this research could not have been done were I *not* female *and* Christian *and* an anthropologist; being white-haired helped too. My two intellectual hats meant I could lightly challenge discussants who insisted it was 'my religion' or 'my culture' which forced whatever behaviour they were excusing. Mentioning family and cooking interests in initial conversations, wearing interesting earrings and usually skirts, and smiling gently appeared to assuage any anxieties. Yes, that was a blatant and intentional 'presentation of self', but sufficient to quiet the assumption that any woman interested in marital violence must be a man-hating, abused, childless feminist, *none* of which attributes apply. Divinity School teaching carried a certain respectability, coupled with crucial affirmation during research by current and former doctoral students. Ordination in the Scottish Episcopal Church in 2009 facilitated access to churches across the world, irrespective of attitudes to female ordination.

Without such multiple ties, it would have been impossible to engage with church workers or access groups of women and men linked to the various churches. Being accepted as a fellow church worker meant 'sisters and brothers in Christ' talked openly, assuming that we shared more than might be the case.

Their attitudes, actions and silence, as well as the voices of survivors, lie at the core of this research, along with those complicit lay observers willing to watch others' lives shrink under the intentional abuse of a partner.

The fact that I am ordained, yet interested in talking about violence in marriage, women's lives and griefs seemed significant for many women. Moreover, and this was important given first world visitor privilege, the views and abuse experiences of women and men and the silence of churches in countries previously visited became part of each discussion thereafter. This interested discussants, as did material on marital abuse in Britain, including clerical and survivor comments. Holding joint meetings with laywomen and their (often male) ordained leaders was not easy but was sometimes the only way to gather a group. Some women were naturally inhibited in such a situation, though the vocal might nevertheless take the risk of offending their leaders. Moreover, offering a generally calm challenge to assembled church dignitaries did allow listening laity to hear *firstly* that all are made in the Image of God and *secondly* that violence against one half of creation is therefore a sin.

Take a meeting of female farm workers, with some nurses and primary teachers, and four male elders and pastors. One pastor interrupted a woman who had been hesitantly explaining how poorly the church deals with marital violence by saying, 'If both come to me, I try to counsel them together, and get them both to see their faults: the wives don't usually say much.' Indeed. When another woman ventured that the beaten prefer to go to the police rather than a pastor, another pastor intervened:

> The media empowers women, so they go to police, *especially those committing adultery*. If there's a problem, I convince the wife of her faults, saying she should try harder to please him and keep him happy. And if he hits her because he is irritated, she must bear it and pray in her heart for him to stop.

He completed this misogynist view with, 'It is because of sin. Violence will continue till the Second Coming.' Irritated, I suggested that waiting till then would leave many wives dead or maimed. He countered with a moral tale of a newly married young woman who, beaten by her husband and his mother and unwanted by her parents, left for the city where she became a prostitute. He blamed the girl, who 'shouldn't have left her new home, because it's too hard to be alone'. He ended the meeting, somewhat sanctimoniously, with 'I have learnt today that we need to keep God's word on love foremost in our minds to tackle violence at home'. Several women came up afterwards with a quick word of thanks and comment about specific points. They were indeed constrained by arrogant patronizing leaders but, attentive and responsive, talked among themselves about what they had heard from another sort of church leader.

The topic evoked anger, joking, enthusiasm and sad memories: remaining cool could be demanding. One pastor repaid my agreement that he could attend the meeting if he remained silent (using a different tack from that outlined above) by asking me publicly at the end of the meeting how I managed my sex life as a single. He lost face in that exchange, to the women's amusement, but it did suggest how he dealt with 'unruly' female parishioners. Overall, the more testing discussions were with clergy, whether male or female.

A discussion in a Pakistan seminary challenges a common assumption that field workers remain neutral. Had I not been Christian, and a priest, ready access to this group of future church workers would not have been possible. Had I not engaged bluntly with the issue, the row of silent female listeners would not have heard marital violence opposed, as several quickly said afterwards. Yet were I not ordained, I may have felt less compulsion to oppose furious male students and staff so strongly with theological and biblical argument. I had made the distinction between a *sin of necessity* which was *not* counted to the person, such as taking food to avoid starvation or (despite Pakistan's *huddud* laws) being raped, and a *sin of conscious choice*, such as an abusive husband insisting his wife's behaviour or failure 'made him hit her', which *is* counted to the sinner. This and my ensuing argument visibly angered male students, who demanded: 'How can you suggest separation because of abuse when Matthew says marriage makes us one flesh? (Genesis 2.24; Matthew 19.7). It is a covenant before God.' I suggested an abusing husband has broken any covenant by not treating his partner as one flesh, rebutting a local defence of wife-beating that 'because St Paul beat himself (1 Corinthians 9.27), and as I am one flesh with my wife, hitting her is hitting myself, so cannot be abuse.' Not to have countered those and other vain attempts to validate violence would have betrayed my vocation. This session was anthropological in terms of wanting to understand the other's position and view of life, although the 'dynamic interaction' (a beater himself, the attending president's anger with me on leaving was briefly frightening) was perhaps less usual.

Unlike much anthropology research, much of this work was done in bursts of two to four weeks in each site, with the world considered as one field. Such intensive work has certain benefits, as I was aware from earlier research on 'that which shouldn't be'. Firstly, abused people tend to cut out everything beyond the limited picture they can manage. Highlighting awful aspects is possible for a time, but the images and memories expressed in a sentence or a flood must return to the shadows as well as circumstances allow. Secondly, churches as institutions are not keen to risk their darker sides being discussed at length, lest things become too challenging: organizations want to endure. Thirdly, the researcher has to manage his or her life. The cumulative impact of multi-site work should not be underestimated. In the short-term, negotiating yet another appropriate demeanour, making and extending links, and starting a series of often ad hoc meetings and one-on-one conversations left little time. One meeting in Trinidad began just two hours after touch down, and everywhere, each hour was filled. Giving a lecture or talk at the end of a research block could help shed the particular tension of each place, as did re-reading my well-thumbed copy of *Pride and Prejudice* in German each evening of a four-month research trip: the language and orderliness were so tranquil, even tranquilizing.

There were difficulties peculiar to this research. Discussants from violent families, in areas where such violence is shameful, might deny that fact. 'Of course,' said a close friend, 'we deny it: we're ashamed of having a parent who felt no shame'. A woman might empathize with victims then in the next breath scorn them. Maybe they were fending off the horrors of potential violence by stressing *their* virtue and the *other's* shortcomings, much as women may insist, despite evidence, that modest dress and demeanour prevent rape, especially if they fear for distant daughters. As ever, memory plays tricks: a sixty-year-old friend deriding 'those beaten women who don't leave' had clearly forgotten that at sixteen she too stayed with an abusive husband until, to her relief, he died.

Discussions sometimes had to stop abruptly. At a meeting in a Christian-supported women's shelter in Korea, the first to speak, a sixty-year-old Buddhist woman, described the years of violence and her decision to leave. I asked what her parents had said when she went: 'I didn't tell them why, as they would have been sad to realise what had been going on.' The next woman, a young conservative Presbyterian, calmly explained that she had left when, after years of violence, her husband had broken her skull, eye-socket and teeth. 'What did your parents say when you went?' I asked. She wept: 'They disowned me for opposing the head of the household. But I will not go back.' It was impossible to go deeper into her situation because the third woman, a Buddhist sitting just by me who had only been in the shelter for two days, began to shake, clutching my arm. A fruitful session ended.

One formal research tool, a survey developed in 2011, was used especially, but not only, in tertiary institutions to allow individuals to comment on or expand their thoughts on violence in Christian marriage. Three surveys were done in single-denomination settings: an Episcopal congregation in Scotland, Methodist ministers in the Caribbean and female Church of South India priests. Two were in state universities in Ghana and Kenya, respondents being from many denominations. The remaining five were at Christian universities and seminaries run by though not entirely filled with students of one denomination. Around 60 per cent of respondents in two Anglican universities, one in Korea and another in Kenya, were Anglican, with a similar proportion belonging to the Church of South India in a seminary. All respondents at an international Christian university in Kenya were Protestant, no one denomination predominating. The majority of those attending a Presbyterian-linked university near Seoul were from many of that denomination's many separate churches.

Memories remain of excited or tearful women who felt able to speak about the unspeakable, and a good deal of mocking laughter about clergy ineptitude, always easier than facing that of lay peers. More than is perhaps usual in field research, there was an obligation to console with words, touch or quiet silence, to offer context-appropriate advice if requested, to pray when asked to do so by a hurting person or, if asked, to suggest Bible verses with which the other, man or woman, could fight, or at least mentally oppose, marital violence. Refusing to respond to such requests would have been unethical, though acquiescing perhaps increased exhaustion through role conflation.

The reality of violence

So much for the research purpose and process, but what about the reality of violence in marriage? Discussants, both men and women, seemed to use three conceptual categories, Level I representing the 'milder' form, although people are aware that violence may suddenly escalate. As a Kenyan man pointed out at a large meeting attended mainly by women,

> You [women] should get the point, see his anger, and take off. If you stay, and he thinks you can fight, he will hit you behind the knees so you fall and then you will be kicked. It is not safe. You can die at Level 1 if you hit something on falling.

Level I would be shaking, pushing hard, slapping with a flat hand or hitting with a thin stick with the shoulder down or level, or swinging her against a wall by her hair. Level II involves the victim being hit very hard with shoulder raised, perhaps with a long 2" × 2" length of timber, punched or kicked, especially when she has already been floored. Level III involves a 4" × 4" length of wood, a knife, axe or gun, attempts to strangle or choke, or actually killing.

A Kenyan lady summarized the order:

> Kicking or punching hard with a closed fist, that is battering, so Level II. Hitting with a stick, that is discipline, so Level I. Hitting with a piece of house timber, that is battering, so Level II. If she slept out at night with somebody else, hitting her with a long piece of 3" x 3" or bigger, which is Level III, might be seen as acceptable, but not for getting up late.

Talking of levels can be helpful when discussing scenarios. For small-town Scottish-born Roman Catholic and Presbyterian women, the general view included sticking to marriage vows made before God. However, all agreed that that did not include risking death or maiming: for them, Level III violence should mean the end of the marriage. Level I, if the violence stopped there, was seen as 'an unfortunate part of the marriage contract with that partner', and Level II left the individual to decide what to do, with the majority opting to leave. *None spoke of 'staying to save him'.*

Largely West African-born Scottish city women, on the other hand, initially responded to my question about what an abused wife should do with the blanket statement: 'If he hits me I should stay because the power of my love and the support of Jesus will change him.' However, in discussing hypothetical cases in relation to the above levels, they insisted that Level I commonly fitted in with 'staying to save him', but potentially fatal Level III attacks did not, their life being more important than his conversion. Reactions to a Level II situation for *both* groups depended on several variables: income, attitude of the church to divorced members, family pressure, and increasing incidence and severity. When violence began, having children may keep women in marriages, yet real fear of death amid Level II or III violence could push them to leave, irrespective of background, lest their children be orphaned. But for all the groups of Scottish women, as elsewhere, the topic of spousal violence is rarely if ever spoken about publicly, especially in faith communities.

Responses among Methodist, Anglican, Roman Catholic and Pentecostal subsistence farming women in the Kenyan Highlands were clear:

> Those who say, stay if it's Level II? No! He had hit me often before, then it got worse: he broke my thigh with a chair. Now I cannot walk well. I am alone, but I am safe. If he kills you, you leave your children suffering: it is better to go at Level I. Had I carried on being patient I would be dead now and my children would be orphans.

And from another woman:

It can easily move from Level I to Level II very quickly. And Level II goes for the eye, the head, the teeth and the limbs, so the woman cannot see, cannot think, cannot eat. If you run away when Level I began and he sat in silence while you were away, he might explode when you eventually return. Better stay away!

In discussing violence, men tended to highlight dramatic Level III events of violence, or even 'women's wish to be hit', women more often cited the regular incidence and the continual anxiety. Four ordained men in Ghana explained:

Me:	If we look at violence between husbands and wives, what is the pattern of violence here irrespective of the reason?
Informant A:	Near here, a woman felt a misunderstanding was resolved, and they both left the house for work. He returned with petrol, but someone saw him. When the wife returned later, the man took the petrol, sprinkled it in the room then called her. That neighbour saw the man pushing his wife, penning her into that room. She was saved.
Me:	That is not everyday violence: what is?
Informant B:	Beating.
Me:	Hand or stick?
B:	Anything. When there's anger, anything that comes to hand 'for her to learn a lesson.' Some women said if he doesn't beat me, he doesn't love me.
Me:	Oh, that mythical group on which abusers rely so much? That surely doesn't mean punching, kicking, slashing.
C:	Some women want to provoke the man, because she will only be sexually satisfied if she's been beaten first. It might look like violence, but maybe they are demonstrating love.
Me:	Is that common?
C:	No.

As I remarked, they had produced three unusual acts of violence against women, ignoring the flow of regular abuse which they perhaps did not register as unacceptable.

But let us leave levels of violence and turn to the incidence. Figures for 'that which should not happen' are clearly difficult to ascertain, but the annual country-by-country UN figures find violence over the duration of 20–40 per cent of marriages. There are pockets in one country with radically different rates. In India, for example, women in matrilineal Meghalaya are nineteen times less likely to be abused than in patrilineal Tamil Nadu (Menon and Johnson, 2000:15). This book is not the place to discuss this or that method of estimating incidence rates, but numbers cloak as well as clarify. An unknown proportion of women do not report violence for fear of being hit more, because they deem reporting pointless and because it may shame them and their family. Abused men may under-report through shame.

Moreover, certain denominations may pressure members not to report cases, giving an unrealistic view of peaceable living. Such is the case for Assemblies of God members in Tonga, with the statistically lowest marital violence rate on the island, denomination being included on all police charge sheets. An Assemblies lady in her sixties explained:

> People like me, we don't go to the police. People might look up to me but if I go to the police they will be shocked. My church says 'Don't go to the police or the government when you have a domestic problem. Matthew says deal with problems yourselves (Matthew 18.15–17),' and 'How can you take your problems to an unsaved person?' And yes, only Assembly people are saved!

Women from her church rushed into her house to seek sanctuary several times a week. But only Assembly abused *wives* are restrained from using courts against violent husbands, other members freely bringing varied cases. The Presbyterian Church of Taiwan also advised dealing with dirty linen internally. However, its Gender Justice Unit managed to exclude marital violence from that policy on the grounds that the reputation of the church must take second place to the safety and dignity of the woman. Churchgoers may assume there is more marital violence outside their group than within. A recent study in Cumbria, England, reports that while 71 per cent saw such a violence as a problem in the area, only 37 per cent thought it was in the church (Aune, 2018). Nason-Clark (1997) found rates in Canada only marginally less among churchgoers than in the general population. Yet in a sense numbers are irrelevant: violence against a partner is wrong.

But does even a single attack mean that the entire relationship is violent? If violence occurred once, the assailant was filled with true remorse which the victim accepted as real in perpetuity, then neither I nor women in any of the places researched regard him as an abuser. For example, a gentle drunken man in Borneo hit his wife in 1974. The next day, filled with shame, he went to the headman requesting punishment. His wife, my friend, fully accepted his contrition. There was no other such incident in their marriage, nor did she fear one, until she died in 2003. Some readers may say one such act renders the assailant an abuser: I take informants' views seriously. If the survivor of a single sort-of-but-not-really-apologized-for attack does not feel confident about the future, she may, if she can, decide to leave.

A drunken attack within a pattern of violent control counts as much (though not always legally) as one by a sober assailant. However, while the survivor can 'blame the drink', thus feeling less personally assailed, being hit by a sober husband leaves just three explanations: She can blame her own deficiencies as a wife and woman; blame the inherent nastiness of her spouse whom she may have chosen; or, the least likely, blame his decision to hit. Drink does not *cause* violence but may be used by an assailant and also by observers to excuse it even though, as informants repeatedly noted, the drunk aims primarily or solely at his wife or other intended opponent.

Are all attacks just part of that so-called human anger which, I have been assured by devout Christians, just explodes now and then due to human nature, or the Fall, and 'can't be helped'? A simple response, as above, is: husbands (drunk or sober) hit their wives, rather than their bosses, friends or mothers, *because they can*. Violence against wives is less about 'poor anger management' (in which case an irritating boss should be the victim) than about the ongoing exercise of power over another human being. Taken 'too far', her death may bring consequences: but even that neither is nor was certain. In thirteenth-century Spain, a 'good' husband who 'inadvertently' killed his wife while reproving her was exonerated, a habitually bullying husband being executed for murder (Dillard, 1984:92). Shortly before my 2016 stay in Pakistan, an older Christian woman was killed by her husband after visiting her local Christian lover who just beat his wife when she asked where he'd been. The community accompanied the murderer to the police station to insist he be let off because, my Christian informant explained, 'he was right to kill her'. The judicial minimizing of 'crimes of passion', or rather 'crimes of thwarted possession', has a long history the world over.

The othering of violence

And here we return to the initial question: why is violence in Christian marriage ignored? Are lay and ordained people deliberately blind and theologically ignorant? Does the wish for institutional respectability take priority over damage to people caused by wrong or ineffective teaching?

One reason is the human propensity to attribute spousal violence to generic 'Others', perceived as qualitatively different. Borneo villagers insisted (against evidence) that men in *their* kin-cluster of the 700-person community were not violent but those in the next were, a statement repeated to the end of the village where the beater was 'not from here so it's not us' (Koepping, 2003), just as wealthy people lower down a New England river eagerly attributed violence to 'those up-river people'. White Euro Americans readily imply only Africans, Asians and Latin Americans beat their wives. The poor were blamed by the influential eighteenth-century lawyer Blackstone for their 'predilection' for marital violence and, compared with the better off, for their apparent 'unwillingness to abandon their [wrongly] assumed right to hit' (Chapter 15, 1765).

People of higher castes in South Asia attribute violence just to *dalit*, while at the same time accepting that middle-class Christian women with too much to lose suffer in silence. Nurses in a rich South Indian Christian hospital insisted 'only the poor' hit their wives. I asked if domestic violence cases came to their hospital: 'Yes, regularly, but they are logged in as accident, and no, poor people never come here'. A Malaysian Anglican priest insisted, against evidence, that 'Christians don't have a problem with that, unless they mix with Muslims and so on'. A Taiwanese woman felt her father's violence to her mother came from 'Taiwan's occupation by Japanese: he learnt marital violence from their attitudes', while a female English priest insisted only non-churchgoers hit wives.

Persistent and intentional violence against wives, just as living in peace and mutual respect, appears in every place and tradition. European and North American Christians may insist that Jews do not beat their wives (doing a disservice to those Jewish women who are beaten: Graetz, 1998 and Adelman, 1996), whereas that same fantasy decides Muslims *do* beat their wives, maligning peaceful Muslim men (Lefkovitz, 2015:176). Marital violence *is* a little more common in some groups than others, and economic or indeed football stress can temporarily increase the incidence, *provided the attitude is there*. Sudden relative poverty for a wealthy family can feel as acute a stressor as that endured by a poor family living in one room with no predictable income. Yet neither stress nor drink *creates* violence for, like war, that necessitates reducing the victim to a lesser object.

If attributing violence to 'others' cannot wish the problem away, one common ploy is to reframe it as a merely social or personal issue. Certain church leaders in my country, as elsewhere, know ordained men under them beat their wives yet say nothing, sometimes renaming it 'poor anger management' or, wringing hapless hands, explaining how hard it can be to sack such a man. A last-ditch universal strategy, associated with clear membership boundaries, is to insist a Christian (or member of another religion) who beats his wife is not really a member and is therefore of no concern to faith-leaders, irrespective of the contribution faith had in developing his views, or the wider public's view of him as a member.

However, this research makes clear that the simplest strategy is collective complicity through silence: the sin of violence against wives is just not mentioned in public or among 'nice' people. And silence, whether puzzled or anxious, was the most common first response to this research especially, but by no means only, from clergy. Yet while church silence makes church workers culpable, the silence of their peers, those other laywomen who know but turn away or excuse the abuse, is *especially* debilitating for survivors, explored in Chapter 6.

Silence is not neutral and inaction is agreement, the conclusion reached by a young Baptist woman whom I was teaching in Yangon:

> Culture, the military, church leaders; they silence us. We do not like that, and we are angry. But we do the same: we preach and teach on peace and justice as if other people should make it happen. *We must stop being silent, for that it is active and colludes with power.* Our society does not count domestic violence as a sin; our church does not act on that issue. It doesn't support violence against women, but *because it does not see it as a theological problem, and is often silent, it looks as if it does.*

Christian readers may at this point already be denying such attitudes in *their* church's practice or protesting that they do not know of any abused women members. People without a faith attachment may feel the hypocrisy of faith is clearly upheld. But *all* people with mental capacity make use of texts, whether written or otherwise absorbed, as the following non-faith examples show:

In 1975, the headman in a largely Christian Borneo village encouraged a quite wealthy woman to send her handicapped child for treatment. In an increasingly tense discussion, he suggested that supporting her healthy children more generously at school now would ensure they could support her in old age. She exploded: 'They might be dead by the time I am old, so I'll eat my money now rather than give them more.' The headman was startled when she continued: 'It is right in Kadazan tradition for exchanges to be balanced. I give them as much as they give me now.' Yet 'balanced reciprocity' is not right within the family: she was playing games.

Atheist Chinese trained volunteers at a government-supported hot-line 're-victimize' abused women calling in, saying 'it is considered right for a man to beat his wife for her misbehaviour' (Liu, 2001:79). The researcher continues: 'Women's tolerant and silent attitude in the face of their husbands' abuse is viewed as a cause of their further abuse, comprising a further way in which women are blamed and held responsible for being abused' (Liu, 2001:81). Reflecting and self-criticizing are a current Chinese value, yet counsellors suggest men beat due to family tradition and stress, being victim of their situation (Liu, 2001:83–7).

The result, supported by the Chinese saying 'Beating is intimacy and scolding love' as well as residual Confucian ideology merged with current Marxist thought, makes a straitjacket as firm as that of any religion. Whatever the context, it is always possible to find a text, pull the rabbit out of the hat and validate any and every intention of the actors.

Reflection

Taking the world as one fieldwork venue may have given the impression that men and women, and therefore husbands and wives, are fixed entities therein: that is not the case. Theologically, humanity is one (Genesis 1.27, Galatians 3.27). But in relation to violence in marriage between males and females, this assumption of oneness (an assumption only patchily followed, as we shall see in Chapter 3) is woefully inadequate.

Life is lived at two levels (Gittins, 2004), the superficial level of dress, gesture, worship-style, which parallels the *words* of a language and the deeper *grammar* of being, which conveys meaning to those unconsciously sharing certain assumptions. We therefore need to ask what *is* a man and a woman, what *is* a human being, in this or that context. The underlying grammar of being offers humans as either two separate categories, one male and one female, or just one, human, with merely superficial male and female differences. Arguably the latter comes closer to the initial 'God made man and woman in God's image,' while the former is more often reflected in the outworking of life.

In Europe, North Africa, much of the Middle East, South Asia and China, the ingrained view of male and female resembles two distinctly different beings. The pivotal place of the first three regions in the development of early Christian theology privileges this double image. However, from then onwards, an assumption of fundamental ethnic, status or gender difference usually implies ranked order, 'different and less', rather than indifference (Thucydides 2: Ch.39ff). Various less-privileged contexts see male and female embedded in a fundamental *oneness* of creation, sex-linked difference being just superficial lexical items of a deep unified grammar. Arguably occurring indigenously in all continents, such a region has been the main focus of my work in Borneo. There both sexes are (or increasingly were) understood to have the same soul, needs and inner bodily system, the same traditional legal rights, and broadly speaking the same capacity to see beyond the immediately visible world (Koepping, 2008). Such equity in unity, which forbad but did not eliminate marital violence though affected the outcome, has not been widely influential, being overwhelmed by incoming, dominant, less equal traditions.

Being models, these categories of single or double versions of humanity are neither rigid nor agreed by all in a context, yet they should be borne in mind by those assuming 'The West' is intrinsically more egalitarian and particularly more individualistic than 'The Rest'. It is only recently that women in the regions from which the main Christian denominations originated or became embedded, areas which retain much influence and ecclesial power, became jural adults, a status which their sisters in certain other regions never lost.

Silently condoned or openly accepted violence against wives is an unpleasant example of contextual manipulation of words and ideas which occurs in all contexts. Some readers know of it first-hand, because they have been attacker or attacked, or because parental violence was a frightening part of their own childhood. Yet all, of any faith or none, should be aware of the issue. Few seem to be, other than at the superficial level of dealing with each event as, let us say, a separate slice of bread. This book puts those slices together to make one loaf, labelled 'institutional and individual inadequacy'.

This is the case whether 'church' is seen *solely* as the institution or *also* as the individual followers *(ekklesia)* making up the church. Protestant and Pentecostal churches since their inception, and Roman Catholic since Vatican II, all see (on paper at least) both the institutional *and* the individual nature of 'church'. However, it is unacceptable for members to say on the one hand, '*We* are Church, the people of God', when things are good and grassroots change they like is emerging, but on the other, if the (institutional) church is in bad odour, to wash our hands of it saying, '*They* are Church.' To the extent that the latter version makes known wrongdoing a sacred secret, that may be reasonable. But *all* people of capacity who see violence against the (female) spouse as proper behaviour by manly men towards unruly wives, rather than an insult to the Image of God in all persons, are colluding in wrong. This statement does not touch the 'headship of husbands', but rather the violence wrongly derived from it. Even where violence appears to be accepted, both women and men may quietly despise it, not through Enlightenment ideas of the reasonable husband nor modern human rights, but because people in urban Scotland or rural Kenya, urban Korea or rural Tonga *know* it causes distress, incapacity and inter-generational damage.

Church-led change can happen and the picture from top-down and especially local initiatives gives some hope. Let us now therefore turn to the legal and sociological aspects of marriage, power and culture, Part One ending with an assessment of marital violence in historical theology.

2

Legal and sociological approaches to marital violence

Having set out the need for and process of research on the physical abuse of Christian wives by Christian husbands, this chapter explores the changing international conventions and secular laws concerning violence against woman as wives; global options for monogamous marriage – contract, covenant or a varied mix of both; the position of women in their natal or new family and after divorce; and culture, power and its abuse by individual abusers and institutional colluders.

Some informants felt state 'interference' in the process of marriage was wrong, that international organizations were anti-religious, that modernity and feminism rather than faith lay behind interest in the subject, that power was irrelevant and that anyway things had been perfectly manageable before. Other discussants held partially or wholly different views, applauding state intervention and hoping churches would follow suit. A Trinidadian pastor insisted that 'the church should not be seen to support violence by opposing or remaining silent about national legal changes regarding domestic violence'. An Ethiopian student explained that her country's legal changes were pushing her church to develop 'a little interest' in the topic; a Kenyan student advised others: 'Do not waste time talking if an abused wife is bleeding: call the police and arrest him.'

Some general points first. National laws may increasingly affect the conduct of married life, but localized controls have always existed, forbidding or allowing the drawing of blood in marital quarrels and punishing or allowing 'excessive' or even fatal damage to wives, irrespective of what states or faiths decree. Thus areas in which early Christianity was embedded had their own expectations of marriage and individual rights, whether Orthodoxy in South India, southeast Europe and the Middle East, or Roman Catholicism in Western Europe and North Africa, joined after the sixteenth century by varieties of Protestantism. These expectations concern both control over *and* respectful treatment of wives, initially dealt with in Europe by church courts, which ruled against 'excessive' marital violence to keep the peace rather than defend the God-given equality of persons. States began to take over that task, though still accepted wives' subordinate role, enabling Agnes Sudley in 1891 to say of marital violence: 'the law allows it, our church consecrates it, and the brute takes full advantage of it' (in O'Faolain and Martines, 1974:167). Changes to prevent attacks on otherwise obedient faithful wives took off in the nineteenth century in various countries, increasing from the 1970s. However, the demeanour, virtue and housekeeping diligence of a female survivor may still affect legal decisions regarding attacks by a husband.

Counteracting what at times seems church collusion in violence against wives have been distinct church-linked movements against marital violence, influenced by when not clearly sourced from secular thought. Taking heart from the feminist movement of the 1970s, itself building on earlier secular movements, women in some church contexts began to voice clear opposition to male dominance in the family. Members sprinkled across the world took part in the World Council of Churches (WCC) 'Thursdays in Black' movement from the 1980s against sexual and gender-based violence. The WCC 'Decade of Solidarity with Women' from 1988 to 1998 saw Protestant, Pentecostal and Orthodox churches include family violence in meetings and writings throughout the period. Roman Catholic response was more diffuse, although Pope John Paul II did note that 'Genesis 3:16 "He shall rule over you" represents a corruption of the good order of creation' (Vocation of Women, 20, 1996). The Centre for Violence against Women founded by Revd Marie Fortune in Seattle in 1977 initiated practical action in America and beyond. Texts such as Aruna Gnanadason's *No Longer a Secret* in 1997 and the Lutheran World Federation's 2002 *Churches Say NO to Domestic Violence* were clear stages on the way, supporting the writing of established individuals such as John and Phyllis Alsdurf, Nancy Nason Clark, Sister John Manazan, Evelyn Monteiro, Elisabeth Schüssler Fiorenza, Mercy Odoye, Catherine Clark Kroeger, Isabel Phiri, Musimbi Kanyoro and many others.

Yet, and this point will recur, even the most helpful texts can moulder in drawers, unlikely to seep into everyday church consciousness. Courageous in that it gainsaid behaviour and attitudes of a good many participants' forebears in this in-married church, a 1993 Synodal Declaration by the Lutheran Church of Australia noted that 'domestic violence has been defended as Christian discipline and the legitimate exercising of Christian authority. Be it resolved that the Convention of the LCA now condemns all forms of violence in the family' (LCA, 1993). Violence against wives was known by Lutheran social workers in the 1980s, who dared not address it publicly lest it limit their chance to work with needy women. Citing this text in a 2011 lecture in Adelaide, several embarrassed people remembered it being 'put into a drawer' to dampen down the explosive reaction by some attending that Synod. The church's focus on its own structural integrity rather than that of abused women is just one more instance of privileging institutional survival above godly leadership.

Any initiative by universal churches needs to be followed by reoriented theological education, preaching and pastoral practice, along with respectful attitudes towards abused women and constructive engagement with abusing men. Unfortunately, that necessary step to fulfil the spirit and letter of the United Nations Convention and later Declarations (never mind the Bible) is usually piecemeal unless pressured by NGOs and more especially governments. Where churches do move, it tends to be limited, helping to ameliorate past damage rather than prevent future harm by teaching from a firmly theological basis. Certain churches, such as several in the Congo and the Fellowship of Christian Councils and Churches in the Great Lakes and Horn of Africa (FECCLAHA), which have seen extreme state violence, are engaged in doing just this and, as already noted, individual leaders across the world are also committed to this approach, as is the United Church of Australia. These, though, are but drops in the ocean amid a changing legal background.

International conventions and secular approaches

The recognition that women and wives should be free from marital violence has underlain moves for their protection within the United Nations over the last forty years. The pivotal 1979 Convention on the Elimination of Discrimination against Women (CEDAW) includes (Article 16) the statement that 'both partners to a marriage have the same rights and responsibilities during the marriage and at its dissolution'. Albeit with some exclusions, this has been signed by almost all countries. The 1993 UN Declaration against Violence against Women (DAVAW) defines such violence as

> any act of gender-based violence that results in, or is likely to result in, physical, sexual or psychological harm or suffering to women, including threats of such acts, coercion or arbitrary deprivation of liberty, whether occurring in public or in private life.

This includes hitting, killing, raping (irrespective of the woman's status) and imprisoning. Important here is Article 4 (italics added): 'States should condemn violence against women and *should not invoke any custom, tradition or religious consideration to avoid its elimination*.' It is easy to dismiss the UN as a secular organization, irrelevant to people of faith, despite the 1948 Declaration of Human Rights having been drawn up mainly but not entirely by practising Christians, together with one Jew and one Confucian-Buddhist. Readers may have heard such dismissive comments from North America and across the globe, especially but not only among Evangelical Christians or conservative Muslims. The Vatican has ratified neither the 1979 nor the 1993 Declarations.

The 1993 UN discussions and the Beijing 1995 Women's Conference had demonstrable repercussions which filtered down to national legal systems in the face of custom, religion and tradition. A swathe of countries enacted or updated laws to criminalize or at least restrict marital abuse, mandate reporting rules, educate about responsibility and rights in marriage, and criminalize violence in marriage. Picking out just some of the areas researched for this book, we find legal changes in Kenya 2014; Ghana 2006; India 2005; Korea 1997; Malaysia 1996; Pakistan 2012; South Australia revised 1994; Tonga 2015; Trinidad 1999; United Kingdom revised 1996; United Sates revised 1994. The 2014 addition of domestic violence to the list of protected attributes in the Australian workplace further strengthened the role of that state in curbing such violence.

Such declarations support the just treatment of all, including those in faith communities. Christians and Muslims are specifically enjoined to obey the state which they live unless that offends their belief. Christians should note Augustine's fifth century comment that household rule should follow that of the city, so it 'may be in harmony with the civic order' (CG 19/16). However, recent comments illustrate ongoing opposition. A parish priest placed a notice outside his church linking 118 wife-abuse deaths in Italy to:

> The fact that women are increasingly provocative, they become arrogant, they believe themselves to be self-sufficient and end up exacerbating the situation. Children are abandoned to their own devices, homes are dirty, meals are cold or fast food, clothes are filthy. (*The Journal* 2012)

Women appear responsible for their own murder, which makes a comment of Toma Holladay of Saddleback Church in 2007, that marital separation is only allowed 'if he is in the habit of beating you *regularly*', seem rather mild. Both countries have criminalized violence within the family.

Have these legal changes reduced the level of violence against wives? The impact of a legal change depends on the institutional capacity and will to monitor adherence and punish breaches. That they may occur *after* social or situational change suggests law is lagging behind praxis, even if violence is still accepted in parts of a country. However, legal revision may intend to change *future* behaviour by nudging individual and community thought towards behavioural change, which will not alter behaviour without information, education and, concerning marital violence, changing socialization practices of children. Moreover, *any* legal change, whether reactive or proactive, demands consistent effort to educate, prosecute the violent and ensure plaintiff safety. Criminalizing domestic violence without such efforts salves law-makers' conscience but not the lives of those attacked: their prime need is for predictable socio-legal support. Let us therefore see how legal processes related to marital violence play out in three countries – Poland, South Korea and Kenya – all of which signed the 1979 Convention, agreeing to be bound by its rules, Poland in 1980, South Korea in 1983 and Kenya in 1984.

Kenya criminalized domestic violence in 2015, and although abusers could be arraigned after both CEDAW and DAVAW had been signed, few women followed that path. Marital violence does not figure in premarital counselling for the large Anglican and Roman Catholic churches (though did in the Presbyterian church, very effectively) and was apparently never spoken of publicly. That changed in 2010, when a wife attacked and injured her feckless husband who, failing to provide food for the meal, sold their one cooking pot for alcohol while she was borrowing food. She scalded him, and he quite properly went to the police to complain of grievous bodily harm. The case fed legion sermons against marital violence the following Sunday, sermons referring only to *female* marital violence as wrong. No discussant in any of the four research sites in Kenya had heard sermons against the abuse of wives: all had heard of and were rather irritated by the 'poor beaten man' sermon, women's daily plight being ignored.

A more complex case occurred in Korea, where domestic violence was criminalized in 1997. Advice and referral centres set up by the government with support from mainly Christian religious organizations in cities apparently worked well. However, rural church-run government centres prioritized an abused wife staying with the head of her household, in keeping with Confucian as well as conservative Christian family values (Song, 2008). One rural-based foreign Christian woman, however, knew her rights from urban-living compatriots and took her older and violent Korean Christian husband to court, past caring about family honour. He suicided before the trial. There *were* other ways for him to learn, and hitting *was* his choice, but neither the shelter nor the church had explained the new rules, regarding it as theologically and culturally inappropriate.

The final example of law and faith shows the interweaving of church and state in Poland, a signatory of the 1979 UN Convention and the (Council of Europe) Istanbul Convention on Domestic Violence in 2011. A Polish woman sued for divorce on the grounds of her husband's violence, but her application was rejected first by the lower court and then the appeal court. This contradicts the rights of the individual itemized in the 1997 constitution: Article 33 states that 'men and women shall have equal rights in family, political, social and economic life'; Article 32, 'All persons shall be equal before the law'; and Article 47, 'Everyone shall have the right to make decisions about their personal life'. However, the judgement made clear that the rights and benefits of the *family* unit count for more:

> Abuse may be recognised as committed through necessity imposed by the desire to preserve marriage or justified by the well-being of children or the alleged victim or any other value protected by law and more important than the *dubious dignity of misconducting victims*. In such circumstances, even if violence amounts to domestic abuse, it may still be recognised as not meeting the criteria of an offence. (Dominiczak, 2010: italics added)

This ruling was by the state rather than the church. However, the fact that some church-supported legal institutions provide free advice for victims of violence, but 'require volunteers to sign papers forbidding them to advise divorce as a solution as this goes against Christian values' (Dziewanowska, Khomuk, Krawczyk, 2010), suggests agreement between church and state on the irrelevance of abuse in certain circumstances. The crucial issue is the integrity of the family, to which end individuals should subordinate themselves, as Pius XI explained in his *Casti Conubii* of 1930: 'In other things, there must be a certain inequality and due accommodation [between the parties] which is demanded by the good of the family' (Vatican, 1930).

Apart from blaming the plaintiff, there are at least two problems with the Polish judgement. Firstly, unless divorce is followed by intentional parental alienation, children are damaged by covert as well as overt parental squabbling and violence long before a marriage has ended. Divorce did not break that family: it *was* broken. Secondly, 'family' is not an idol before which members should be sacrificed: it may be caring or loathing nuclear, caring or loathing extended; it may uphold each member or demolish the weak; it may be a safe nest for growing children or a disaster. Likewise, an extended family can assist a feuding couple to sort out marital problems but may exacerbate them, especially for wives living with their husband's family. Families are neither holy nor wholly perfect.

However, it is not only in Poland that a wall is erected around each family, violence within being a 'private family matter' or where the maintenance of the family outweighs the legal rights of individuals to live free of violence. The designation of 'private' to violent acts within the family, even if these take place in public, allows outsiders to ignore the fact of violence. This goes against the suggestion in an early cross-cultural text on marital violence (Counts, Campbell and Brown, 1992, 1999) which assumes that wives are safer in 'face to face societies'. Violence *may* be facilitated when couples live in isolated houses, but the pretence of privacy can produce collective blindness in the closest-knit community.

The way of being a person: Marriage

Culture and power are basic to the acceptance, condoning or rejection of spousal violence, and crucial in creating and defending the behaviour and expectations on which it relies. Ethnicity too: neither Koreans, Indians nor Americans are portrayed primarily by *baekjeong*, *dalit* or rednecks, nor are their ways of being. Louder privileged voices seek to speak for and thus control 'lesser' people, however so defined. We must therefore always ask: 'Who says or thinks what about whom?' But first comes marriage, creating husbands and wives and informing their ongoing relationship.

Marriage is the intentionally entered into 'bed and board' relationship between one man and one woman. (Other forms, such as ghost marriage, levirate, short-contract or same-sex, have long existed. Violence within such marriages would be as offensive as in ubiquitous male-female marriage.) Each marriage in a polygynous or polyandrous context is between a man and a woman, and though forbidden for most Christians, its regional availability may silence abused wives reliant on a husband's support if he can easily add another wife. Marriage defines affiliation of children born to the union and rights to resources of family members during and after the marriage, whether that ends in death or divorce. It commonly includes a degree of affection between the spouses and support by both families.

Marriage *always* includes a list of expectations and responsibilities for each party which, depending on area and income, traditionally sees husbands providing the family with raw food and shelter, and wives caring for children, cooking and being exclusively available to husbands. Shortfall on either side may cause problems. The failure of the wife to produce children, cook on time or look pretty easily 'validates' attacking her, failure in the husband being dealt with differently if at all. A seminary chaplain in Yangon, for example, felt it correct that 'a husband he knew hit his wife because she doesn't cook or look after the children properly'. My suggestion that a short-changed wife might have some come-back horrified him. Tongan men should provide food for the table. But if he doesn't, the wife does, finding taro, borrowing, going together with other women to forage: 'If she doesn't find food, her in-laws blame her for not cooking but they do not blame their son'. Many a wife in modern cities knows that line all too well.

In many regions of the world, a married woman was wholly or partially subordinate to though not owned by her husband. Legal and social changes over the last fifty years have ameliorated or ended that, yet vestiges of past expectations remain. Marriage in patrilineal systems transferred responsibility for and control of the woman from father to husband, the wife thereafter being subject to his discipline and that of his family whose honour she may be expected to maintain. The husband lost that honour, however, if he hit his wife in public, both in Europe or further afield: if ordained, publicly abusing his wife may see him sacked, private sin apparently counting less. A pastor's son in a Franco-German parish explained the honour process:

> Our family knew she was being hit by her husband, an Elder, and that afterwards he would sit outside the bathroom where she'd taken shelter, loudly reading certain passages from the Bible to make her more obedient. People who heard him told us, but she never said anything because she knew she'd be accused of 'dirtying the name of his family', making life in the village impossible. Officially my father 'didn't know', and so the husband carried on being an Elder.

An important point for any discussion of marital violence and the need for sanctuary or support is: does the woman as wife remain a full or partial member of her natal family, in which case she may have a place of retreat, or is that tie cut, rendering her more dependent on her new family and therefore more vulnerable? Perhaps the clearest retention of birth ties occurs among matrilineal communities in Northeast India, Indonesia, North America and pockets elsewhere, where identity and assets are inherited directly through the mother: divorce is neither uncommon nor particularly disruptive. In Christian matrilineal Meghalaya, for example, fathers may officially be heads of households, a role more than balanced by the wife's superior economic and social status and perhaps not coincidentally by a low rate of spousal violence and, despite its Roman Catholicism, the third highest divorce rate in India. The other end of the natal-tie spectrum, in which a married woman moves totally to her husband's family, affecting her choices in a crisis, is found in China and other East Asian regions, much of South Asia, and to a varied extent in the Middle East and parts of Africa.

The unwelcome return of a married daughter may shame her parents, especially her mother who 'failed' to train her in proper wifely demeanour. Stories abound of 'a young woman whose mother sent her home to her husband again only to have him kill her'. Typical is this abused woman's experience in Pakistan, where Christian and Muslim expectations overlap:

> A Muslim taxi driver picked up a pregnant bloodied Christian woman, taking her to her parents' house: she'd left after a beating from her husband, angry that she'd found out he already had a wife. Doubtful about her reception, the driver waited outside and when, as expected, she was quickly flung out, took her to his own family until she found a safe place. It was not a matter of money as she had a regular job, but her parents' shame.

Retaining links may give the chance to 'go home' if the marriage becomes unbearable or, if space or money does not allow, to receive actual and emotional support, although variations are legion, even in one region. In Ghana, women of the broadly patrilineal Ga retain their membership in their own family, whereas Tallensi women, a little further north, lose it. Women of the Akan people, where inheritance is indirectly through females, retain their membership, readily quoting the Akan proverb to a departing husband: 'If you divorce me I shall not eat stones' (Dolphyne, 1991:9). From the West Indies (depending on class) to London's East End of old (see Wilmott and Young, 1957), mothers and daughters retain very close and even daily links, with marriage somewhat irrelevant to family survival. Unless the natal break is total, the gender make-up of a family, local expectations, personal relations, economic needs and absence of violence in the parental home will all affect a married woman's capacity to retain or revive her natal family ties. Yet leveraging her way out of a violent marriage, assisted by retained natal ties, will only be half the battle if divorce and remarriage exile her from her church.

Marriage: Contract or covenant?

So much for relations between a marrying pair and their natal families, but practically and theologically what *is* a marriage? Is it a *contract* between two people, or a *covenant* between them and God, or a melding of both, and are the man and the woman, both children of God made in God's Image, equally or unequally ranked within the relationship? The latter thread continues throughout this book, so let us here examine 'contract or covenant' more thoroughly, for the difference can affect not only an abused wife's decision to stay or leave, but also her chances of retaining full church membership. First, what *is* contract or covenant marriage?

A contract, and this excludes short-term marriage contracts occurring in parts of Africa and the Middle East, is an agreement between two parties, commonly seen as equal, primarily for the ownership of or access to property, the exchange of goods and services, and the ordering of social relationships. A negotiated contract commonly forms the basis for all pre-marriage discussions between the individuals or their families: who gives or pays for what, what property each brings to the marriage, where or near whom the new couple will live. Where a marriage is seen primarily as a contract, both parties are also expected, indeed obliged, to hold to the conditions agreed, such as fidelity, support and respect, an unacceptable breach voiding the contract.

A covenant will also commonly be preceded by contractual discussions and carry the same expectation regarding conditions. However, while contracts are normally between equals, a covenant or treaty which defines the relationship between two parties, their responsibilities and rights, is either between *equals*, mutually agreeing the terms, or *unequals*, where the stronger asserts control over the weaker. In the Christian and indeed in certain other traditions, a covenant to live in justice and love is made by the marrying pair each of whom is equally inferior to God. Biblically, a breach of a contractual covenanted agreement made before and 'supervised by' God causes God to withdraw care until the defaulting party recants. In marital violence, therefore, the assailant should lose God's protection. However, breached expectations in a covenanted marriage commonly works differently in practice. The couple are clearly not equal to God, but nor is the wife equal to the husband: the covenant is therefore unequal.

One problem with such a marriage is that it easily lends itself to the idea that the 'superior' has the right and even the duty to keep the 'inferior' in line for the good of her soul. As we shall see later, this occurs in some Church Fathers' writing, becomes even stronger in the medieval period and was clearly evident in this research. Where the 'inferior' is committed to God and the church, she may be constrained (as in the Polish case) to remain in a violent marriage (see Starr, 2018).

Let us see how informants perceived the covenant-contract basis of marriage, and what effect it might have on decisions. Older Scottish women, whether Presbyterian, Roman Catholic or Scottish Episcopal, tended towards 'keeping the vows within reason'. Marriage was a covenant and, for most, this included the word 'obey', put in the Presbyterian service in 1564 on the model of Calvin's Genevan 1542 text and continued in all three churches until recently. Scots law made clear that marriage was a contract, though the merging of the secular with the religious is indicated in Lord Stair's seventeenth-century comment:

> It is a divine and not a human contract; the obligations arising from it are not like those which 'take their rule and substance from the will of man'. It cannot, for example, be arbitrarily limited in its duration [nor] so framed as to invert the relative position which nature has assigned to the sexes. (Stair, 1675)

In other words, Scots marriage is a contract with strongly covenantal elements, including the 'natural' subordination of one party. However, for almost five hundred years it has been rendered void by adultery or desertion by *either* party, with re-marriage fully accepted. Younger Scots women of all three traditions were less likely to feel controlled by obedience, no long in marriage liturgies, nor to see marriage as a covenant.

A 'covenant with contractual elements' likewise held in early New England, exemplified in the 1760 diary of Abigail Bailey, whose violent husband also committed incest and adultery:

> Gladly would I have remained a kind, faithful obedient wife to him as I had ever been. But I told Mr B he *knew* he had violated his marriage covenant, and hence had forfeited all legal and just right and authority over me. (Taves, 1989:78)

A female Roman Catholic church worker in Tonga felt strongly that 'for better for worse' is used against women, yet each had promised to love and care for the other. She explained:

> Both the men and the church say it is a covenant, and I agree it is sacred, but both say to her 'but you promised to obey me/him'. The church says it when they go to counselling, and the police say it if she goes there.

Both Roman Catholic and Methodist women in the local Women's Centre in Tonga insisted marriage is also a contract, 'though church people pick out lines from the Bible to tell her it is a covenant and she will turn her back on God if she leaves'. No mention is made of the man turning his back on God by breaking his vow.

Discussions with Presbyterian ladies of Indian origin in Trinidad (from a Hindu background which abhors divorce) evinced both versions. Setting up the scenario of a husband who repeatedly hit his wife, I asked whether seeing the marriage as a contract or a covenant affected the woman's course of action. An initial response was: 'It is a covenant with God, so she cannot leave just because he hit her.' Another lady suggested they needed to think about it: silence ensued. She then said: 'It maybe a covenant but it is also a contract, and the agreement is to support and help each other. If one side fails, the contract is void: that's how business contracts run.' Her view was upheld by most others at the meeting.

In Korea, Presbyterian churches and their pastors saw a marriage contract as not traditional (marriage under Confucianism being for life) and therefore accepted only a covenant view of marriage. However, a few female pastors and active laywomen recognized the excessive power the covenant-only view gave an abusing husband over a devout wife. Moreover, not all male pastors rejected the contractual element of a covenant. One shocked his audience by saying: 'If a lady comes to me and says, "I am being hit and hit and hit," I say to her: "Leave him and divorce him, because he is not keeping his agreement."'

Some Roman Catholic and Presbyterian leaders in Taiwan felt discussing violence might increase divorces, though were equally aware that the human rights of each person counted, Presbyterians being at the forefront of the human rights movement in Taiwan. One clarified covenant and contract:

> Most churches are not keen on divorce. People see it as a covenant, but it is also a contract. Both parties have to sign. If one side breaks the agreement, a contract is normally void. Clearly, there's an extra issue in a marriage contract because it is also a government agreement. But the man by beating his wife has broken his sacred agreement, his solemn contract.

A group of nuns in Pakistan shared that view. Despite hoping for reconciliation amid violence, 'We say that both adultery and violence break the covenant of marriage: *insisting it is unbreakable oppresses abused women*.' A leading Roman Catholic theologian in Taiwan accepted divorce was best in cases of persistent violence, with an annulment a possible next step, yet diocesan Roman Catholic priests and older True Jesus Church men there insisted that marriage was an unbreakable covenant, cancelled only by an annulment. Younger people from both churches veered to the 'covenant with strong contractual element, voided by violence'.

During a long discussion with Kenyan theologians, I asked whether a violent husband has broken the marriage covenant by abuse: 'Isn't a marriage also a contract between two people and families?' The informant responded with: 'That is the difference between the West and Africa: we see marriage as heavenly,' despite the bargaining over dowry or bride-price, cattle and feasting beforehand. More usefully, the male discussant then pointed out that 'marriage as contract is seen as temporary. African Christian marriage *could* be seen as a contract, but it must be permanent.' This touches on the point made above of alternate local forms of marriage affecting the attitude to and process of Christian marriage.

Marriage is now a sacrament and thus essentially a covenant in Roman Catholic and Orthodox theology, although for the latter only the first marriage, a second being just 'sacramental'. It has only formally been a sacrament in the Roman church since 1439, the first widely accepted liturgy stemming from 1570. Church marriage may well be a sacramental covenant, but for centuries, by no means all followers actually married there, each saying 'I marry you *now*' before family and friends or a prelate. In the Reformation, Protestant churches adopted the civil rather than the sacramental nature of marriage, allowing divorce and stressing the contractual and equal nature of the relationship, explored further in Chapter 3. The 'equal' element soon slipped back to earlier patterns. However, a 'contractual with varying degrees of covenantal but not sacramental' view of marriage has remained for Protestant churches although, as we have seen, a Presbyterian tradition in Korea and Trinidad became firmly covenantal in accordance with specific local expectations. Anglican views, as Roman Catholic, veer to the covenantal, although each may follow a rather more contractual view in practice.

Precepts and practices change both within and across churches, explained by an Anglican priest in Ghana, a supporter of divorce for abused women:

> Leaving a marriage is seen as breaking a religious sacrament, or covenant. Most people don't see it as a contract which can be abrogated, because they think that is not of God, and it separates from God. They think they must try everything possible and that divorce is the last resort. But that is changing. Vows are not felt as strongly. Both men and women have the same vow. And the theology of marriage is changing. It's increasingly seen as companionship. Creation of children is less important, which is good because it removes the 'right' of the man to get another wife if she hasn't produced.

Roman Catholic practice, discussed in Chapters 5 and 6, varies from rejecting those who have left violent marriages without an annulment to the generally quiet advice from a number of priests to 'get out, get divorced and live'.

Divorce is affected not only by particular church rules, but by the place of the married woman in her natal family which, as we have seen, varies considerably. As subsequent chapters show, the possibility of divorce radically affects abused women's choices and safety. Family support, wealth or poverty has long affected decisions, the rich getting annulments or divorces, the poor grimly cohabiting or moving for a fresh start with a new partner or alone (see Luther 1970:234 and Dillard 1984:95).

Marriage and culture

Talk of the social context in which a particular marriage begins or indeed ends brings us to 'culture' as instrumentally used. The term covers collective ways of acting in, understanding and seeing the world which are considered appropriate for males and females among peoples of or from a very loosely defined region, or other visible or less visible community whether intentionally created or given. Earlier social science saw 'cultures' as clearly bounded entities, all within behaving in one way and all outside in another: internal variation meant deviation if not plain deviance. The 'pure' core of a culture was thus readily defined and simply described, rather than seen as fuzzy, multi-layered and conflicted. Yet neither now nor in centuries past have people held to a hermetically sealed closed tradition, with each member part of a tightly fitting jigsaw. People may still insist *their* 'culture' is unchanging and sovereign, as did this irritated pastor in India: 'It may well be that man and woman are made in the Image of God, but my culture allows me to hit my wife, so I do.' Worshipping culture offends the Second Commandment and is no friend of faith.

A multi-cultural situation such as at a Baptist-Presbyterian church in the Congo, attended by Hema, Biva and Alur, brings other complexities. Biva do not punch wives, as that dishonours the abuser, though a slap does not; Hema hit readily; a hit Alur wife complains to her father. Hema are the richest group at church, but Hema women prefer marrying out into relative poverty than being treated 'worse than a cow'. My clerical informant pointed out that the church sees itself as dealing with spiritual things, leaving marriage and marriage relations to culture. The ensuing silence about marital violence, he agreed, not only reduces the chance of offending rich Hema, but prevents sound teaching.

In subtler forms, this scenario is present wherever those of different ethnicity, race, class, caste or wealth join a church, a situation commonly managed or avoided by self-selection. So often, both 'culture' and 'ethnic' are applied to generally poorer others, neatly exemplified by certain richer mission-supporting agencies in North America, parts of Europe, and increasingly Nigeria and Korea which assume *they* live in a 'culture-free true-faith zone'. *No* context is free of the constant subliminal interplay between faith and cultural context.

But this is not a game played just by those in faith communities, as indicated in Chapter 1. Fighting with 'culture', whether the arena is religion or employment or marriage, is just using an available weapon – 'cultural', scriptural, philosophical – to bring a whiff of validity to actions, intentions or arguments. Our negotiating and bargaining backcloth is primarily that of the locality or segment within which we function and, unless we have been immersed in other ways, we tend not to see much less accept it as peculiar to our social context and milieu. The local version of any supra-local faith tradition becomes the norm, texts being massaged to comfort or maintain face rather than confront. Nineteenth-century English churchgoers sang 'The rich man in his castle, the poor man at his gate, God made them high or lowly and ordered their estate', totally ignoring Jesus' strictures on wealth in their support of a class-based society. This example from a Muslim woman in Accra illustrates a similar twisting of the text:

> I went to the imam because my husband had attacked me when six months pregnant. On hospital advice, I said I couldn't have sex. He was so angry he raped me twice that night: my two babies died. The imam said it was my fault for rejecting him, that the penalty would be one thousand angels descending on my head, and that was why men needed more than one wife, to use another when one was unavailable.

Apart from appalling care of a bereaved woman, the imam's comment is theologically wrong, ill health removing any sexual obligation of a Muslim woman to her husband. Both perpetrator and imam were relying on Ghanaian male norms, *exactly* as would any Ghanaian ordained or lay Christian abuser. Indeed, talking to several married ordained men in Ghana, their first response to my asking about spousal violence was to voice their suffering, 'because if we want sex and our wives deprive us of our rights, it is painful, and some men become so depressed by such abuse they die'. Having 'paid for the field they had the right to plough it', a view shared by Roman Catholic men, irrespective of their wife's discomfort. Callous inexactitude to fit local norms and personal inclinations, part of the Christian as of any tradition, easily trumps love and justice.

Marriage and power

Contract and covenant, natal links and culture, leads to the nub of the problem. The exercise of power over wives by husbands is commonly condoned by religious authorities as well as social contexts, although death or permanent damage is usually excluded. Cited in Chapter 1, common biblical verse fragments used to validate 'power over' wives include Ephesians 5.22 'Wives obey your husbands', 'Adam was not deceived but the woman was deceived' (1 Timothy 2.14), Genesis 3.16 'Your husband shall rule over you,' and 1 Peter 3.1 'wives accept the authority of your husband'. But what *is* power? At one level, power is necessary: the police have the power to stop dangerous drivers, a great music teacher the power to enthuse a school choir, a transport company the power to ensure drivers are where they should be. That is power *for* something, not primarily power *over*. However, if the company boss starts exerting power *over* by keeping drivers away from families *just because he can*, drivers may leave; if the teacher's determination for a great choir oppresses, pupils may sing less sweetly.

But how does 'power over' work without weapons of mass or minimal destruction? A customary approach sees power as the probability that A can get B to do what A wills, using force if necessary. Such naked power is exercised whether or not it is authorized by the institutional context in which that power is exercised, be that state, church or whatever. This is essentially 'power over', which in the context of spousal violence is shown in the kicking, slapping, knifing, killing and other forms of abuse set out in the previous chapter. Authority legitimates power, and apparently authoritative texts 'validate' violence against wives, even if their props stand on sand. The fear of brute force, and the probability of its exercise, leads potential victims to take evasive action. However, if one person wishes to attack the other, walking on eggshells rarely helps if she is just *there* for the more powerful player to vent his spleen and assert the proper order of things. Interestingly, the idea that marital abuse involved power over the victim was strongly opposed by a number of (male) English clergy on a recent domestic violence safeguarding course. However, an abuse survivor from a conservative American Christian background insisted that where 'theology promotes a power differential between men and women, it fosters the sort of abuse of power that devolves into abuse' (in Haddad, 18 November 2018).

Yet a more refined use of power is so internalized that those being controlled neither recognize nor therefore oppose it. The issue here is thus not only how power in husband-wife relations is *overtly* exercised than how it is secured through wives' *internalized* consent. But why would a sane wife freely consent to being hit, or be so subordinated she does not resist or even realize? The Italian sociologist Gramsci and his followers (Lukes, 2004) insist that the (hegemonic) power exerted by the husband relies on cultural or religious expectations about society's ordering, sadly relevant where active personal faith is malignly recruited to accept violence. In the context of marital violence, the husband gets the wife to accept both her subordinate place and punishment, a common process within social relationships, and far easier to achieve if such social norms are underpinned by particular readings of scripture.

These two modes of explicit and hegemonic power are not as separable in everyday life as the models suggest and this example from South Australia illustrates. At a Lutheran marriage in South Australia, the groom's uncle drew his nephew aside:

> A word of advice. Early on in your marriage, when there is no problem at all, hit your wife, and when she says, 'Why did you do that,' raise your finger and say, 'Because I can.' The horrified nephew said, 'Why would I do that?' The uncle replied, 'If you do that at the beginning, she'll learn, and that'll keep her in order.'

When that uncle was young, a wife would have known her subordinate situation so well an 'educative' slap would have been unnecessary. However, she may still have received it, some husbands at that time seeing their wives as good for 'bed, board, and beating' as one very old and gentle informant, a local bread delivery boy in his youth, explained in 1990.

Such advice is not rare. A Kenyan pastor from the Jesus Christ Victory Church advised a discussant's boyfriend about his forthcoming marriage:

> 'She has to know even if you do not beat her that you can.' My boyfriend was annoyed about such words, but he knows the pastor had told his wife on their wedding day, 'I can beat you if I want to,' and all the older men at the wedding thought that was fine.

Abused wives who have not yet 'lost their self' may use what agency, power and room for manoeuvre their context, status and interests afford. Apparent consent may long have masked inner dissent, leading some abused wives to leave apparently on a sudden whim: circumstances may have changed; a now-married daughter offers refuge; a support network is found; a sudden appreciation that domination is illegitimate, as with the 63-year-old confirmand in Chapter 1; the realization in later life that life is too short to be ruined, as an abused divorcing Taiwanese woman of seventy-four jubilantly told an applauding Synod; or the strengthening of state laws. Staying does not necessarily mean the woman recognizes abuse as legitimate, though she may if that makes enduring more bearable. Leaving may mean the woman has ceased to police herself, and can recognize that many. separate acts of violence make one continuously violent relationship. Assumptions can so easily patronize.

Reflection

This foray into marriage, its purpose and process, its starting and finishing, has indicated ways in which marital violence runs through lives and therefore also churches across the world. Local understanding of the person, and of the way to live, informs and shapes the blinkers through which inevitably inculturated faith is seen and biblical texts are reshaped to suit. It has ever been so. Yet while marriage, culture and power are always present, so is change, and we must be careful not to fossilize assumptions. Two centuries and more ago, the position of women both socially and spiritually was high in Tonga but that is largely a memory; a century ago, divorced people were excluded from the Eucharist in many churches; arguably women bishops are creatures just of the last fifty years.

Power runs like a rope through the entire discussion, whether exercised by the institutions organizing faith communities and doctrines, by international organizations establishing rights-based rules which may irritate if not offend locally interpreted faith traditions, or by individual abusers. It is present in social media, spreading knowledge about the failures of faith institutions and individual leaders as well as alternative doctrines and views. Power *could* be exerted by church members to oppose marital violence and support the damaged. Choosing not to act is itself an act of power over the person whose needs are thereby ignored.

Power can work for good and, equally, power can support evil. The theologian Wink said some years ago that 'with some thrilling exceptions, the churches of the world have never yet decided that domination is wrong' (1998:11). Evidenced in this chapter, domination over wives by husbands will be examined historically in the next as we consider the contribution of churches to the abuse of women.

3

The disciplining of wives in church history

Marital violence is often dismissed as occurring 'elsewhere' or among 'those people'. That sense of a 'wholly foreign country' can also be the case for the past. The fact that Christians have supported as well as rejected violence against wives for at least the last 1600 years should stop us assuming that a little tweaking, a little teaching, will resolve the issue. *Every* faith community, *all* faith teaching, *all* faith practice, is embedded in specific cultural and historical assumptions, ready to harness the Divine for the worship of Our Way. Moreover, historical assumptions and ideas do not stay in the past but reappear in response to a somewhat similar set of circumstances or anxieties. An accepted view of the Trinity, with the three persons 'co-equal and eternally present', in contrast to internal ranking for example, was more or less settled by the fourth century. Yet for the last century, and increasingly since the mid-1970s, this doctrine is again being challenged by those who wish to subordinate Jesus permanently to the Father and women to men.

This chapter considers two threads of thought and teaching in the early Christian, medieval and early modern periods, one being that of Chrysostom and Laurence Hispanus and the other Augustine and Huguccio of Pisa. The first pair opposed and the latter accepted violence against wives. Aquinas contributed to the argument, but it was Gratian's legal code of 1140, following the Augustinian line, which more or less set the rule, via the Council of Trent, until 1917. Sixteenth-century reformers in Europe increasingly stressed the companionship aspect of marriage, facilitating the legal end of violent or adulterous marriages or those where one party had been deserted. Subsequent changing attitudes to violence in marriage were part of secular developments of the later European Enlightenment, based on the ideal of the reasonable man scorned for vulgar violence: theology played little part.

The early and medieval church

The theologian Sister Mary John Manzanan noted some years ago:

> Even though Christ showed a remarkable breakthrough in his relationship with women, his apostles did not seem to learn this aspect of his message, and very soon there was a repatriarchisation of the Early Church. (1994:51)

Such a process is arguably exemplified in Augustine, who towers above others in early Western Christian thought but not Eastern, where Chrysostom holds sway. Of his mother Monica, often assumed to have been abused in marriage, he wrote:

> When many matrons who had milder husbands than hers appeared with marks of beating on their faces and began to complain about their husbands' behaviour in their chats, she would tell them seriously that once they had heard the matrimonial tablets read, they should have considered them as a document that made them slaves of their husbands, and they should remember their status and not think of insubordination against their lords. (Confessions IX.9)

Such pre-Christian tablets, clarifying the rights and duties of each party to the marriage contract, were long retained in the North Africa of his birth (Hunter, 2003). Their intent is still a point of reference, an abused English vicar's wife being unimpressed when recently advised by a female parishioner to 'model yourself on St Monica who was abused but stayed and produced St Augustine'.

He does not explicitly support his mother's treatment. However, his Roman views on rank within the family make clear the man as the head of the household carried the right, indeed the moral duty, to save the unruly in the family from mortal sin by chastising them, other than in *sine manu* marriages (Power, 1995:26) in which the wife retained natal benefits. Writing of Christian domestic life, Augustine notes that although the Christian longs for heaven, 'where there will be no further need for giving orders to other human beings';

> Those who are true fathers of their household desire and endeavour that all members of their household, equally with their own children, should worship and win God ... and if any member of the family interrupts its peace by disobedience, they are corrected by word or blow. (quoted in Power:80)

A Christian husband, Augustine said, should love his wife like Jesus' command to 'love our enemies' (DeConick, 2011:123). He cannot unequivocally be said to have supported the hitting of a wife by her husband, although he outlined certain patterns of thought which enabled it, especially the maintenance of peace in the familial whole at the expense of the parts. He states, in opposition to 1 Corinthians 11.7 ('a man is the image and reflection of God, but woman is the reflection of man'), that women *were* created in God's Image at creation, rather than just through any salvific benefit gained through Christ. However, he qualified that by insisting that in her role as her husband's helpmate, a married woman does *not* image God, marriage changing both her legal and spiritual status. The spiritual subordination of women as wives is as inevitable as their socio-legal subordination under husbands.

He uses the abstract spiritual marriage of Christ (male superior) and the church (female inferior) as the paradigm for actual human marriage which, if the first is accepted, puts pressure on the parallel roles in the second. Seeing the persons of the Trinity and their internal relationship as indicative of relations between husband and wife can run into serious problems. The Trinity for Augustine was an interweaving trio of equals, although that had been rather challenged by the hierarchical nature within the Roman family, exacerbated after Constantine, when the entire church imitated the hierarchy of the state. Strands from this early period, some linked to neo-Platonic non-Christian schools of thought, have been adopted by certain modern church groups which break the Oneness of the Trinity, with God as the authority over Jesus the functionally submissive Son, just as women are subordinate to men. It was this which an ordinand in South Asia put forward as the reason why the bottom-rung wife is bound in obedience to a superior, if violent, husband, who is under Jesus who is under God, the Holy Spirit losing out in that scheme.

Basil of Caesarea, another significant writer of influence from the Eastern church, wrote explicitly on the proper response of a beaten woman. Just as the wife of an adulterer, thief or unbeliever must stay married, so too must a beaten wife remain with her abuser, her faithful witness turning him from sin, still an expectation amid abuse (see Chapter 6). Husbands, on the other hand, may leave adulterous wives and re-marry. Basil continues: 'In the case of her being beaten, and refusing to submit, it would be better for her to endure than to be separated from her husband' (Basil, Letter 88). Basil's view of active women was firmly negative. Explaining intended and unintended consequences, Basil judged men whose wielding of a cudgel killed the opponent to be guilty merely of *unintentional* killing 'for all he had in his mind was to give the man a thrashing not do him to death' (Letter 88). However, the woman whose seducing potions inadvertently killed her love object was guilty of *intentional* killing, even though neither intention nor act was aggressive, because her means were illegitimate.

Ambrosiaster, while saying nothing directly about abuse, sets the scene for it. For him, women *could* mirror God through Christ, but were not equal at creation, and thus definitely not made in God's Image (Hunter, 1992:447). A Roman aristocrat and churchman, he defended his view by grasping at straws: 'For how can it be said that the woman is the Image of God, when she is subject to the dominion of the male and has no authority? For she is not able to teach, nor be a witness.' He was using a fact from the secular world to support his interpretation of the sacred, a domestication of the Gospel which was no less problematic in ancient Rome than now. Moreover, man, any man, 'holds the imperium of God as his vicar, since every ruler bears the Image of God, and that is why the woman is not made in the Image of God' (Hunter:452). Husbands as the pastor of the family, recurring from the early fifteenth century and still including 'correcting wives for their salvific benefit', have a long pedigree.

John Chrysostom opposed Augustine's often negative-view of marriage in what was both a more complex and yet more pastoral approach. For Chrysostom, both male and female have the same origin, soul and substance: 'He made the one man Adam to be the origin of all mankind, both male and female' (Homily on Ephesians). However, man's authority over her means she is not made in God's Image, her role being useful but subordinate, although the making of Eve as Adam's helper (*ezer*), which as Chrysostom rightly says means superior, inferior, or equal, gave her a good start. His pastoral interest included the behaviour of partners in marriage.

This orientation was integrated with his theology, his Homily on Ephesians noting that 'husband and wife are one body in the same way as Christ and the Father are one' (in Ford, 54). His commitment to both parties as equally made of God was clear:

> Adamant that no husband should hit his wife for any reason, he exhorts husbands to rule their wives gently, without resorting to physical and emotional threats, and while encouraging persistence by generic abused wives, several times advises Christian women who have left violent husbands not to go back. (Schroeder, 2004:414)

Talking more directly to women, he notes: 'If he beats you every day, constantly picking fights [over the issue of immoral or idolatrous acts] it is better to separate ... Such a partner is as much to blame for such a separation as a partner guilty of fornication' (Homily on Corinthians). As a last resort, he allowed divorce on the grounds that 'we see many who come to be together for evil, even by the law of marriage, and this we should not ascribe to God' (Homily on Romans).

Of marriage, he writes:

> One's partner in life, the mother of one's children, the source of one's every joy, should never endure fear and threats but love and kindness. What kind of marriage can there be when the wife is afraid of her husband or in dread he does not love her. The husband who does not make his wife the loved one in the family has failed as a husband and as a man. (Homily on Ephesians)

Chrysostom makes clear both that a wife is not a slave and that loss of control leading to violence is childish and unmanly, in phrases borrowed a thousand years later by Protestant writers in England and New England. Particularly important in both the field research and the historical development is: who is shamed by beating, the aggressor or the victim? This long extract from his Homily to the Corinthians gives a clear answer:

> For a wife to be beaten is the extremest affront, not to her that is beaten, but to him who beateth. And if the shame be great for a man to beat a maidservant, much more to stretch forth the right hand against her that is free. And this one might see even from heathen legislatures who no longer compel her that hath been so treated to live with him that beat her, as being unworthy of her fellowship … There is the shame too: I would fain know who can endure it. And what description can set it before us, when shrieks and wailings are borne along the alleys, and there is a running to the house of him that is so disgracing himself, both of the neighbours and the passers-by, as though some wild beast were ravaging within? Better were it that the earth should gape asunder for one so frantic, than that he should be seen at all in the forum after it.

His rejection of 'real man hitting' has clearly failed to sink into Christians across the world. However, the Augustinian view that a husband discipline and control his wife lest her rebellion and lust increase has cast a long shadow.

A key contributor to that shadow was the medieval theologian and Doctor of the Church Thomas Aquinas, whose understanding of power influenced church life. In his discussion of domination in 'The production of the woman', a category of human which he saw as not quite made in the Image of God, Aquinas sees 'servile subjection' as problematic, 'because a superior makes use of a subject for *his* own benefit … but in the other kind of subjection, domestic or civil, the superior makes use of his subjects for *their* own benefit and good' (1952:489). Sadly, he ignores one consequence of the 'Fall' which affects all, whether made correctly as Adam or incompletely as Eve. Humans lack perfect dispassion and disinterest for more than a fleeting moment, especially if their own interests are involved. This affects the capacity of any 'superior' to separate what benefits accrue solely to him or her, and what to those she or he dominates. The slippery relationship between 'my personal need' and 'your salvific benefit' becomes a charter for abuse.

Yet as with the early Christian discussions, Aquinas's was not the only voice. There was uncertainty in church law about a husband's right to chastise his wife. Civil law had not allowed a man to attack his wife violently, but neither did it say he could chastise her 'moderately': hitting a free-born person was unacceptable. Gratian developed the rule of moderate chastising in his 1140 first volume of what eventually became canon law: 'A man may chastise his wife and beat her for her own correction; for she is of his household and the lord may chastise his own, so likewise the husband is bound to chastise the wife in moderation.' Whether that meant with a stick, a slap or until blood flowed depended on local custom: that it excluded manslaughter and permanent harm was clear. The influential canon lawyer Huguccio of Pisa drew vivid pictures of marriage:

> If she is to be judged in matters of behaviour, because she does not cook and prepare food well, or she does not tend her husband's goods properly, or she is very troublesome and does not clean her nose, and minimal things of this sort, she can certainly be judged and corrected and beaten by her husband ... she is judged by the law to be almost the husband's servant. (quoted in Kelly, 1994:359)

Huguccio's views, incidentally, evoke those of the Hillel party of Jewish thinkers at the time of Jesus. He naturally did not support their view on 'divorce for any reason', but his 'poor cooking' or 'burnt food' or 'finding something unseemly in her' as a reason for beating parallels the former's reasons for easy divorce (Bavli Talmud, Gittin 90a).

Against Huguccio, and writing a little later, Laurence Hispanus of Spain allowed the husband to beat his wife for minor misdeeds, but *not with rods, or by blows* (Kelly:358). Despite the conundrum (a tap with one finger?) he clearly opposed physical aggression. Huguccio's words, with his wrong or dull food cooked by an irritating near-chattel, are *still* used to 'validate' marital violence, whether Elders giving a Kenyan preacher permission to beat his wife for not having enough food for five surprise guests, an English vicar upending the spread dining table when annoyed with his wife, or countless wives hit for making the 'wrong' food, making it too soon or too late or not to her master's taste. Gratian's Canon Laws were revised in 1917 but segments referring to wives enduring abuse for a greater good were still in twentieth-century encyclicals and twenty-first-century practice.

Setting out these differing views on women evident in both the patristic and medieval periods is important, because those two threads are woven into the attitudes and arguments on marriage from then until today. A Luccan court case of 1308 in which 'the ecclesiastical court had to decide which was more important, preserving the indissolubility of marriage or protecting a member of the diocese from cruelty' (Wieben, 2010) underlay the Polish ruling in Chapter 2. Church courts in England seemed less concerned about faith than that the troubled couple live reasonably amicably, telling a violent husband to 'treat his wife with marital affection' and 'not to wound her in her limbs', or asking the wife to 'treat him peacefully and quietly and obey him humbly and not provoke him to anger' (Poos, 1995:299). These are all phrases we shall meet below.

By the later Middle Ages, it was felt time to improve the education of the average follower in part to douse the fires of heresy springing up across Europe. Fathers (that thread of Ambrosiaster again) were increasingly nominated as pastors to their family, charged with teaching and disciplining their wives and children. As Bailey noted in her discussion of the English priest Whitford's matrimonial advice book of 1515, 'The household in the sixteenth century was developing a civic arm, articulated through a programme of communal religious instruction' (2016:345). The growth of catechisms in the Roman Catholic Church clearly supported this, making clear not only that hitting wives was in order, but that where a husband had to do this because his wife's opposition was 'without good and legitimate cause', she must understand that 'she committed a mortal sin, being the cause of his evil deed' (Bast, 1997:75). The victim's opinion was not part of the above assessment.

That a husband was spiritually in charge of his wife is clear in Friar Cherobino's late fifteenth-century Rules of Marriage, which encouraged gentle teaching rather than violence, although not for wives with a 'crude and shifty spirit'. Unless their offence was just a minor failing, *they* should be beaten soundly 'for it is better to punish the body and correct the soul'. For serious sin, 'readily beat her, not in rage but out of charity and concern for her soul, so that the beating will redound to your merit and her good' (in O'Faolain and Martines, 1974: 190–1). Similarly, in Spain the benefits of wifely suffering were spelled out by Juan Vives in 'Instructions to Christian Women' of 1523, dedicated to the future Mary I of England:

> If he laid hands on you for some fault of yours or in a fit of madness, imagine that this is God punishing you, and that this is happening because of your sins, and that in this way you are doing penance for them. You are fortunate if, with a little suffering in this life, you gain remission of the torments of the next. In fact, very few good and prudent women are beaten by their husbands. (Elizonda, 1994)

In this, Vives manages both to extol suffering and to make clear that *had she been a truly good wife she would not have been hit*, still a common view. The guilt of the victim not the perpetrator, who bears little or no responsibility for his freely chosen sin, is still strongly represented in churches across the world, the first question a pastor, priest or minister often asking the woman being 'What were you doing *to make him hit you?*' Represented today too is the theme of Christ-like female suffering in marriage leading to heaven.

John Chrysostom and Augustine took different approaches to women, with Augustine's heritage staining subsequent centuries while John's bided its time, just as Huguccio and Laurence beat different medieval drums, the latter's being long-muffled.

The Reformation and beyond

Appearing sporadically in earlier centuries, regular criticism of male violence appears in texts of the Reformation. Protestants saw marriage as a good in itself and essential for the avoidance of sin, rejecting earlier views of sexuality as filthy or women as seducers. Divorce and remarriage rather than just separation were therefore necessary lest essentially single people be led into sin. The Ordinances of the reformer Zwingli in Zurich allowed divorce not only for adultery and permanent desertion but also for endangering a partner's life, two cases citing the wife being beaten 'almost to death' and breaking the woman's hips (Areen, 1999:47).

Martin Bucer in Strasbourg went further in his view of marriage, seeing it primarily for love, fellowship and mutual service. In 1533, he therefore allowed divorce for various reasons, including a partner's brutal violence and cruelty (Hopf, 1946). Early on in Geneva, Calvin was likewise willing to allow divorce and remarriage, his marriage Ordinances of 1542 forbidding wife-beating, although by 1559, an older Calvin exhorted women 'not to deviate from the duty which she has before God to please her husband, unless in danger of her life' (quoted in Tucker, 2016:90). Witte (2013:245) combed the records for cases in 1546, 1552 and 1557, finding one case in the first year, dealt with by admonition, three in the second, similarly dealt with, and twenty-two in the third, including nine admonitions, five exclusions from Communion with a degree of ostracism, seven removals from the area, and one excommunication: the authorities did actively pursue wife-beaters in that year. Philipps (1991:98) notes that between 1564 and 1569, sixty-one Genevan men and two women were convicted of spousal abuse and excommunicated or exiled. The 1546 Ordinances cite Genevan church-run state practice:

> If it is known that a husband mistreats his wife, beating and tormenting her, or that he threatens to do her an injury and is known to be a man of uncontrollable temper, let him be sent to the Council to be expressly forbidden to beat her under pain of certain punishments. (Areen: 51)

Ozment suggests that the fact that Zwingli and Calvin turned Luther's Reformation theology into law was crucial for its success and for a new phase in theological opposition to spousal violence. Without that, as Ozment puts it, 'it would have been confined within the minds of preachers and pamphleteers' (Ozment in Areen:52). Yet did this revolution unequivocally recognize that all humans were made in the Image of God, that marriage is a partnership of mutual service and love which excludes violence, and that divorce totally frees an abused partner? And if so, to what extent was this carried through in churches of Western Europe?

This is an important point for the simple reason that Roman Catholic countries such as Spain and Portugal totally integrated church and state rule in parts of Africa, Asia and the Americas from around 1500. Although French and later British, Danish and Dutch colonies had no such integrated intention, the overall outcome was that the already domesticated Western European version of Christianity spread across the world, *including marriage*, 'with the belief that a new morality would emerge if Christian marriage took the place of traditional' (Martey, 1996:64). If I might leapfrog time, a priest-friend who helped convert a region in Borneo from the late 1950s explained the process in 2000:

> 'Initially, men confessed hitting their wives, as it was wrong in Kadazan law, but after a few years they stopped confessing it but I know they still hit a bit. I had taught the English Christian way of marriage, as my teachers had taught me, not gone into the Kadazan system even though it was similar to my own. I would not do that now.'

Given the extent of world colonization from Britain, its inculturated faith has influenced many global attitudes and laws, those of Scotland being largely set aside. Let us therefore focus on England.

Following changes in marriage rules by Zwingli, Luther, Calvin and especially Bucer, whom the English cleric Cranmer knew, Cranmer prepared an initial and limited programme of church reform in 1534, which in its much altered and expanded final form was formally presented to the House of Lords in 1553 as the Church Law Reform (*Reformatio Legum Ecclesiasticarum*). It offers detailed comment on spousal violence and even better protection for women than under continental reformers. However, the Protestant King Edward died before the law reached Parliament. Marital violence was grounds for divorce, by either 'deadly hostility' (attempted poisoning) or 'ill-treatment of the wife'. This last clause reads:

> If a man is cruel to his wife and displays excessive harshness in word and deed, as long as there is hope of improvement, judges might reason with him, but if he cannot be restrained by bail and refuses to abandon his cruelty, then he must be considered his wife's mortal enemy, and a threat to her life .... In her peril recourse must be had to the remedy of divorce, unless she also was rebellious, petulant or displays evil behaviour. (*Reformatio* in Areen, 2014:51)

There is nothing here about the family good, nor of any faith advantages accruing from remaining in an unsafe marriage, the respectable wife (no slatterns, shrews or whores) being an individual with a claim to justice in her own right. Earlier judgements in church courts had taken a man's 'excessive harshness' into account: the *Reformatio* text codified both fact and remedy.

Would Cranmer's views have won had Edward lived? There would certainly have been opposition. A new edition of Matthew's 1537 Bible was published in London in 1549, with notes by Becke. Commenting on 1 Peter 3.7, that a husband should behave kindly to his wife, Becke wrote:

> He taketh his wife according to knowledge that taketh her as a necessary helper and not a bond servant or bond slave. And if she be not obedient and helpful unto him, [he] endevoureth to beat the fear of God into her head, that she may thereby be compelled to learn her dutie and to do it. (quoted in Tucker 2016:75)

'Beating the fear of God into her head' may not mean hitting her. Yet any version of beating seems a poor basis for relations between two adults pledged to honour and love each other. Becke's view brings to mind the comment of a South Indian pastor: 'You are educated so will understand your husband, but my wife isn't so I have to beat proper ideas into her head.'

Although Cranmer's hopes of changing marriage law failed, its tenets may have endured. A decade later, the Anglican Homily on Marriage of 1563 rejects violence in marriage by either party, echoing Chrysostom in saying the perpetrator should be ashamed. Moreover, the victim should be free to leave if her or his life were threatened, with the *abuser* being guilty of desertion by reneging on the agreement, as should be the case with a godly covenant. Again we hear Chrysostom in the 1563 view of the proper man:

> To beat his wife is the greatest shame that can be, not so much to her that is beaten as much as to him that doth the beating ... The common sort of man ... thinks it is a man's part to fume in anger, to fight with fist and staff. And yet a man may be a man although he doth not use such extremity .... Who would not think that it were better for such a man to wish the ground to open and swallow him in, than to go out into the market place again.

The writer has clearly experienced the arguments ('real men beat') abusers commonly use, for he responds to them point by point in the full text, later picked up by Cotton Mather in New England who makes clear (like Goodman in Chapter 1) that beating a spouse is a sacrilege (1692/Wing 1487:41). A particularly interesting point is that, after explaining that Chrysostom's heathens (here called Paynims) allowed an abused wife to leave, this 1563 homily writer says, '*Surely it is a shame that the Paynims who do not have Christ should be wiser than we*, who are commanded to resemble angels or rather God himself through meekness' (1563; italics added). Far from attributing violence to others, this text not only compares Christians to heathens unfavourably, but insists the Christian has a *greater* obligation to behave with equity and kindness.

Moreover, in discussing struggles in marriage, both husbands and wives are dealt the same hand, being advised to see the heavenly rewards. Advice is offered first to the wife: 'But if by some fortune thou chancest upon such a [bad] man, take it not too heavily, but suppose that thereby is laid up no small reward hereafter and in this lifetime no small commendation to thee, if thou canst keep quiet.' Then husbands are told:

> Peradventure thou might say [your wife] is a wrathful woman, a drunkard, a beastly, without wit and reason. Chafe not in your anger ... Furthermore, consider what reward thou shalt have at God's hand if thou abstain and bear patiently her great offences.

Such advice must be set against the near-impossibility of divorce. A lone man might risk finding another 'wife' if he moved elsewhere, state control over new partnerships in distant places being inconsistent. However, a lone woman departing with children might have at least as frightening and unsure a life alone as with all but the most violent husband.

For some years, this 1563 Homily, which in intent if not word harks back to Cranmer's attempt to reform marriage laws, seemed to fall on deaf ears as people negotiated church life in Elizabethan England. If wives did bring their husband's cruelty to the court, judges increasingly demanded formal witnesses, the mere declaration of problems by the couple being outlawed from 1604 lest they 'damage the sanctity of marriage' reinstated after the initial Reformation disruption (Ingram, 1987:184–5).

However, reform-influenced members of the Church of England, including clergy, were still expected to sort out problems, the Vicar of Wootton Rivers often 'blaming' a parishioner for beating his wife (Ingram:180). They would advise how marriage could best be managed and enjoyed by each partner, implicitly picking up on the first reason for marriage of 1563, that of living in 'perpetual friendly fellowship'. Whately, the reform-minded Vicar of Banbury, saw marriage as based on 'fidelity and due benevolence', in the absence of which separation was acceptable, a view his church vainly ordered him to rescind in the second edition. He had made clear in the 1617 edition (though not the 1619) that, while the man must be in charge, violence against a wife was totally unacceptable for 'we dare not allow him to proceed so far as to correct by blows' (Whately,1617:22). He also demanded (following Colossians 3.17) that husbands 'must be not bitter towards their wives, reviling, striking, or using other furious words and gestures' (Whately, 1617:49), maintaining authority 'not with violence but skill' (Whately, 1617:48). Richard Baxter, taking a similar approach, upheld earlier patterns of wifely subservience to authority:

> As an arch to support his church, God had built the family. The keystone of that arch, paternal authority, derived from divine commission, so that just as the several justices in the countries do govern as officers of the king, so every magistrate and master of a family does govern as an officer of the king. (1673:512)

The reformer Thomas Gataker, on the other hand, insisted that 'the wife must resolve to give herself wholly to him as to her Owner, on whom God has bestowed her, a disobedient wife being a wart, a cancer, a gangrene' (in Koehler, 1980:39).

This period is of pivotal importance not only in setting the direction for the following centuries but also because attitudes to spousal violence in New England and other parts of North America settled from Western Europe in this period are so clearly linked. The move across the Atlantic by people opposed to the English state church was soon followed by local laws on marriage. The 1630s saw Connecticut initially allowing divorce for cruelty, defined as repeated abuse over a long period threatening permanent bodily harm or death, grounds similar to permanent separation in English common law. In 1641, Massachusetts prohibited a husband from 'bodily correction or stripes' against his wife unless in his own defence. This might seem a new chapter, albeit with old phrases, yet as Dolan (2008:53) notes, North American wives were far from secure even though, having tossed off Anglican rules, divorce on the Genevan or Strasbourg basis was allowed. By the next century, such equity before the law had dwindled, accusations of family violence disappearing from Plymouth courts in response to the decline of Puritan interest in the enforcement of morality (Pleck, 1989:28). An American woman who left the family home to escape cruelty may have been seen as a rebellious deserter, but not particularly a sinner.

In the same period as Connecticut's liberal divorce law, largely Roman Catholic Maryland allowed none, nor were its abusers particularly chastised. Meyers (2003:40) cites a clear case:

> Her husband beat her ... his choice of weapon was usually made of wood, such as the cane he beat her with until he broke it all to pieces, and the oaken board that snapped in two pieces on her. She had a miscarriage, the child bruised on one side: Mrs Brooke said her husband caused the death by hitting her with large metal fire tongs.

The earlier view (still extant) that abused wives should endure what God had sent was evident in Abigail Bailey's diary from the late eighteenth century:

> God had seen fit to make use of Mr B as a rod for my awful chastisement. He had seen fit to suffer him to go on from one act of singular cruelty to another. It was impressed on my mind that God's anger was not yet turned away ... I deserve all this and infinitely more from God. (Taves, 1989:120)

Ambivalence about divorce in early America is clear, but was that universal among Protestants? Looking eastwards to Lutherans in Germany and beyond, eighteenth-century marriage sermons made clear both that wives must be obedient and that a husband's violence gives firm grounds for divorce. As a Lutheran wedding sermon put it: 'Tyrannical and bad husbands ought to be forced into exile, subjected to corporal punishment and their wives permitted to marry other men' (Karant-Nunn, 1999:35). Two specific examples of clerical advice by Lutheran pastors in different countries suggest a common social order tinged with faith. In 1755, we read of a husband in south west Germany who, angry because his wife had taken a small amount of money from him, 'choked her, threw her to the floor, tore off her dress and beat her with a stick. He was fined largely because he did it on Sunday. He was also warned to live in a Christian manner' (Sabean, 1990:135). A decade earlier in Madras, Fabricius, a Lutheran missionary from the Halle mission heard from his Dutch assistant that a woman in the Portuguese congregation (marital abuse in Indian congregations is not mentioned) had been living apart from her husband for ten months due to his harsh treatment. She wished (or needed) to return home from her friends' house. Fabricius wrote,

I *warned* her here in the Mission-house that she should subordinate herself quietly and peacefully to her husband, and I *asked* her husband to receive her with kindness and without angry accusations, [requesting] they both promise that, on an agreed day in the presence of other people and with witnesses from the congregation, they would set aside their quarrels. (HB 65C:934, my italics and translation)

New churches may have been established in every direction, but old narratives of household violence, male control and general collusion endured.

The modern world church and marital violence

The two ecclesiastical threads, one opposing and the other condoning violence against wives, continued throughout the eighteenth and nineteenth centuries and, albeit with some opposition, well into the twentieth. Personal choice apart, the right of a man to discipline errant or irritating wives was part of much Christian life irrespective of brand, with the possible except of Congregational and Salvation Army churches, both of whom ordained women from the nineteenth century based on a shared Image of God. Worldwide, the latter currently has more women than men in each officer cohort (Strickland, 2020).

Yet the world context for church life has moved on, irrevocably changed by two world wars, internet and social media, and the expansion of Buddhism and Islam, as well as the legal changes set out in the last chapter. Extra-territorial church influence and power remain, that exerted by Europe from the sixteenth century and America from the twentieth being joined by electronic preaching from East Asia and West Africa. Texts written in the American Midwest become teaching texts in Tonga: Christian material originating in Nigeria, the United States or Korea is beamed across the world, with wifely submission and attacks of the Devil exonerating husbands vying with mutual marital submission and the active care by husbands for their children. These radical changes affect church consumers and will increasingly have to be negotiated by church leaders.

Let us pause before moving to the more ethnographic Part Two and see how the two threads of Augustine, Huguccio, Gratian and Cherobino on one hand and Chrysostom, Laurence Hibernus and Bucer on the other present themselves in the contemporary world by focusing on female submission in marriage (Ephesians 5.23). Clearly a wife's submission does not mandate or even allow a husband's violence. However, within a faith context (and contexts influenced by faith) any imagined or real shortfall on her part may contribute to it.

Since 1987, an Evangelical group from the United States, the Council for Biblical Manhood and Womanhood and Women (CBMW) has had worldwide influence with a *complementarian* view of relations between partners in Christian marriage, based on the 'Natural Order' and the will of God. Women as wives should live out their inborn fixed gender-specific roles and submit to husbands like Jesus submitted to his Father, not only during his incarnate life on earth but permanently. This teaching seems to have chimed in with local faith-and-culture views in more places and churches than has the Evangelical *egalitarian* alternative, the Council for Biblical Equality (CBE), founded in the United States in 1988. As the name suggests, CBE sees roles in marriage, and indeed in church and society, as equal and open to any person, rather than being inborn attributes restricted by gender. The CBE approach has had a more restricted global influence than that of CBMW, the latter appealing to those contexts which favour male authority. After briefly examining these two Evangelical groups, we shall consider the Roman Catholic leadership's contribution to this quandary.

CBMW states:

> The Bible clearly teaches that men and women are equal in value and dignity and have distinct and complementary roles in the home and the church. If churches disregard these teachings and accommodate to the culture, then the members ... will be less likely to submit to God's word in other difficult matters as well. This hinders the sanctification of married couples.

There is a problem here, as 'accommodating to culture' is how *everyone* reads their world *and* their Bible, whether in Minneapolis or Madras. Anxiety about 'accommodating to the culture' is usually when a particular idea is objected to: I wrote some years ago of a Malaysian Anglican Archbishop barracking strongly for faith 'being part of culture' in Borneo but speaking vehemently against any such accommodation to culture in the United States (2008). A South Asian minister who fully accepted the above CBMW thesis said: 'God made us equal in his image but as he gave authority to men, women must follow that. We must follow God's orders, and if we do not discipline and even hit our wives, we sin.' Was he truly responding to God's word, or doing what he wanted and felt culturally allowed to do as a 'real man'?

The Danvers statement of 1988, essentially CBMW's founding charter, affirmed that 'Adam's headship in marriage was established by God before the Fall, and was not a result of sin', although no verse is given for the first point. The next affirmation states that the Fall distorted relations between men and women. CBMW bases marriage on Ephesians 5, *starting from verse 22*:

> Ephesians 5 calls husbands and wives to relate to one another as a picture of Christ and the church. The picture involves the humble, sacrificial leadership of the husband and the joyful, intelligent submission to that leadership by the wife. Husbands and wives who model this improperly portray a distorted and false picture of Jesus Christ, the Head and Saviour of his bride, the church.

The first CBMW statement against abuse in relationships came in 2018, making clear that it was a criminal offence and a hallmark of the Devil. Oddly, however, only two of the seven biblical verses condemning relationship abuse cited are actually about male-female abuse. The first (Proverbs 12.18) is about badly behaved men, and three more (1 Tim 3.3, Titus 1.7-8, and 1 Peter 5.3) about church leaders' behaviour to their flock: perhaps the choices assume the husband is the pastor of the family. Ephesians 5.25-9, which are cited, do talk of a husband's duty to his wife (though CBMW omits the awkward verse 21 on mutual submission) and while Colossians 3.19 expects husbands not to be harsh to their wives (as does 1 Peter 3.7), only verse 18 is cited, 'Wives be subject to your husband as is befitting to the Lord.' The pattern they expect is clear as is the allocation of responsibility.

One CBMW-influenced text is *Created to Be His Help Meet* (2004) by Debbie Pearl, with her husband Michael, who wrote much of one chapter, 'To Obey or Not to Obey' on the position of wives in especially difficult and abusive marriages. He makes clear that 'wives are to obey unreasonable and surly husbands, for they retain their headship unless they cross the bright line of criminal acts or imposing immoral behaviour on the family, bringing God or government to intervene'. Michael then (262–3) quotes 1 Peter 3 verses 1–23 *omitting* verse 7, which advises husbands to treat their wives gently lest God not hear their prayers. In place of Peter's 'servants and employees' in verse 3, Pearl inserts *wives*, 'ready to suffer in marriage for the chain of authority must remain intact even to the point of allowing some abuse … because it is acceptable to God and brings glory' (262–3). He continues:

> Lady, when God put you in subjection to a man whom he knows is going to cause you to suffer, it is with the understanding that you are obeying God by enduring wrongful suffering … [when] you bring great glory to God in heaven. You were called by God for the very purpose of suffering for him just as he suffered for you … Women who do their own will may flee from a marriage that is no fun, but women who do the will of God will enter into a plane of blessedness known only to the obedient.

Do men not need to suffer as much because, as in some schools of Buddhism, men start a rung closer to heaven or nirvana? One wonders.

Independent Baptist and Holiness churches, with which Pearl is linked, replicate such views from the West Indies to Korea, Taiwan, Queensland and Accra, where this book is regularly found, as it has been on the bookshelves of newly married couples in the United States. CBMW views are meticulously set out in Wayne Gruden's many books, and also in the popular *Happily Ever After: Finding Grace in the Messes of Marriage* by the Reform Baptist evangelists John Piper, Frances Chan et al. from 2017, in which Ephesians 5 again starts at verse 22, 'Wives obey your husband' rather than 21, 'Live in mutual submission'. Similarly, the mention of 1 Peter 3 includes verse 1, bidding wives obey husbands but, like Pearl, omits verse 7. One contributor, Kim Tate, insists that 'the god of this world has waged war on submission in order to supress the truth', which is that 'submission in marriage bears witness to our risen Lord who reigns supreme' (2017:36). In *Desiring God*, Piper explained that

> for decades Christian and non-Christian egalitarians have argued, have assumed, and have modelled that those peculiar roles and responsibilities among men and women in the home, in the church, and in the culture should emerge only from competencies rather than from a deeper reality rooted in who we are differently as male and female. (quoted in Haddad, 21 March 2018)

The second Evangelical strand from the United States, holding the more egalitarian marriage thread, is the CBE, which includes churches of an Evangelical persuasion within a wide sweep of denominations. CBE feeds strands within hierarchically-organized churches such as Methodist, Lutheran, Roman Catholic and Anglican, although each church, along with others, has clergy and members preferring the CBMW line. The CBE current mission statement says:

> CBE exists to promote the biblical message that God calls women and men of all cultures, races, and classes to share authority equally in service and leadership in the home, church, and world. CBE's mission is to eliminate the power imbalance between men and women resulting from theological patriarchy.

It is clearly opposed to domination of a wife by her husband which is seen as a potential or real problem in CBMW and similarly minded groups and churches, who oppose CBE for 'giving in to culture'. Yet as has been made clear, the interaction between culture and faith, context and belief, is continual yet rather subtle. Moreover, the CBMW's attempt to break the unity of the Trinity in order to make Jesus eternally submissive to his Father, as women should be to men and wives to husbands, may be a faith as well as culture reaction to the Women's Movement of the 1970s. It was at that point that George Knight, a CBMW precursor, began publishing books which are foundational for such 'Bible-True' approaches.

CBE's core statement on marriage and family life, written by the first president, the late Catherine Kroeger and maintained by her successor Mimi Haddad, reads:

> In the Christian home, husband and wife are to defer to each other in seeking to fulfil each other's preferences, desires and aspirations .... In so doing, husband and wife will help the Christian home stand against improper use of power and authority by spouses and will protect the home from wife and child abuse that sometimes tragically follows a hierarchical interpretation of the husband's 'headship'.

Individuals from all denominations, whether laity or clergy and particularly Roman Catholic nuns, draw on these parts of the CBE statement as a valuable contribution to their struggle against that violence which some theologies appear to enable. As we shall come across further into this book, CBE identifies the problem with a hierarchical interpretation of headship. Husbands as household pastors, being human, ignore the unwitting intrusion of human egoism into apparently 'dispassionate' decisions. This underlies much male violence within Christian marriage. It may be useful here to quote from an American ethnography of Evangelical Protestant women. Moving between CBMW and CBE approaches, they suggest a middle way. 'Jane' describes her marriage as an 'exercise in mutual submission':

> I am definitely feminine and my husband is definitely masculine, but that doesn't necessarily mean that I'm the domestic homemaker and he's the breadwinner. We have a mutually submissive relationship. He gives everything he can. I do everything I can. (Brasher, 1998:149)

Women in the two churches Brasher studied considered marital violence a serious and even intractable problem for which divorce is one response. One woman noted that God works to stop violence in a marriage by 'putting people in the couple's path that pull the two apart, because the abused person needs you to step in for them because they can't. They can't make decisions because they're frozen' (ibid.:153): No talk here about staying in danger to fulfil God's will. Groothuis, in her *Good News for Women* (1997), puts forward the egalitarian theology of relationships in daily life, marriage and faith, and is joined in her approach by other conservative evangelicals such as Myatt, Erikson, McCormack and Sanders.

The tension within the largest single church, the Roman Catholic, seemed almost palpable at times in this research, especially among nuns and church workers. We have seen the attitudes and rules set out from Augustine to Pope Pius IX, so let us now examine the institutional Vatican view in the late 1980s, when CBMW, CBE and the WCC Decade of Women began or became prominent. Felisa Elizonda writes:

> Even tracts on married life published in the years approaching Vatican II [1959–62] are written in terms of greater tolerance for a husband's neglect of his duties and greater 'understanding' for his harshness or the excesses of his authority as head ... leaving women excluded from the equality and real reciprocity that the best texts on marriage have called for since apostolic times. (Schüssler Fiorenza, 1994:104)

Thirty years after Vatican II, Pope John Paul II still had interesting things to say about women in section 10 of his 1988 Letter 'On the Dignity of Women'. Following a complementarian view, he saw them as wives, mothers or nuns. Unlike CBMW, which stresses male headship with few provisos, he writes that although male and female were made in both Genesis 1 and 2 as a 'relationship of communion expressing the unity of the two', Edenic sin then threatens this 'more seriously for the woman, since [the husband's] domination takes the place of being a sincere gift' indicating the 'loss of stability of the fundamental equality'. The sincerity of the gift is not unpacked, nor are the implications of domination for spiritual health examined. Unlike CBMW, he sees men and women as initially if briefly equal, but like CBMW and unlike CBE, unequal since the Fall. He cites the Ephesians passage on wives and husbands in marriage as beginning at 5.21 (unlike CBMW) but starts his discussion at verse 22.

Like CBMW, he strongly opposes theological feminism which will prevent women 'reaching fulfilment but will instead lose and deform what is their essential richness'. Indeed, he insists, 'even the rightful opposition of women to "He shall rule over you" must not lead to the "masculinisation of women ... contrary to their own feminine "originality"' (1988 Letter). Moreover, in canonizing abused faithful wives such as Elisabetta Canori Mora in 1994, critics suggest that John Paul continued to valorize the suffering of women. Rossi writes, 'The most insidious inculcation of this [martyr mentality] is the Vatican's canonisation of women who reflect the misogynist teachings of the church' (Rossi in Cruz, 2005:64). The views of priests and especially of nuns discussed in Chapter 5 suggest considerable divergence from the teaching promulgated in the Dignity of Women.

Choosing modern somewhat or clearly conservative material from two evangelical groups, CBMW and CBE, and the Vatican is intentional, because it is *such* material, and the underlying ideas therein, with which the majority of Christian people across the world live, wrestle, or indeed reject church. Part Two of this book includes many views supporting both complementarian and egalitarian points of view, sometimes in the same person, and regularly within in the same church.

Reflection

The legacy of the early and medieval church is still with us, not only in ideas about men and women in relation to God and each other, but in the very words used to advise and control them, whether that is their taking the blame for their men 'having to hit them' because they are rebellious, didn't cook the right food or were just unpleasing to their superior. I have pointed out some links between 'then and now' at various points but could have done so on every page and virtually every paragraph. Readers will find more links in the next three chapters: my head resounds with them.

That violence against wives is still not openly and consistently opposed suggests a degree of complicity of *all* the people of God, laywomen and men, not just those standing up to represent them. There will thus be no quick fix of deep-seated issues deriving, as I have asserted in the first two chapters, from power *over* people in the moment rather than life-enhancing power *with and for* people for the future. Yes, a woman *could* say, 'My husband has hit me because he wished to and that is *his* sin', just as she could tell him 'what you ask me to do is sinful, so I will ignore your wishes'. But what abused woman retains such a sense of self to do that, and to whom does she turn?

Let us now explore violence in Christian lives across the world and the response of church teachers, leaders and people, discussants being the major resource. After setting out the biblical concept of church leadership, Chapter 4 sets out the reality of violence against their wives by ordained men and husbands as household pastors, arguing that if a leader is also an abuser, he can no longer pray on behalf of his family nor make decisions untainted by his sin. Chapter 5 discusses the teaching and advice which church workers – priests, ministers or elders – feel they give, with a critique by nuns. Chapter 6 considers what laypeople, especially women, feel about the church advice and teaching they receive on marital violence. Crucially, it discusses the collusion of unbeaten women as well as non-abusing men in violence against Christian wives.

Part two

Views from the field

4

Church leaders as abusing husbands

'It's been a long road, because the church did not seem to have any answers for one of its [violent] ministers and his family' (USA, quoted in Alsdurf, 1988:72).

'Any Salvation Army pastor who beats his wife would lower the spiritual temperature of the church, and there will be no church growth because abuse is an ulcer, a cancer' (Pakistan, 2011)

'It was the theology of headship that did it' (abused clergy ex-wife to Bishop, England, 2017).

'If the pastor or elder is an abuser, even if what he offers people is good, people will not hear it because it is tainted by their knowledge of his abusing (Trinidad male elder, 2011).

'I stayed with my abusive pastor husband because the Bishop said it was shameful for the church if I left: but after 14 years I'd had enough! (West Indies, 2011).

'A new curate rang her Bishop to say her Vicar hit his wife. The following Sunday, the Vicar announced, "It's been good having X, but this is her last Sunday"' (England, 2009).

'My husband constantly reminded me it was my wifely duty to obey his every command. As parish priest he was protected by the church: I was shunned' (Australia, 2018).

There are three sound reasons for starting Part Two with clergy violence against their wives. Firstly, a leader's personal attitude as well as practice affects the willingness of women to seek consolation or advice. Secondly, as an abused survivor in Scotland pointed out, theologically trained people are best placed to twist Bible verse for their own benefit. Thirdly, such a person's personal life lacks integrity as, therefore, does his public prophetic voice, affecting both teaching and preaching.

Moreover, the pastoral and spiritual repercussions of clerical abuse suggest that while all intentional sin is blameworthy, the clerical abuser's sin is heinous.

Let me give one reason. The ordained commonly preside at Christian marriages, which include promises to 'love, respect, cherish and honour each other'. Even where women still promise to obey, the cleric will have explained in marriage preparation meetings what mutual respect, love and honour mean. An abusing cleric must therefore be either a blatant hypocrite ('I'm in a special category') or adept at 'moral re-framing' ('but my wife is neurotic') to validate 'disciplining' his own spouse.

Certainly it is clerical spousal abusers, among all Christian abusers, who were most often named by discussants in this research as hypocrites, exemplified in this comment from a Korean Christian student:

> If a pastor hits his wife then gives a sermon to young people on proper behaviour between the sexes, he is a hypocrite, and if the young people know what he does, they will not follow what he says.

The topic rarely comes up in sermons or other pastoral contexts there (as elsewhere) in part, as several Korean pastor-friends have said, 'because so many pastors beat their own wives'. There are of course more reasons for pulpit silence: acceptance or sheer ignorance of violence, fear of opposing church rules, not knowing what to say to survivors, a feeling violence (though not adultery or contraception) is private, or anxiety lest abusers and their money leave the church.

However, before discussing *ordained* abusing husbands, let me highlight their *lay* counterpart. As the last chapter made clear, married fathers from at least the fifteenth century could be expected to fulfil the role of pastor to the family, leading prayer and intercessing, teaching and admonishing, and being responsible to God for the spiritual welfare of wife and children. This is the case in various contemporary churches across the globe. In relation to his family, the household pastor plays a role similar to that performed by the ordained person to his/her congregation, with similar responsibilities and duties of care. This chapter primarily discusses the impact of abuse by an *ordained* person on his family and congregation. However, where husbands play a lay leadership role within the family, readers should hold abusive lay household-pastors in mind.

The role of pastor-husbands, abuse and the Bible

In James and Phyllis Alsdurfs' 1990 book *Battered into Submission*, which alerted interested Christians to the overall problem, the first case is of a Baptist minister in the American Midwest. Basing his views strongly on Ephesians 5.22, he so abused his wife spiritually, physically and psychologically that when she killed him in response to his calm threat to end her life, she was declared innocent by the court. The quotes at the start of this chapter make the point: from the United States to Australia, from Kenya to Korea, a number of those who vow before God and their church that they will support and minister to all nevertheless intentionally attack the body and soul of their wife. There is a sound theological and sociological argument that such a person loses the right to represent their congregation before God. Is there also biblical support for such a stance?

James (3.1) writes: 'Not many of you should become teachers, my brothers and sisters, for you know that we who teach will be judged with greater strictness.' Timothy spells out leaders' roles thus:

> They must be above reproach ... sober-minded, self-controlled, respectable, hospitable, able to teach, not a drunkard, *not violent but gentle*, not quarrelsome, not a lover of money. He must *manage his own household well*, with all dignity, *keeping his children submissive*, for if someone does not know how to manage his own household, how will he care for God's church?' (1 Timothy 3. 2-4, my italics).

The inclusion of 'not violent but gentle' would seem a decisive rejection of violence by a church leader. Indeed the (conservative Missouri) Lutheran Study Bible says of this verse: 'The Lord would not approve of a church leader who deals forcefully, using verbal or physical violence, towards family or congregational members' (2009:2072). The Lord may well not approve, but abuser or institution readily use the 'manage his household well' exhortation to avoid action. The 'orderly household' of Roman law still rules many a manse.

Slippery though the word 'submissive' is, it does not mandate violence. However, some Christian groups and individuals disagree, quoting 'those who spare the rod hate their children' (Proverbs 13.24) and 'If you beat them with a rod you will save their souls from Sheol' (Proverbs 23.14) to validate violence against the wife. This implies only the father is an autonomous adult, exemplified by the English cleric who slaps his wife 'to keep her in order', the Ghanaian pastor for whom 'women are like children and need correction', or the Caribbean minister who says 'Spare the rod and spoil the wife.'

The view that the attitude and behaviour of religious leaders affects others has a long history. Malachi (2.7 in The Message translation) says bluntly,

> It's the job of priests to teach the truth. People are supposed to look to them for guidance. The priest is the messenger of God-of-the-Angel-Armies. But

you priests have abandoned the way of priests. Your teaching has messed up many lives.

Abusive leaders indeed 'mess up many lives' not only of their family but of the congregation they serve. Discussing the husband in his role as house prayer leader, Peter implies that an abusing leader would be unacceptable:

> Husbands, in the same way, show consideration for your wives in your life together, paying honour to the woman as the weaker sex, since they too are also heirs of the gracious gift of life, so that nothing may hinder your prayers. (1 Peter 3.7, New Revised Standard Version)

This passage, addressed to husbands, comes after several verses addressed to wives. The Greek allows the final injunction on prayer to refer to both husband and wife, picked up in the Missouri Lutheran Study Bible footnote: 'Disrespect and mistreatment would prevent husband and wife praying together. Such sins would also cause God to refuse *their* requests' (2009:2153, my italics). Equally, and more logically, the Greek allows the final 'your' to be addressed to the *subject* of the verse, the husband: 'If *you* mistreat *your* wife, God will not hear *your* prayers.' If such a husband prays in church *on behalf of* all as their representative, or the lay abuser acts thus *on his family's behalf*, his prayers are null and void. Each may well still have authority, but it is a travesty to assume either can speak for those on whose behalf they pray.

There is a temptation for leaders to assume their carefully managed front stage version of themselves leading the congregation at prayer will be equally effective in controlling knowledge of the backstage of their life, the personal stuff. Yet this can be a delusion. Phrases such as 'the minister's wife never smiled near him', 'she was always so pale and silent, we didn't know she could laugh till she worked with some other women here on a project', or 'pastors are the worst wife-abusers', make knowledge and sympathy clear, even if ineffectual. In a world context where violence against wives is increasingly judged illegal, why would congregation members not speak openly to local or regional church authorities about their leader's abusive behaviour?

Congregational collusion in clergy family violence

Reasons for silence about clerical marital abuse are complex, but one point is significant. Congregations, like families, do not want their leader's image tarnished because *his* image is also *theirs*. That a congregation is prepared for others, or a *particular* other, to be sacrificed so that its own image and reputation are not damaged could imply elements of group worship. Let me give two examples from rather different situations to clarify this point. Living in Germany, my devout Roman Catholic neighbour explained none of her sons were altar-boys, as the local priest abused many who were. Most parents knew and held their sons back, though some, she said, 'may not know his habits, while others didn't mind much'. But *no one* spoke out lest the reputation of the church in that town be damaged. In Australia, a woman reported her pastor husband to church authorities for his 'very close relations' with at least one parishioner. To the surprise of the church hierarchy, the members were angry *not* with their adulterous pastor but with his *wife's* damaging of their self-image by making his behaviour public (Koepping, 2008).

A pastor in an Evangelical church in Ghana explained the pressure on him to keep abuse secret. He was first called out some years before at 2 am because a church Elder was beating his wife, early in their marriage. They separated and came together again, but the violence continued. The pastor wanted to demote the man, but the church council did not, despite a psychologist's negative report:

> I was again called to the Elder's house, to his mother's surprise. The Elder kept saying his wife is useless: 'if I say sit, you sit, if I say lie down, you lie down'. His mother agreed, and was annoyed when I said, 'Your son wants a robot for a wife'. I told the committee that the report said his attitude to women was abnormal, but they refused to act *to avoid public scandal.*

This point, about who is shamed by such acts, was noted in the last chapter, and occurred repeatedly in spousal violence discussions. As a Pentecostal theologian in Ghana said, 'Everyone covers things up, especially if the pastor is attacking his wife. They want to maintain the perfect image of the pastor representing them.'

It is thus not just the church as an institution which may be keen to cover up clergy violence, of which more later, but also his congregation and, given tied clergy housing, his wife. Should it come to separation and divorce, some clergy wives feel they have been conditioned to see it as bad taste, indeed unchristian, to insist on their rights resulting from both their marriage and their contribution to the church. And everyone needs a roof. Exactly this reason led to a female Kenyan priest silently divorcing her violent priest husband: had the bishop known he was an abuser, he may well have lost his job. That she lost hers for desertion at least meant that her children could remain in his town at their good school: she returned to her parents' place in the bush.

What do churches say about violent clergy?

Do churches have written policies and rules and if so, do they sanction the abuser and support *both* the abused person *and* the congregation? If churches have neither policies nor rules, is such violence accepted, or regarded as private? A female Baptist student in Myanmar is sceptical:

> It is good to talk about spousal violence. It is physical and verbal. In the theological college I attend, one staff member's husband is a pastor and lecturer and she is often hit. We all know she is hit: we hear it and we see the evidence. Should the church be silent? We are: we do nothing. Everyone holds back, because we know he'll just say, 'I paid for her so she'll do what I want.'

In South India, an ordained male lecturer has been known as a wife-beater for at least the past decade, attacking his competent but frightened wife in full view of students and staff. Attempts to support the wife backfire, the culprit hitting his wife more under the misapprehension she has spoken up, and verbally attacking those seeking to intervene. He continues to climb the academic ladder. In a Tongan seminary, several staff hit their wives publicly and harshly. Two offending ordinands, one the police commissioner convicted of abusing his wife and another a man whose wife went back to New Zealand to avoid the beatings, were subsequently ordained as ministers. Not all seminary staff or future colleagues were happy about either decision. However, the institution, indeed all these institutions, ignored the sin of abuse.

In contrast, a church may decide to oppose violence against wives. Take the Baptist church in the Congo where, amid the violence of war, churches have made clear efforts to stop pastors abusing their wives. An Elder or pastor will lose his position if he hits his wife because, as a Congolese pastor said in an echo of Timothy:

> If he cannot run his own house, he cannot help other people. You must be irreproachable. Such an Elder must sit back in the pew. We will unpick the problem: 'Where are you coming from in your mind? Why do you think you can do this?' And he cannot become an Elder again for at least three years: most people would not bother trying again. For the pastor, as for an Elder, when and if you sin, *it is not like the sin of a simple person*, because as a leader you must give an example. Therefore, we must take time to be sure your attitude is not a stumbling block to others, for *a pastor does not belong to himself anymore*.

This pastor makes several important points. First alerted to the issues by a group of women who graduated from Bible School in the early 1990s with no immediate chance of ordination, he began not only to think but to act. His starting point is that an abusive leader is a stumbling block to others, a key point which recurs throughout the research. Then he engages with the miscreant, asking just what rights the abusing elder or pastor is relying on to support his action. Finally, and strongly, '*A pastor does not belong to himself anymore* but to God and those for whom s/he works.' The three points together give a rock-solid foundation, irrespective of context, to exclude the unrepentant ordained from ministry.

Yet not all his peers supported his approach to the hitting and beating of clergy wives. Indeed, as he sadly explained, some tell others to 'hit your wife if she doesn't seem submissive enough'. Occasionally, he explained,

> a fellow pastor will look sad when saying their mother or sister was beaten, but such passing sentimentality seems enough for them. A good African man doesn't want to show he is moved by emotion. He covers his feelings, to look stoical. To deal with this is tough. It needs an intentional decision to say something, whether in preaching or premarital counselling or ... I don't know what. We just don't talk about it.

I pointed out that the Church of England, of which I am part, has clear rules but far from clear responses. 'Yes,' he said,

> we have rules, but the higher-up leadership will say that X is doing a lot for the Church, so we can set aside the damage to his prophetic voice caused by his abuse of his wife. And anyway, they say, it will cost us money if we suspend him, so let's just close our ears and hope it will go away.

The 'prophetic voice' point will be picked up below but let us see first if the clear rules and weaker processes of the Congo are repeated in the Church of England, or churches in the British Isles. Do they have similar ways of managing or ignoring marital violence by ordained and licensed ministers or elders? The 2006 Church of England report makes clear that:

> If a priest, on a marital break-up, is respondent to a petition for divorce or judicial separation based on unreasonable behaviour (which includes physical or mental abuse), then the bishop ... will have power ... to remove the priest from office and/or impose a prohibition, without going through the normal complaints procedure.

However, church leaders seem to avoid using their power, whether in recognition of the abuser's past work for the church, which just happened to include attacking their partner, his future prospects or because they judge his actions trivial. A church lawyer, aware of the extent of the problem, pointed out that such a divorce 'could easily be used to lever out an abusive priest'.

One divorced ex-clergy wife went to the Bishop to discuss her former husband's regular violence, accepted by the divorce-court judge based on her evidence and that of medical services. She was concerned that both that and other issues would continue to affect his ministry, especially to women. She was told that 'the threshold of evidential acceptability in a divorce court is lower than that for the church, and it would therefore be unfair to restrict his ministry just on such evidence' although 'the fact of his violence would stay on the books for five years'. Given that the man is officially living alone, and that even if he re-marries it commonly takes several years for an abused person to complain, he'll probably be safe. Future parishioners may be less sanguine.

Naturally it *is* delicate for a superior, a presbytery or other relevant authority to question an ordained person about his private life. How much easier to reframe suspected abuse as 'he's got a problem with anger management' or 'she gets stressed very easily'. However, an ordained person no longer has total privacy. Moreover, where there is suspicion that adultery or malfeasance is happening, there appears less reticence to dig and question, sex and money winning over intra-family violence. Indeed, sex offers a far easier means to get rid of an abusive pastor or priest. Asking a group of Taiwanese Presbyterian women in 2005, for example, if their pastors could be sacked, the response was immediate: 'Yes, for adultery.' 'And for hitting their wife?' I continued. After a silence, the slightly puzzled answer came: 'No.' 'What should a beaten wife do?' I pressed. 'We are taught to be gentle and sensitive, and as Christians, marriage is sacred.' In Ghana, the Assemblies of God Church insists that a violent pastor, who should 'portray a Christ-like life', will be

> investigated by an elderly pastor, and if the claim is upheld, he will be disciplined for at least a year and to an extent retrained. Usually, such a pastor leaves to go to, or to start, a new church, but if he continues with us, and continues to beat then he will be kicked out. *But in that first year, he is watched, and if he commits adultery, he is sacked.*

One case of continual violence in a South Indian manse, violence which the congregation knew about and heard, led to a long-drawn out court case 'dragging on for years', with the pastor refusing to leave. Luckily for the institution, he began an affair with a married woman in the congregation and had no choice but accept a rural transfer, adultery trumping violence. Removing an abusive minister is not something any church embarks on easily, although a good many do not bother, are not interested in the issue or, as one bishop said, 'If I had to sack or suspend all the priests and pastors in my diocese who hit and beat their wives, I'd be running this diocese with only two men and the women helpers.'

The reader may recollect the reference at the start of this chapter to the curate sacked by her vicar for reporting his violence to the bishop. An oddity of English Anglican life is that a dwindling number of vicars still have 'freehold tenure', which can give job security for their working life. Discussing the case of the above curate with another English bishop, one sensitive to the personal and prophetic problem of clergy violence, I said that the first bishop colluded in the vicar's sin. The second immediately said: 'Well, it can be very difficult to get rid of a vicar who has the freehold or even common tenure of his parish.' I then asked, 'But were the said vicar to have hit your wife, which he wouldn't as he doesn't own her, you would have got him out, wouldn't you?' He agreed. A clause of the Common Tenure legislation of 2008 states tenure can be ended by disciplinary procedures in cases where, among other problems, there is a 'breakdown of pastoral relationships'. Does the vicar's wife not count?

Clearly, rules for dealing with marital abuse by clergy can be reinterpreted to suit the occasion, as illustrated in the following story from Kenya:

> Five elders of a Pentecostal church went with the pastor to his house, although he had neither warned his wife they were coming nor [as he should] provided food in advance. The surprised wife said, 'we have no food in the house' at which the senior elder, with approval of three others, told the pastor, 'if it was my wife who did that, I'd beat her: we give you permission to do so.'

The fifth elder and informant was shocked but remained silent. Given that that Pentecostal Church opposes violence which kills or maims the wife, the elders were giving their pastor permission to 'beat reasonably' without being sanctioned by church law.

Yet the reader may with reason be asking how, in the absence of a criminal case or imprisonment, are church authorities to *know* an ordained or licensed person is violent to his wife, for surely innocence should be presumed. There are two elements to this. Firstly, do abused church leaders' wives refrain from informing on husbands through fear of him and the common anxiety that 'if he is sacked he'll have nothing to give to help support me and the children,' or are there other reasons? Secondly, might church authorities be assumed to give more credence to the minister's version, a man in whose career they have invested and whom they know, or to his wife, whom they may well not?

Why do clergy wives not speak?

First, unwillingness to admit being hit happens in most abusive marriages, not just those involving clergy, resulting in a problem of evidence which can make it easier for an institution to ignore the problem, as explained by a Kenyan man:

> My father's sister was beaten very badly and taken to hospital, where she said, 'He didn't beat me: there was a problem in the cowshed and the cow hit me'. But he was seen running after her at night and running into the coffee plantation and he was seen beating her. You *know* he beat her, but if she says no ... It's the same for a bishop: how many actually find out what his priests are doing, even if they want to, unless he breaks the door down and sees it?

Accusing anyone of wrongdoing without a statement from the victim or evidence from witnesses is tricky if not plain unwise: yet enabling an abuser to continue damaging the victim and the wider community is a sin. The position of clergy wives, her private versus public persona, is part of the problem. A woman who marries a man after he was ordained usually knows she will have a particular status within a church. (Late vocations are another issue.) That was certainly the case in Europe and regions initially populated from there and is still the case in regions of church growth in Africa and Asia. That can pressure the wife to keep silent both to maintain her status and, especially if she is devout, to support his public role and their mutual faith, a feature of manse life across the world. The need to maintain a pastor's public honour at the expense of the wife's mental and physical health was referred to often in the research: 'People would rather cover up than let other people know especially if they are a pastor's wife: they try harder to keep it secret, for the sake of the church.' In Taiwan, where the image of the virtuous wife is strong, a pastor wife's shame at being hit usually keeps her silent. Yet she may be pushed to speak. An informant visited such a woman in hospital, where the patient's worried sister told the visitor that for the last ten years, her sister had been badly hit and was in hospital after yet another such event. The sister's voice merging with that of the female church visitor led the wife to speak up: the husband resigned.

If a clerical abuser is sanctioned, much of the family income would go unless she works for money outside the house, which may have been actively discouraged. Keeping violence secret thus becomes crucial, the abused wife turning frightened children into innocent colluders by saying: 'Never tell anyone about what just happened, or we might be turned out of the vicarage and you'll have to move schools.' Should she speak up, she may be blamed both by the community and by her wider family for 'putting her family into poverty'. A frequent comment was: 'She should have endured for her family's sake, because now there is no food in the house and soon there'll be no house,' or 'She should have endured for all our sakes,' sacrifice clearly being the duty of clergyman's wife.

Moreover, in areas of high divorce, the fact that the woman has married an ordained man who cannot easily leave the marriage and get another woman may be seen as a benefit which 'gives the wife a foundation from which to be kind to her husband', according to a group of pastors from a charismatic church discussing spousal violence. Their assumption that 'kindness and wifely goodness' will avoid violence is not borne out by the facts: an abuser will abuse because he can, irrespective of her efforts to avoid trouble. The banning of divorce may constrain ordained men from attacking the present wife to encourage her departure before getting a new one or installing the new 'wife' into the house while the first wife is still there. However, forbidding clerical divorce may cause disaster. Evidence from southern India, reported both about and by local Pentecostal clergy (and in Anderson-Kumar, 2010), is for the pastor to strangle his unwanted wife, hang her up for the summoned police to view the 'suicide', and then swiftly acquire a replacement.

Clear though the loss of social status may be for an ordained person's wife if she leaves a marriage, it may also mean a loss of religious purpose, especially but not only in contexts where women cannot be ordained or a woman does not feel so called. Marrying an ordained man offers a clear and semi-official degree of involvement in church life, which in some churches is formalized in the role of co-pastor. The ending of such a marriage can be especially miserable and spiritually damaging. As several British women put it, 'In marrying him, I knew I was marrying the church and doing what I could for it: now there is nothing.' Another said:

> It is so hard to keep that sense of vocation which was lived as part of a couple when the marriage ends. I wouldn't have minded becoming a deaconess, the option in those days, and in fact I very much saw myself as a handmaid to his and others' work. But I couldn't stay with him any longer: he was so uncaring and cruel.

For one priest and ex-wife of another, staying was partly pragmatic:

> For the first twelve years of our violent marriage, I was frozen, blamed myself for having chosen badly, and tried to be an exemplary clergy wife. But anything set him off, and then he'd hit me, pushing me into a corner, yelling and hitting. I wanted to be ordained and reckoned I'd get no support if I exposed him, so I stayed long after I was priested, and financially and emotionally strong enough

to leave. It affected my ministry: still can't read Ephesians 5. I was glad at a weekday service in Rome when that was the reading for the day and the priest said she wouldn't use it as it was too painful for some people. Help from the bishop? Frankly, the policewoman I saw one wet night when my husband had once again kicked me out gave me far more kindness and practical help than my bishop had ever done.

There are reasons to do with status and faith why abused clergy wives do not readily turn to church authorities. The core one, shared by *all* abused wives, is summed up in a comment from a Scottish Presbyterian Elder's wife in a 2016 Church of Scotland report of violence:

I was in a living tomb of fear and isolation; so constricted, so fearful. I just lost myself really ... I wanted to try harder and harder all the time to be good, to be a proper wife, to please him, to stop him hurting and humiliating me. And the more I tried, the worse it got. There was no 'I' left in the end – just a shadow fading into walls.

A body that has ceased to be a person has neither voice nor strength, nor does it feel entitled to be fully alive: how much more acute can this be when the abuser is also a means of approaching God.

Might clergy be seen as favouring their own?

The second point is: if church authorities receive a complaint, directly or indirectly, that an ordained person is beating his wife, is their response more likely to favour the short-term reputation of the institution and their employee, or his partner? If the former is perceived or even assumed to be the case by potential complainants – 'they're all blokes together' – might this affect their readiness to complain?

This is a delicate point, yet the evidence available suggests defence of the institution comes first: remember the pleasant bishop above, whose first response was to exonerate the church for not defending a sacked curate?

Another British clergy wife explained:

I went to the bishop, as I knew my husband, G, had seen him, and I said that. He said: 'Yes, your husband came to see me and said you were having problems. What can I do?' I explained that G hit me, but he just fobbed me off ... 'known G a very long time, he's a fine priest' and so on. It was clear G was fine and I was crazy.

As we have seen in recent worldwide cases of the sexual abuse of young people by clergy, exemplified among others by the 2018 Church of England Inquiry and by Vatican admission, some rational faithful church leaders believe the word of an ordained colleague with whom he may have a long history against that of a lay complainant. The West Indian pastor's wife noted at the start of this chapter endured fourteen years of violence, staying to avoid embarrassing the church, or rather the bishop who had appointed her violent husband. Did he really think no congregation member knew, and that the church was not thereby placed in daily disrepute? A Baptist pastor's wife in southern India spoke about the abuse she had endured. When no change was evident, she told the church that she would seek a divorce. Rather than controlling the *man* by suspending him, an available option, they put their effort into damaging the *woman's* reputation to stop her going to law and 'shaming the church'.

Where violence was judged 'sufficiently serious', however, church leaders and structures may well support a plaintiff against an ordained person, especially if imprisonment has taken the decision from them. In general, however, 'serious' appears to mean breaking limbs, slashing faces or eyes, putting into hospital for more than a quick visit, all of which should face criminal assault charges in countries covered in this research. Support is thus hardly a mark of merit. Whether it was people in the congregation who wanted to uphold their icon and maintain the happy church family image, or church leaders who either could not be bothered with complaining wives or indeed hit their own, the research suggests that abused clergy wives could expect little support, even if they reached beyond their own commitment to God and the church and spoke openly.

Moreover, there may be an implicit, perhaps unconscious, tendency to prioritize the ordination vow and subsequent status over the marital, even when that means ignoring what may be a deep commitment on the part of a clergy wife to God, marriage and husband. This seems the only way of understanding a recent (2016) Church of England otherwise sound publication 'Responding Well to Domestic Violence'. In the section 'Clergy and domestic abuse' on page 14, we find the sentence:

> Clergy may see marital breakdown as a failure of their ordination vows and therefore be particularly vulnerable to staying in abusive relationships for many years. In such situations, dioceses should not put fear of scandal above the safety of vulnerable people.

If abused clergy are assumed to be female, why would leaving the marriage signify failed ordination vows, and not a violent husband? If clergy are male, they are far more likely to be perpetrators than victims of abuse. Asking for comment from the bishop overseeing the text, his reply of 'one cannot include everything in a short text', rather missed the point. Clergy wives, just as frozen by violence as any other survivor, and egged on by congregations protecting their own image, their personal commitment to marriage and the ministry linked to that marriage, are *very* vulnerable to staying in an abusive relationship for many years.

Faith and forgiveness: Why abused clergy wives stay

This brings us to the question: 'Why does she stay if it is so bad"? As much as many abused Christian wives and more than most, the abused clergy wife stays because she is subject not only to the usual existential anxiety of homelessness and the disembowelling of her being, but also to relentless spiritual abuse. Pressure to stay may be exerted by the abusing husband, by faith twisted to oppress, by the church and by her devout family. An English clergyman, knowing his ordained brother-in-law abused his sister, insisted she was 'chosen to carry a heavier cross', in an echo of Michael Pearl. An English clergy-wife in a strongly Evangelical church was advised by her brother, also a leader in that denomination, to stay:

> My brother said I had to stay – but I couldn't. The constant cruelty, the hitting, the total lack of empathy, the "who are *you* to complain": horrible, especially as so many people loved him in the congregation. They didn't know the violence in the house, so I got the blame. My brother cared more about the church than me.

Clearly in an argument, we assemble what we have to make our point: but these abusing husbands and their relatives were employing 'obedience' as a long-term strategy to control partners, as did this Nairobi pastor:

> He came in late and woke me. I said: 'Please be quieter, you are disturbing me'. So he began to beat me, and I ran outside, hoping he'd be shamed into stopping, or that someone would help, but he carried on hitting, saying 'You are a bad wife, you should obey me but you don't so you force me to hit you.' But I stay: I promised.

Evident in the last chapter, the aggressor demands the *victim* accept the responsibility for *his* violence. This is common practice (Collins, 2019:176), though it is exacerbated for deeply devout Christians by damaging theology which oddly fails to insist on the sinner's full responsibility. The above pastor was suspended because the attack was public.

The experience of ordained leaders' wives is similar to that of any woman, a point taken up again in Chapter 6, yet it is very different. The personal commitment to lay ministry which the clergy wife may have; the tied housing; the often rather closed network, with dramatis personae in the household of daily life and the local household of God being the same; the kneeling before one's abuser at Communion in some traditions: these all add an intensity and an increased salvific anxiety to the experience of the abused church leader's wife. The ex-wife of an English Methodist explained his skill at twisting texts in that church's 2006 report on domestic violence:

> Repeatedly I was told by my Methodist Minister husband that it was my duty as a Christian to forgive, told that as a Christian I had promised in my marriage vows 'For better, for worse'. Initially I strove as a Christian very committed to marriage to forgive but I came to see that although apparently there was a duty for me to forgive, there was no mention of repentance or sorrow on my husband's part or if there was, the words would prove to be insincere and abuse would soon start again. (2006)

Exactly the same demand for forgiveness without repentance was cited by Cynthia, an American survivor and pastor's wife for sixteen violent years. Left naked and bleeding on the cold tile floor of the bathroom floor after being thrown through the glass shower doors, her husband, Bob,

> ran out to the bookshelf, came back with a Bible and started quoting scripture: 'For if you forgive men when they sin against you your heavenly Father will also forgive you'. Bob also told her if she didn't forgive him, she was not practising Christian love. (Miles, 2000:132)

Clearly this pastor lacks integrity. If a church leader ignores Ephesians 5.21-32, why should pew members bother with mutual respect, mutual love and mutual honour in marriage? The Australian Anglican was shunned for speaking out; the English Methodist was expected to offer cheap grace to her husband, no follower of Christ; the German Elder's wife suffered in silence. They represent all abused clergy wives who keep quiet, support the church and follow Christ, sickened every Sunday when their abuser mounts the pulpit, preaching the love of God, and all those wives of household pastors who must compose their face for family prayers led by the man who assails her, body, soul and mind.

Congregation-wide implications of an abusive leader

But let us leave the plight of clergy wives and consider the wider congregation of an abusing pastor priest or minister. If the institutional pastoral care offered to an abused clergy wife is uncertain or lacking, might that also be the case for abused women in congregations where clergy are hitting their wives? And if so, would that affect not only the prophetic voice, as the Congolese pastor pointed out, but also the capacity of that person to offer pastoral care, leaving women in such a congregation with nothing but an ordained stumbling block? Here we get to the nub of the problem. The abuse of clergy wives is not just an embarrassment but a blasphemy when their abuser clutches the lectern to speak of God's love, and a scandal when his behaviour leaves needy congregants in the lurch.

Abused women seeking advice or solace try to keep away from ordained ministers who are known or suspected of abuse, or who insist that 'discipline' meted out by the husband is a proper way of conducting a marriage. This means, of course, that some clergy have never had a woman coming to talk about violence, making it easier to dismiss the issue as 'not relevant here', as did an abusing pastor in a small Australian town with immense intrafamilial violence problems known to social services. There might conceivably be congregations and contexts where marital violence is truly unknown to any member, although even a congregation of ten ancient single ladies would surely have at least one with such memories from childhood. However, the suggestion that if no one has ever spoken about it 'there is no violence here' can say more about the ordained person than local reality. One abusing minister, who proudly told me no one had spoken to him about spousal violence in forty years of ministry, was also the person who, to the shame of his abused wife, asserted publicly at a weekend meeting on marriage enrichment that 'some women ask to be hit'. In choosing carefully whom to speak to, abused women rule out not only abusing priests and pastors, but those known to judge and chastise complainants. They may go to non-violent kind neighbouring leaders known to be less judgemental, and, in places where women are ordained, may choose to confide in a woman, *provided* she is known to be kind and open. Not all are.

As women across Kenya put it, 'You can't go to a pastor who beats his wife to complain about your own: even if he seems nice, you know he is a liar because you've heard her scream.' 'If my pastor does wrong, hitting his wife or chasing other women,' explained another Kenyan, 'people lose confidence in him and the church, and they don't seek him out.' In Ghana, a Presbyterian teacher who had said 'pastors are the worst at wife-beating of anyone in the church' told the following story:

> A Baptist friend of mine wanted to talk to a pastor other than her own about her husband's violence as he was friends with both of them. An Assemblies of God friend of hers – with no experience of abuse – said: 'Come to my pastor, he's really nice.' As they approached the pastor's house, they realised he was beating up his wife, so the Baptist lady ended up taking her home. The Assemblies lady couldn't take the woman to her own house, or it would have shamed her pastor. It's happening a lot, but it is even more serious because we pretend it isn't happening

A Kiribati Protestant pastor explained that women decide which pastor they will go to, normally the one to whom they are more closely related. However, 'even if they are related, they won't go if they know the pastor is not sympathetic to women or beats his own wife'. This man, strongly against any abuse in marriage, estimated that at least three out of ten Kiribati pastors beat their wives, qualifying this by saying 'but maybe that's too conservative, it's probably closer to half'.

A telling objection to clergy violence came from the Kenyan Highlands:

> An elder was beating his wife, and the neighbours knew. They told her to tell the pastor, but she said 'No, he also beats his own wife, and he says wives ought to be beaten if they misbehave.' When it became public, that brought a lot of controversy and my neighbours left that church: the husband would never beat and has never beaten his wife. He said it is from tradition that people are beaten, not from the church, which should be a refuge.

The impact of the reputational damage to faith represented by an abusing pastor is significant. As one South Asian priest said of another:

> The congregation knows he hits his wife, because he's even done it in front of them. He hit her with a shoe, an incredible insult here. And nothing happened. No one said anything to the bishop: it's like a sacred secret they keep.

An Elder in Trinidad explained:

> Violence by a Minister or Elder affects the church because, well, suppose we have an elder who was abusive: in preaching you reveal God but also yourself. If he is an abuser, even though what he is offering is good, people will not heed it because it is tainted by their knowledge of his abusing.

Even if the leader's violence is reported to church authorities they, as we saw at the outset of this chapter, may prefer to close their eyes to the sin of spousal abuse unless new laws make this a risky choice.

The effect an ordained person's violence towards his wife has on a congregation emerged clearly in Pakistan at a two-day workshop for male and female participants. Most men proclaimed conservative family views, but *all* responded clearly to the question: 'If a pastor hits his wife, what theological and pastoral impact does that have on the congregation?' In their collated words:

> Pastors who hit their wives have dual personalities and give a bad example. *Their jealousy, anger, and attitude towards dispute might be wider than just with the wife.* They make such a big difference between preaching and practice there is a spiritual flaw in their leadership. It is hard enough to put our spiritual and daily life together, and such a pastor will not help that. The church has to be protected from such a pastor because he is an impediment to the church. He may provide counselling for people in the congregation, but he should not be allowed to: he needs counselling. People stop respecting the pastor and will say he lies all the time. Sometimes such bad ones are moved to another congregation: they should all be suspended. Violent people will be encouraged and justify their violence by his. The congregation's faith gets shattered. Women feel unprotected.

The highlighted comment that an abusing leader may exhibit that attitude in dealings with the congregation has already been noted in relation to English clergy and is relevant everywhere. While one abused person is one too many, the ripple effect of clergy violence against wives is incalculable.

Survey responses: Sack or support the clerical abuser?

Let me approach this from another angle by turning to the multi-country survey noted in Chapter 1. One question asked if an abusing clerical husband should be sacked immediately marital abuse had become known or only if he did not change his attitude and actions after counselling. A third option was that an abusing unrepentant pastor should nevertheless keep his job. One hundred and eighty-four people answered this question. The greatest number of omissions (seven) was in a conservative Christian University near Seoul which, I am told, may derive from cultural Confucian-linked controls against even anonymous bad mouthing of a pastor. Limited though the survey is, it makes clear that a majority of well-educated lay and ordained followers, most between twenty and forty, object to a cleric attacking his wife and expect decisive action.

Of the 184 responses, 79 indicated a leader who abuses his wife should be sacked immediately, 87 that he should be sacked if he refused to follow guidance and mend his ways, and just 18 that the church should not sack him. In that last figure, however, and it could also be placed in the 'sack if doesn't reform' response, were two responses from India suggesting the wife leave her husband and seek divorce, whereupon the church could more easily sack him for being divorced. As we have seen, such ways of avoiding direct ecclesial action against abusive priests are not uncommon. However, passing the burden of decision to the abused wife for the convenience of the church is unsatisfactory.

In analysing the figures by area and institution (Scottish Episcopal congregation in Scotland, Church of South India (CSI) women clergy; Anglican universities in Kenya and South Korea; state universities in Ghana and Kenya; a Presbyterian University in South Korea, an ecumenical College in South India, and a Protestant University in Kenya), some interesting patterns emerge. None in the Kenyan Anglican and State Universities or the Scottish congregation accepted that an abusive and recalcitrant church leader should keep his job. This contrasts with the six at the Korean Presbyterian, three CSI clergy and four lay people at the CSI College, and three at Kenyan and Ghanaian Universities who would not sack a continuing abuser.

Responses at the Anglican and the Presbyterian Universities in Korea showed marked differences not only between the institutions but also between those attending each. Thirteen at the former insisted on immediate dismissal of abusive ordained leaders and four if the miscreant continued to abuse after counselling: all would dismiss a recalcitrant offender. At the Presbyterian University, thirteen respondents agreed an abusing pastor be dismissed immediately, with a further four voting for dismissal after failed or refused counselling. However, six insisted a pastor should not be dismissed even if the violence continued. This is not, however, a simple difference between the attitudes of two tertiary institutions, or of two faith traditions, one seen as more liberal than the other, but also of who attended which. The three Presbyterian students responding from the Anglican University were for immediate dismissal, while of those at the Presbyterian University who would refuse to eject a delinquent pastor, three (one female) were from the Holiness Church, with two Presbyterians and one Independent. If access is open, people may select the institution best fitting their own attitude.

Among those choosing immediate severance of an abusing leader, there was no overall gender difference although further evidence of what I am suggesting is culture before faith may be provided by the South Indian College. There, the three insisting a pastor be retained were all CSI male ordinands, whereas of the seven who would sack him, six were Baptist females from Northeast India, where women have a considerably higher status than in South India. Yet tradition and background are not all: good teaching helps. Both the Kenyan and the Seoul

Anglican universities based their teaching on 'all are made in the Image of God', the latter explicitly rejecting the local view that 'on Christian marriage a woman loses her own head, thereafter having only that of her husband'.

Concluding this discussion of clergy violence in marriage are these comments on abusive clergy made by young Christians:

'Such a person is insane!' (South Korea): 'He should be excommunicated' (India); 'He should be sent back for re-training and re-think his calling' (India); 'Judgement belongs to God but the institution must sort it out here on Earth' (India); 'He must be a role-model and if he isn't he must go' (Ghana, Kenya, India); 'The church should feel ashamed to ignore it' (England); and 'How can he preach, consecrate bread and wine after hitting his wife!' (Kenya).

Reflection

The Congolese pastor pointed out that marital abuse by a leader *is not like the sin of a simple person*, because he must give an example and not be a stumbling block to others, for *a pastor does not belong to himself anymore*. The first point was discussed at the outset of this chapter: the second will come up again. All are equal before God, man or woman, lay or ordained but, as James's Epistle pointed out, putting oneself forward to support, care for and represent people in a congregation or around the dinner table demands particularly honourable and loving behaviour. St Teresa's dictum that 'you are the only hands and feet Christ has on earth' is the case for every person linked in any way to faith: how much more might one say that for the ordained and for the house leader. Their hands belong to God and must be so used. Using the hands, the mind and the body intentionally to abuse another person is a particular blasphemy.

Accepting and acting on the awkward reality and extent of clerical abuse of their partners in marriage would transform theological and pastoral approaches to faith life for all. This would not only benefit the abused *partners* of such people, but also give abused *members* a greater chance of finding proper support and solace from their leaders, not just those known to be sympathetic non-abusers, a point taken up in Chapter 6. No clergy wife should be terrorized spiritually and physically, nor sacrificed for the self-image of the congregation or the wider organization, and nor should abused members have to traipse around to find a listening ear, an issue for all churches.

Worldwide, neither most married clergy nor most household pastors abuse their spouse nor would they dream of so doing, either as loving human beings or as Christians. Yet their silence is sinful. *They* need to speak in their own churches about the Image of God in all, and the blasphemy of attacking *any* person, especially those one pledges to love. If that means speaking against marital violence knowing another brother-in-Christ nearby is abusing his wife, that is the price of integrity. Loving a partner can *never* include sustained deliberate abuse through power over a person in an ecclesially weaker position, whether that is an ordained person vis-à-vis his wife, or a father-as-pastor in his family. A sound model was offered by a married minister: 'Ministers, *all* people, need to model relating to partners like we relate to God individually, not following a narrative that Eve seduced Adam, but that we are all made in God's Image.'

We have dissected the unacceptable behaviour of some ordained people who speak of the love of Christ while intentionally damaging their wife, and the equally unacceptable behaviour of 'family heads' who similarly treat their position as licence to abuse. The fact that little is said about their abuse of those they vowed to honour is a theological problem for the world's churches, stemming in part from earlier and still present dismissive attitudes towards half of creation. Exactly the same must be said of the complicit silence of the non-abusing majority. What (hopefully non-abusing) ordained and lay church workers think and say they do is the subject of our next chapter.

5

Ordained, professed and appointed church workers: Mixed views

How people recognized as church workers – ministers, nuns, pastors, priests, elders – talk about, teach and advise those in abusive marriages not only affects those needing help, but defines what wider society assumes 'the church' thinks. Worldwide, the vast majority of ordained people are male, because Roman Catholic, Orthodox, many Pentecostal and some other post-Reformation national churches do not ordain women. Regarded as 'of the church' by other laypeople, professed nuns' ties to a specific congregation are usually limited, potentially allowing them more flexibility. Elders, both male and female, have defined responsibilities to those they pastor and to their ordained leaders.

Ecclesial authority includes a clear risk of spiritual abuse. A Taiwanese nun explained how her group began to focus on violence in marriage: 'We realised we were part of the abuse: women came to us and we just said, "be patient, be patient, pray and pray for him." We were perpetuating the Church's abuse of women.' Elsewhere, an abused priest told her female bishop that she could endure her marriage no longer. As she explained: 'The bishop was really sympathetic and kind but she ended the discussion by emphasising the *sacramental nature of marriage.*' This left the survivor with 'marriage as a sacrament', *not* her husband's sin and her fragile hold on selfhood. Like the abusing husband, the bishop chose her path. A diocesan male lesser dignitary to whom the survivor spoke some months later, however, insisted living with abuse was unacceptable, supporting her need to get out.

Before delving deeper into views and actions of the ordained, numerically and in terms of power the crucial category, let us pursue those Taiwanese nuns. After the 1994 Beijing Conference on Women, they organized a conference with relevant professionals which marked the beginning of their theological awareness of abuse. They knew the problems single divorced or separated (and not remarried) survivors of violence have with parish priests informing neighbouring parishes about their status to prevent them taking Communion, contravening Canon Law. As nuns said: 'It's no use priests saying it's just lay parish workers who exclude such women, when the whole effort of church teaching is to stop people divorcing and being properly and safely separate'. They explained relations between professed and ordained:

> We have to get priests on side in our work with parishes because they have more influence in the church, but it can be tricky finding the right one: most don't get it. They are taught by priests in seminary. Their closed thinking sounds reasonable until they consider the other half of the world, lay-women and wives.

Some felt the Asian Bishops' Conference tried to dampen critical discussion:

> 'Everything in the garden is fine!' That's what our church leaders tend to think. It's depressing when you know what ordinary women think and how they survive. That's why we focus on the theological and practical side, working with Presbyterian and Episcopal churches to find a caring ethic based on the Image of God beyond the narrow dogma of Adam and Eve on which churches here rely.

Some nuns in *every* research centre were wearily aware of being defined if not maligned by their church hierarchy as feminists if not 'some sort of deviant', whether in India, Kenya, the United States or England.

A number of ordained, professed and appointed church workers respond to spousal abuse in a practical supportive manner, set out more fully below, and a proportion quietly critique church institutional failings and indirectly their own lack of courage. Long-term, proactive faith-based teaching against abuse in personal relationships is vital, even where that challenges local custom and leading abusers. Short-term, capable reactive discussion is valuable, although never with both parties together and ideally with outside help. In practice, proactive and reactive merge in a melange of hope and apathy, ignorance and effort.

What proactive teaching is given both to a couple marrying and to each individual earlier in their church life? How is the wider congregation fed? What reactive advice and support are given when abuse has begun? But first, how is marriage seen by church workers?

Marriage etiquette

We examined the theory and specific implications of marriage in Chapter 2, but what does marriage look like for the bulk of clergy and church workers in their cultural and faith niche? A point to remember, made by the clerical son of a survivor, is that 'marriage ends up being "the woman's job", with everyone ignoring the wife's needs and pain', as indeed he and his siblings did with *their* mother's pain at the hands of their violent father.

There seemed some nostalgia for a more ordered past, even for the 'Natural Order of Being'. A Caribbean pastor explained,

> Women are moving to a place of independence which is defeating Scripture because by nature they want their men to be in control. He is her spiritual leader, and though that doesn't mean he has power over her, God works through men.

As to wifely roles, he explained:

> If I'm treated well I give my wife respect and love back. Make the husband feel good, he'll behave better towards her. When a woman respects her man, he'll do anything for her: if not, sin takes over.

The success of the marriage seems to lie with the wife, her loving respect keeping him from sin to his salvific benefit, the theme of a clutch of advice to Christian women books starting in the 1970s in the United States but, as shown in Chapter 3, rooted in the past. Ghanaian Pentecostal leaders said:

> He is your husband, and you have to respect him because you are one flesh. You must submit so that the husband knows he has a good wife and doesn't go elsewhere. Be humble to your husband, speaking to him as you speak to your father. The man is the priest of the household.

Such views, as we shall see, feed into advice to and admonishing of battered survivors. Different views may combine in one church, as this Australian United Church minister explains:

> My church has never held man as the head of the household. Marriage is between equals, although if people don't know how to have a relationship, they lash out if there's a disagreement. Not much respect here. Some Aboriginal pastors tell abused women they should respect their husbands, then abuse wouldn't happen, despite evidence to the contrary.

Indeed there is rarely one view of marriage in a community which, says a Kenyan pastor, explains silence on the issue:

> We know some in the church have hit wives and still do it, so talking about it opens a can of worms. The man would need to admit he'd done wrong, and he'd never do that, so everyone pretends. No one's hands are clean nor those of their families: it's too big to touch. You might be speaking to a man whose father didn't do it, but his brother might still, and you can't shame him.

Meanwhile, wives are hit. The clash between 'culturally proper' and 'properly Christian' present in *every* social context (remember the Yorkshire funeral) can seem harsh, said another Kenyan pastor:

> If I take a wife, I must follow rules, but the church is blind to that: before God we are equal, but in culture we are socialised otherwise. Culture teaches us values, and so does the church: we men are the victims of both.

Such views of proper marriage echo the historically grounded European expectation (see Chapter 3) that a real man does what a man should do among his peers in pub, locker room or other meeting place, and if that means hitting an irritating wife, so be it. As a Pentecostal pastor in Kenya explained: 'If I suggest to a complaining man that a wife is not a robot, he might say: "I do what a man should do, hitting if necessary. My wife, my kids, are under submission to me," forgetting he is under submission to God.'

A group of Roman Catholic priests in Accra felt marital violence is part of unacceptable inequality in marriage:

> Men boss, women serve. Any time he feels his ego has been tampered with, he hits out. Much pain stays in the house: we see the tip of the iceberg. Men egg others on: 'if she doesn't respect your position, if she doesn't do or say what you want, hit her'.

Having reminded ourselves of key issues in marriages, discussed further below, let us look at the process of church marriage.

Proactive approaches: Pre-marriage counselling and marriage homilies

Pre-marriage mention of conflict and violence seems obviously proactive, yet various discussants were less sure. First, intimate relationships do not necessarily begin at marriage. As an astute Methodist minister in Ghana put it: 'Most of the kids here begin their sex lives at fourteen, and the girls are already used to violence. Nice words in pre-marriage meetings are far too late.' Second, by the time a couple start pre-marriage counselling they are already so committed they cannot imagine violence in their beloved or excuse any such event as an exception: 'Pre-marriage counselling hits closed ears' is a common ministerial comment. A Taiwanese priest helping nuns with abuse issues said, 'Preparation for marriage classes, however good they are, can't teach them much because it is too late: their views are already formed.'

The Roman Catholic Church in Tonga holds pre-marital weekends for the engaged assisted by happily married couples and nurses, together with married people who survived violence. However, a sceptical church worker explained: 'No page is labelled "violence" in the Roman Catholic marriage book, though we have pages about Christian family planning.' She continued: 'Priests themselves don't talk about responsibilities and violence in marriage, which apparently starts with Ephesians 5.22. It's OK to bash her, but not to use condoms!'

Baptists in the Democratic Republic of Congo face the theology of marriage in pre-*and* early post-marriage meetings:

> We have eight sessions before marriage and regular meetings afterwards, starting with Ephesians 5.21: men expect 5.22 and Eve's sin. It is not easy, because women are looked down on in our place. The man will often say: 'why should I submit to her?' We explain Genesis 1.27: she is equally a child of God, so treat your other self as you are treated. But they say: 'I kick her because she commits adultery, but she can't kick me if I do that, because it just happens.'

An Evangelical church in Nairobi teaches ten couples together for ten weeks, people who were expected to stay in touch after marriage to make a safety net for conflict resolution and mutual reinforcement. Sessions, all led by trained facilitators, were for men or for women, and some joint, with couples paired up to be 'accountability partners in life'. Topics included 'Looking for love in the wrong places: Values necessary for marriage', 'From roses to dishes and dealing with families', including conflict resolution. It did not discuss subordination of wives and rejected the CBMW material.

A course based on complementarian views of marriage, such as that taught to Kenyan Anglicans in 2011, notes that 'the man is the priest and pastor of the home ... men are to provide leadership in all areas of the family. The wife is not inferior but lacks an equal voice in leadership.' Husbands were to resolve conflict, defined in 2011 as 'dealing with anger and disappointment': there was no mention of abuse. Yet unless such a 'family-head pastor' fully submits to God rather than his human ego-centredness, he risks behaving unjustly and even abusively towards his wife and children. If pre-marriage counselling of those intending to marry is not done in large groups, the clergy counsellor may shy off exploring the couple's past experience of conflict and violence, especially in small communities, lest that reveal family secrets. A written check-list could ameliorate that problem.

However elaborate or cursory the counselling, the wedding day comes. Wedding readings across the world commonly starting at Ephesians 5.22 (Wives obey) not 5.21 (mutual submission), suggesting either leaders insist that 5.21

has nothing to say to marriage, the couple insist 5.22 is part of the correct ritual process, or no one thinks. Yet it is an ideal opportunity to speak against marital violence for the benefit of witnesses even if the flurried couple do not always take in the words. A Taiwanese Roman Catholic priest said:

> If I mention divorce or violence at the wedding service, most people, including the parents, don't mind because it's a wonderful chance to teach everyone there. The couple marrying won't change that day, but you encourage others to reflect. It's not just food for that day but nourishment for the future. If the bride's father hits his wife he might begin to change, because *he heard it opposed publicly.*

In Trinidad, discussants had heard this done at the Roman Catholic or Anglican weddings of African-origin couples but not at Presbyterian or Pentecostal weddings for Indian-origin couples, 'because everything said and done on the marriage day must be auspicious, and violence isn't'. A South Asian priest, firmly against violence in marriage, explained: 'I would keep it for the premarital counselling phase because I can see the reaction of the two people.' The need to avoid the inauspicious in his high-caste church seemed greater than the chance for the already-married to remember their vows.

However, leaders *can* speak against even the firmest tradition. A Church of South India priest mentioned violence in a wedding sermon to 'stop colluding in sin through silence'. After I had discussed marital violence at a women clergy meeting, she decided to include it in a village wedding homily later that day, which she immediately translated:

> God created us all equal, men and women, rich and poor, and loves us all equally. God loves relationships, and he loves marriage as the recognition of this particular relationship. In future, I hope when someone in this town asks, 'who has a good marriage here?' people will point to you two. Why might they do that? Because in living in a good marriage, you will not talk badly of each other to others, you will never hit, slap or kick each other nor scream at each other, and you will respect, honour and care for each other, the one who is less tired helping the other, the one who is more cheerful helping the other, the one who is healthy caring for the one who is sick.

Those attending stopped chatting and listened with rapt attention. No one expects a 'near-Damascus conversion' of listeners, as the Taiwanese priest above made clear. Nevertheless, weddings are theologically and pastorally important points of potential enlightenment *precisely* because so many are present, a point not lost on those eighteenth-century Lutheran pastors, as we saw in Chapter 3. A Kiribati pastor explained the value of the wedding homily for all:

To the couple, I'll say 'One woman + One man = One made in the Image of God. Treat your partner no differently from the way you treat yourself, because you are one. Think how you would feel if your wife dies before you, think how you will grieve for the bad things you have done to her, grieving not just for her loss but because you can never put it right. Think forward and never behave in a way you will be ashamed of'. I want all the married people there to feel they are at their own marriage, so I say: 'Listen to what I am saying to the bride and groom and give yourselves a second chance to set things right'.

The wedding homily can also clarify the unequal position of each partner. Currently some Pentecostal and Evangelical-influenced churches in *all* countries preach on the headship of the man and submission of the wife, but not necessarily that wifely submission demands a man's consistent submission to and imitation of Christ as *his* head. Poor sermons appear in *any* church, as a professor of systematic theology in Seoul discovered:

> At a Presbyterian wedding last year, the minister said to the woman, 'before today you were in charge of yourself. From today, this man is your head, you do not have a head, the man is your head'. I was so shocked: had it been my daughter marrying, I'd have stopped the wedding and taken over.

This is reminiscent of the reading of the matrimonial tablets in early Christian North African marriages (Chapter 3) which, as St Monica said, make the wife's position very clear. And it is a theological and pastoral issue in *any* church *anywhere* in which Ephesians 5.21 and the subsequent demanding duties of the husband are set aside in favour of 'wives obey your husband as head of the household'. That can make asking for forgiveness, or even apologizing, seem weak, despite being key elements in Christian faith, a faith in which obedience is attentive inner listening to God's loving call, not making the tea on time.

If talking about violence at the marriage is judged indelicate, and pre-marital counselling too late, is there an earlier point in a person's church life when Christian views on inter-personal violence could be taught?

Proactive teaching opportunities: Confirmation, adult baptism, school

In many churches other than Orthodox, for whom baptism and confirmation are one rite, children and young people commit to full membership in confirmation, adult baptism or other official event. Of the 180 responses to the 2011 survey question 'Was violence in marriage mentioned in confirmation/adult baptism classes?' only 7 were affirmative. Asked if it *should* be mentioned, many agreed. Laypeople in Scotland, on the whole older, were less sure, as were male ordinands in South India and some African Independent Churches. Ordained Church of South India women, and some ordained people in Scotland, on the other hand, *were* in favour of marital violence being included. Priests in Hyderabad were ambivalent, because 'our classes focus more on church history and the candidate's responsibilities to Christ rather than "social teaching"'. This view was shared by a cluster of Roman Catholic priests in Ghana for whom 'the focus of confirmation classes is on the doctrines of faith, on right ritual practice to become a defender of the faith'. Some priests in East Asia, however, felt confirmation *was* the right time for such teaching, a pattern already followed by a Ghanaian Methodist minister who urges youngsters to leave a violent friend: 'Act immediately, like people did in Exodus: they prayed, and they acted.'

Yet whether the ordained accepted discussing this issue in confirmation classes or hid behind its absence on the confirmation syllabus, few did it. An Anglican said:

> I want to see domestic violence as a theological issue, not an extra. I teach on it, creation, and a man and woman, but I never link the two properly. I want to see that as part of the theological discipline of catechism and confirmation. I'm trying to develop that, because confirmation is not just about learning to recite the Lord's prayer. But it's hard to start it.

Methodist ministers at a Conference Workshop in the Caribbean with experience of ministry in the United States, Europe and Latin America were, with the exception of some older men, clear on the pre-service training of ministers and of young people, indicated in their collated words:

> An ounce of prevention is worth a pound of cure. Domestic violence training should begin among children. It should be in Sunday School, and in Teens meetings, making clear that violence is not part of courtship or married life. Ministerial training does not include domestic violence as part of theology: it should. We need to empower church workers and clergy to teach about abuse in marriage, to recognise and name it.

The need for teaching about mutual respect in relationships to begin early for the future of marriages as well as the life of children in abusive households was made clear by a young female pastor in Trinidad:

> We need to educate children as soon as they can sit and listen in Sunday School. As soon as a child knows daddy hits mummy and is frightened, as soon as the

child sees that, they are alone. That's where we need to start. *If no one takes the initiative to say what daddy did was wrong the cycle will go on.*

However, considerable opposition emerged, lest talk about relationships and marital violence 'rob children of their innocence'. Yet if there is abuse in 30–40 per cent of marriages, and one partner has already experienced abuse in an earlier marriage, at least half a cohort of children will know of abuse directly or indirectly from their home as well as from their cousins and from their friends. As a group of mainly Roman Catholic teachers in India realized, 'we are not protecting the children's innocence but our shame'.

Teaching in schools and from the pulpit to support the abused and their families plays a part in eliminating such abuse, although few workers and teachers had relevant training. One Roman Catholic worker gave talks in Tongan girls' schools, starting with their rights both as citizens and as Christians, quoting Genesis 1.27.

> No one listened, and when I got on to culture, and that's the big obstacle here, again no one listened, because they know the man is the head of the household and can do what he wants. *The girls quoted Ephesians 5.22 to me.*

She wanted to teach such material in boys' schools but was not invited. This imbalance was also evident in Pakistan, where a nun involved in similar secondary school visits felt talking to teenagers was near-pointless: 'I know girls are taught in Roman Catholic schools and churches to be glad to suffer [in marriage] to imitate Jesus, but boys are not.' Another nun from a teaching order struggled to insist all are made in God's Image:

> We had a Christian brother and sister in primary school. B was six and his sister Z seven. B said he wanted to marry Z, and the teacher asked how they would live. 'I'll go to work, then come home, she will take off my shoes, make my tea, cook my dinner and we shall eat together.' His sister Z protested: 'No, you will hit me if I am not quick or don't smile or say what you want. I won't marry you."

Let me end with a Malaysian nun's efforts to address the sinfulness of violence against a partner by merging the proactive and the reactive:

> I run family counselling. Last week, I acted out domestic violence. After the programme finished we had a time for sharing. One woman is in a very bad relationship. She prays every day for her husband to accept her, even though he has written her a letter to go, and hits her. She has great strength and I make clear to her what happened was wrong. Some men were crying because they could see how their actions affect women. Afterwards men and women talked together. I'd

not realised the failure of the church to give people an opportunity to talk about pain, violence, abuse. Church is a safe environment to talk about it for men too, even those who are emotionally incapable of even hearing about it.

At the same time proactive and reactive, this nun's work ended in that town when she moved, for her successor did not share her approach.

Reacting to violence: The core problem

If *proactive* teaching is fragmentary at best, and too late, what about *reactive*? Are variations when church workers talk about, and to, abused parishioners related to their local experience and their denomination's attitude to divorce, or their gender, personal faith and quirks? Ideally, proactive teaching and reactive advice should be part of holistic theological, biblical and pastoral care for all, well-expressed by a pastor in an Accra shelter for abused women and children:

> Mainline churches do little about marital violence, Independents nothing. We work with churches, saying it's against the Bible, human rights and the law and that they should respond to it, not hide behind culture or just forbid divorce. Too many say 'we give it to God' but *we must act, not hope someone else will*. We realise women talking about abuse might offend abusing top men in the church. Most churches live in denial or say it's a family matter, but it affects spirituality if people say, 'it's the will of God that you are hit: let's pray about it'. 'God is love' but you do nothing? Too many people add the Christian bits they want into culture. Seeing women as lower is part of culture, *but not part of Christ* or the new world.

Seeing women thus has been part of much faith-and-culture since Christ. Failing to teach mutuality before marriage and then just saying 'Give it to God' and 'Let's pray' without naming or acting on marital violence during marriage colludes in sin. The above pastor's, 'Act, not hope someone else will,' together with his points on Bible, divorce and faith with integrity, frames this chapter.

Reacting to violence: Teaching with Bible verses

Using a wide spread of Bible verses related to marital violence *should* be part of consistent proactive teaching, preaching and advice: they rarely are. Asking church workers, primarily the ordained, for verses relating to violence in marriage, they commonly referred to those they would use *reactively* to complainants, not for general teaching. An Australian school chaplain offered Romans 13.8: 'Let no debt be outstanding save that of loving your fellow human: *love does no harm*,' and 'those who abide in love abide in God' (1 John 4.18). 'All sin is sin,' he continued, 'but the consequences of some sin, such as hitting your wife, are greater. Luther said you shouldn't kill. *That includes not killing the soul.*' Teachers in a South India Pentecostal Seminary offered survivors Ephesians 5.22-3 on male headship, James 3.8-11 on enduring suffering, and Hebrews 12.5-8: 'The Lord disciplines those whom he loves and chastises every child whom he accepts,' which unfortunately elevates suffering above justice, making love an inevitable source of pain which survivors should endure. Perpetrators were admonished with Philippians 2.3, Genesis 1.27 or Ephesians 5.21.

Neither cited the commonest texts, Eve's role in subordinating women to men or all being made in God's Image, both verses which three Caribbean church leaders used in discussing texts related to marriage and gender. 'Genesis 1.27,' said Susannah (Methodist), 'because it is inclusive, though not all in my congregation agree.' Peter (Pentecostal) said 'Genesis 3.16-19, the Fall made women desire men to rule over them' to which Joanna (Anglican) said: 'Adam was with Eve and he was as guilty.' Peter disagreed:

> Look at 1 Timothy 2.14 'Adam was not deceived.' Men have responsibility placed on them, but they are vulnerable, and women must be careful near male clergy leaders because they [male clergy] can fall.

Annoyed with that last phrase, both women agreed neither Genesis 2 nor 3 allows men to abuse women or trample on their head, Susannah suggesting some men say, 'If you disobey me I'll treat you like a child and hit you for your benefit.' Missing her point, Peter noted that 'proper correction used very positively is good and as a last resort you can try hitting'. He used Ephesians 5.22 when talking about love and discipline asserting, to the women's disbelief, that 'God gives us freedom to operate, and if the man beats her, he feels guilty, which is difficult for him.' This theme of men 'having' to hit wives recurs.

Is Genesis 1.27 regularly used as the basis for opposition to marital violence and advice about it? This depends in part on the church, mainline using it a little more than Pentecostal. 'I often ask questioners about Genesis 1.27,' said a Lutheran pastor, 'because I like to know if people take it for real or say "yes, but …." which makes clear how they think, which isn't how I see it.' An Anglican Archbishop used it at a Ghanaian women's rally:

> By what authority do we ignore creation? Jesus Christ allowed women followers, and both were created in the Image of God, though men are stronger: they bully and abuse women. There is also Galatians 3.28.

Like Susannah, a Jesuit in Chennai saw Genesis 1:27 as the foundation of marriage, as did a priest in Germany, the former explaining his church did not take it to its logical pastoral conclusion 'in case people use it to push for women's ordination' or, put differently by a Trinidadian Presbyterian pastor, 'in case the implications offend church-going abusing men'.

A Roman Catholic Bishop opposed to marital abuse taught both that all are equal before and made in the Image of God *and* that men stand above women, explaining that 'I work through the theology of humanity based on Jesus' stories grounded on "I made you, man and woman, in my Image." His ambivalence (which affected the reception of his teaching) stemmed in part from being trained, as he said, in 'both equality and male superiority'. Clergy in southern India likewise conveyed a mixed message:

> Made in the Image of God is relevant and we talk about the dignity of the human and equality of the sexes. But we don't name violence in sermons because we don't want to broadcast the inside part of marriage, though yes, parish members experience it.

These and other parishioners, noted in Chapter 1, had no recollection of either the verse or the inherent implications: if taught, it went unheard. On the other hand, Salvation Army Officers in Pakistan, all sharing theology, praxis and the universal impact of cultural context, run a gender justice programme attended by men and women based on 'All are made in the Image of God'. A pamphlet shows a smiling couple on one side with 'Made in the Image of God', the reverse showing fragmented faces criss-crossed with 'hitting, slapping, abuse'. All members receive the same teaching, together and separately.

This is an important point. Teachers should be aware of listeners' lives, but also of what others teach. A South Asian Pentecostal principal insisted he used 'Made in the Image of God' as his basis for teaching Genesis. However, a student said it was 'drowned in male headship with the man's rights over the wife under God with no divorce', taught by the wider faculty. Sensitive to marital horror, the principal's mother having been beaten until his older brother stopped it, even he could not quell faculty opposition. It seems 'Image of God' teaching hits brick walls: either it is not taught, or taught so uncertainly it is lost amid Adam and Eve's antics, or is so contrary to life as lived that it fails to register. A Trinidadian explained the problem:

Female and some male clergy want to preach *against* local traditions of violence using 'equally-made in the Image of God' because it is our duty to speak, and we know violence can affect half the congregation as wives or as children. But we keep silent in church about the idea that all people are made in the image of God lest we upset those hitting their wives.

However, few seem upset by or misunderstand the failings of Eve. A Methodist girls' school chaplain bitterly insisted:

> People use Eve for wives, 'submit or disaster will happen, but never Genesis 1:27.' At home they say: 'You're inferior rubbish: even God knows that. Just submit.' At the wedding, submit. We should use Ephesians 5.21, submitting to each other. I'll preach on it.

The point is, however, that she had *never* preached either on the Image or mutual submission, perhaps unconsciously imitating her brothers in Christ. Being blamed for being 'yet another Eve' is so entrenched, so normal, that opposing it demands coherent Bible teaching challenging abuse and consistent care so the teaching can take root and bloom. As a minister in northern Australia said, 'People here, men and women, favour Biblical verses featuring Eve as prime sinner and wives as subordinate, rather than both as co-heirs in partnership with God, which they ignore.' It is also easy for leaders to ignore signs of distress. As another said: 'Yes, if a woman came and mentioned Timothy and Adam and Eve, I'd reckon there was a marriage problem, as that's how people here (in southern Australia) often introduce a topic: but *it's easy for pastors not to pick it up because we'd have to address it*.'

How might clergy respond to an abuser quoting 'Wives obey your husband' or a similar verse? An older Lutheran pastor said:

> I'll ask an abusing man how he justifies his action. One man quoted [Ephesians] 5.22 at me. I asked what Christ did for the church. 'He established it,' so I said, 'What then?' Silence, so I said: 'He died for it.' Took the wind out of his sails.

A Ghanaian Roman Catholic asked her priest what she should say to her Protestant husband when he demands biblical obedience? 'Say "I'll obey you if you die for me!"' An English Anglican priest explained:

> If the abused woman says her husband demands obedience as a Christian, I'll explain Ephesians 5.21, and make clear choosing to abuse another person is sinful. But the main thing is for her to hear 'you are not useless, you are not alone, you are wonderfully made.'

Interestingly, that last verse was cited several times in various countries by female leaders responding to abused women. Yet it was a female Nigerian Pentecostal pastor who insisted, to the horror of an Assemblies of God female pastor, that 'only *complete* obedience avoids wives being sacrificed to the husband's anger and abuse'. Is this nothing more than utter and dangerous nonsense, especially given the fact that she did not name such violence as sin? Perhaps she is responding to and accepting the edict of certain male pastors who insist that 'the ego in men always wants to control people: it is the effect of sin and of culture, and they cannot live equally with their partner'. The Assemblies of God pastor dealt with the offensive comment by 'othering': 'This pastor used to be Muslim, so that's where that comes from, it's not really Christian.' Indeed it is not: nor is it from Islam. In the ineluctable interaction between context, faith and sin, context-excused sin often wins:everywhere.

Against this, Ephesians 5.21, 'Husband and wife live in mutual submission one to another,' has little chance. Asking a Mar Thoma priest in India if he taught 'mutual submission in marriage', his immediate comment was 'Here in India?' as if Ephesians 5.21 uniquely, rather than commonly, clashes with local understanding of the person.

Reacting to violence: Divorce

The factoring of church attitudes to divorce into abused women's decisions to stay or leave was discussed in general terms in Chapter 2, but what do clergy and church workers say? Asking a Korean pastor whether pastors advise divorce if violence worsens, she said sadly:

> 'No. Many male pastors will just say be patient and patient and patient until he changes.' 'Or dies?' I asked. 'Yes. Marriage should be sacred, and I know if women stay they risk death. I just don't know how much of what the *church* says is true [about faith] is actually what the *people* think. Most won't say, because the church leaders rule people, using ways from the past.'

Presbyterian, Roman Catholic and Pentecostal Koreans *all* oppose divorce, and *all* exert the same firm control over ordained leaders as they do over followers. Presbyterians or Pentecostal leaders who stepped out of line could move to another church of the same brand, but Roman Catholic priests risked being 'sent to the desert'.

A Caribbean Pentecostal pastor recognized death might be the cost of staying in a violent marriage. He advocated temporary separation with counselling, saying, 'I'd pray for them. Some people will get killed. In our church people can divorce for adultery and remarry in church, *but not for violence.*' A Kenyan Pentecostal, on the other hand, was clear that if staying risked death, 'you should leave and divorce, because if you are killed, we cannot bring you back to life'. In other Pentecostal churches such as the Australian Assemblies of God, divorce after violence has been allowed since 2006 (Davies, 2007). However, individual pastors may oppose church rules, as a female church worker in northern Australia explained:

> Our senior pastor opposes women leaving their husbands, 'because God created marriage and it was the will of God this man married this woman'. He once preached about a man who killed himself 'because his wife left him'. From his preaching, he blamed her. We have to accept his ruling, but it is hard for my pastor husband.

Similarly, some Protestants who *can* include the divorced remarried don't and some Roman Catholics and Anglicans who *shouldn't* do, both decisions being personal views on local or universal church rules. A female Kenyan Anglican priest, where the divorced remarried are excluded, insists even a young woman divorced after a violent marriage cannot remarry until her former husband has died, as she'll be 'cut off from the Eucharist and from salvation'. Her male colleague, advising abused women not to stay and risk death, disagreed, though made no effort to discuss the issue with his colleague:

> An abused, divorced and remarried woman wouldn't come to the altar until she's sorted things out in her own mind. I wouldn't keep her away: who am I to reject her? We don't encourage divorce but look for the most economically wise way to go.

A Ghanaian Anglican refused communion to abusers until he has evidence of their contrition, especially if the abuse began in an effort to force the first wife out and take the blame (and financial loss) for divorce. The Roman Catholic position until and in many places beyond 2016 refuses communion to the remarried, although some priests in all countries covered here offer it. As a retired German priest explained, 'I would give communion to a divorced, remarried woman. Her conscience is more important than the Pope's.'

The view that an annulment should be granted if a marriage began with violence, the assailant's intention clearly being suspect from the start, was put forward by Roman Catholic priests in several regions, including a former matrimonial judge. His view on divorce was succinct:

> I tell students, mostly Fathers, to refer cases to competent professionals linked to the church. A woman should first divorce, then go to the church court and

hope it finds grounds for annulment. Even if excluded from the sacrament, divorced people should be welcome in church: few are.

Pastors in two large worldwide West African-rooted Pentecostal and charismatic Evangelical churches stressing female obedience and male headship allowed survivors an annulment-like divorce early in a marriage because 'unrepentant persistent abusers were never believers'.

Yet exclusion from communion is not the only discipline meted out to the divorced. A just-divorced Protestant woman in England was recently told by her church leader that 'if you have sex again, you will be committing adultery, because abuse is not a Biblical ground for divorce': presumably that leader has not read Exodus 21.26, which makes clear that after adultery, desertion or failure to provide food or love, the legally released party can remarry. A Taiwanese Roman Catholic, telling her priest she had to leave a very violent marriage, which he was aware of, was shocked that his first response was: 'You cannot marry again if you leave him.' As she said, survival, not remarriage, was her main concern. People can be so harsh, so keen to throw rules in the face of the desperate, so loveless.

Summing up Christian behaviour and also the place of divorce in Christian marriage, a long-retired and generally conservative Australian pastor explained,

> I've the same reverence for my wife as for my Lord: I do not demand obedience from her. I suggested one abused lady left for a while: he didn't change, so she divorced, and I've no problem with that. Marriage is about mutual support and you can't force people.

Reacting to violence: What clergy say they say

A first point is that church leaders should signal in a sermon that they care. One, whose 'liberalism' found him barred from counselling in the city, explained that in his rural birthplace

> women regularly come by to talk. I sometimes address the issue in everyday conversation or at church: addressing it gives people permission to come and talk. If you are silent about it, people think you agree so they will not come.

Every clergy person and worker actually involved in the pastoral care of abused adults had signalled in a similar way, reminiscent of the Myanmar Baptist woman above: 'The church doesn't support violence against women, but because … it is often silent, it looks as if it does.' An English curate had six women come in one year after such a signal:

Initially we talk very briefly, then meet, but keep it short. I make clear there's no excuse for violence; that he chose to hit her, and she is not responsible for that decision; and make sure she has the police or local refuge numbers. Later meetings are under an hour, lest she fall apart and lose her dignity. Once it was too long and she hadn't enough time to put herself back together.

Along with others, her British pre-ordination training did not mention domestic violence survivors, either in practical or in theological terms, although it now offers two single sessions. A Roman Catholic priest in Germany agreed women must know whom to talk to:

> I was diocesan advisor for pregnant women: they had an address and knew I don't judge. A woman came once, and I said 'Why do you let him hit you again? If he touches you once more, go with your child to the women's refuge'. She is now happily remarried. *I said it quietly to avoid trouble.*

A group of Roman Catholic priests in Ghana were blunt:

> We talk a lot about violence, in church, and we challenge cultural assumptions, using Paul, making the man responsible for loving the wife as Christ died for the church. If a couple have problems, I ask to talk to the man. If he isn't contrite, I tell her to tell her family. If he still hits, tell the police, but divorce if it is life-threatening.

Signalling, and talking openly, is affected by the church worker's context. Jane, abused in her first marriage and now a Pentecostal pastor in a clearly male dominated church in which women pastors tread delicately to keep their footing, felt unable to signal her opposition to some advice given by fellow pastors. Aware some bordered on the abusive, she was clear:

> If the backsliding husband hits, he cannot blame her for letting the devil in, for *his* backsliding gave the devil entry. 'Christ suffered, so I can too?' No way! That is wrong advice! No, the church tells you: intercede with Christ and your man will change. If he doesn't? He will be shamed and repentant if we pray, so all is okay.

Feeling that expected a lot of prayer, I asked what she advises abused women:

> If you love him, make space for forgiveness: love enables you to forgive. Given a long rope, he'll come back. Till then, be normal with him. Tell him the scripture. Apologise for anything you did which caused the hitting. But some men won't listen.

There are clear sources for her ambivalence: she knows the abuser chose to abuse yet feels she must stress prayer's strength and female forgiveness. She was angry to hear 'Suffer as Christ did,' which was said to her in her first Roman Catholic marriage and is still being said. When she got beyond worrying lest she stray from the church path, she was kind and caring, offering precisely what those in trouble want when reaching out for help: a listening ear and a generous heart. A German Roman Catholic priest said:

> Women would talk to me about their husband's abuse so that someone was nice to them, someone believed them, someone was kind. Priests saying, 'Jesus suffered and so you can carry your Cross?' Heard it often, but what a cheek! Thankfully, people would laugh at you now and say, 'You're mad.'

He may feel that, but pious women in his small town had heard it from priests in the past and still use it as a supposed 'comfort' for currently abused women, as we shall see in the next chapter.

A group of Roman Catholic clergy in Accra insisted *all* violence in marriage is serious, and that 'pray, persevere and be patient' is only for everyday problems and irritations, *not* for violence, which may need separation and divorce for the survivor's safety. In the same city, though, another priest advised against divorce for an actual abused woman whose husband has a second family because 'the lapse is just a temporary separation'. This leaves the first wife vulnerable to her still-violent husband if he chooses to visit.

Clearly, cultural tropes, church rules and personal traits are all relevant to how church workers relate to abused women. To listen, to insist the assailant chose to abuse, to make clear the victim is wonderfully made in God's Image and to ensure her safety: any or all of these would make a sound start. What more might the church worker do (beyond not giving advice to women which would not be given to men) if they see their role as one of pastoral and theological support? An obvious point is that all church workers should know the number of any refuge there may be, and of other relevant secular and faith agencies. It would be helpful were they to gather on the local grapevine whether *all* the local police actually support abused women, or whether some rotten apples are liable to mock 'women who complain' or are themselves abusers, supported in their wrongdoing by their colleagues.

Some contexts have clear social rules. If a Kiribati pastor is willing to help, he encourages an abused woman to go back to her home, where he later accompanies the husband to see if she is prepared to come back. However, if he knows the violence is both continuing and dangerous, he will not help get her back, but hope she remains with her parents, her safety and her future being his main focus. An Australian pastor explained:

> Once visited an abusive man: his wife had come to ask for 'prayer in difficult circumstances'. He wasn't offended by my intrusion but rather embarrassed, thankfully as he was built like a brick shit house. I just said, 'This is illegal, it is unchristian, you cannot do it.'

Anxiety about his reception was clear in that man's comment, and rightly so. Intervening has dangers and risks, as an eighteenth-century curate in England found when prosecuted by the husband for advising an abused wife to procure a warrant against her husband (Bailey, 2003:35). There are definite problems in visiting an abused person at home. Even if the assailant is absent, neighbours may report the church presence, causing violence to resume and even escalate. A German Roman Catholic priest echoed the potential vulnerability for helpers:

> A man came to the presbytery with his grown sons to shout at me: they were yelling. 'You have empowered her and she has left us. You must get her back.' I told them: 'She came to me in her need; I must be on her side and support her and I did. I shall not tell you where she is. I wasn't happy not to be able to talk to you about the problem, but she was too afraid of you.'

Certain things should not be done! Three ordained men in Australia and England told abusive husbands they would be 'dealt with directly' if violence continued. All three had had military training, all were big, and two had boxed. Other than to prevent a fatality, stopping abuse with violence without the abuser being transformed risks 'power over' coming out in another way, putting the survivor or other vulnerable persons at risk. One of the three explained:

> I was working in an isolated area: no social workers or psychologists or whatever. I just went to the guy who'd hit his wife, picked him up by the shoulders and threatened to do him over if he did anything like it again. I object to domestic violence on ethical grounds, as a Christian, and from common decency. Did I believe her? Yes.

Believing an abused person is important, and his reasons for objecting to abuse are sounder than his method, even taking isolation into account. Less problematic is urging a woman felt to be at risk of death to leave. Yet even this can arouse questions, in that the *survivor* should decide, assuming abuse has not utterly eliminated her capacity to act, as noted in Chapter 3. As a Methodist minister said: 'I will not encourage people to leave, nor tell a person talking about it that her husband is violent: *she* must say it. I say, "you must seek help" and I don't let her leave the room till we've talked about her safety.'

Encouraging a survivor to leave might nevertheless be appropriate in certain situations. One pastor from a cultural background which rejected divorce explained:

> If murder is likely, I'd tell her: 'you must leave now,' and send the husband for psychiatric assessment so she can sort things out and decide if she wants to leave. I've been telling an abused 36-year-old woman with one son: 'Staying encourages your son to think hitting is okay. That'll make a bad life for your future daughter-in-law.'

Creating such a safe zone by removing the assailant may be seen as intruding into the woman's decision-making domain, whether this is done by police taking him to the cells or by this canny pastor with good connections. Yet provided the survivor is safe and has effective support in that time, she may well be able to decide if she wants to leave or await his return. Being there to help a woman frozen by abuse, even being there to give blunt advice, may offend her dignity: dead, she has none.

To act, to visit, to protect may be a decision of the moment and the context: but to teach, to speak, to name the sin, to listen, to sit in warm silence with the desperate must become part of daily reflection and practice. These comments by South Indian women priests make the point:

'Life is a gift from God and no one has authority to damage or destroy it'; 'the church must no longer keep silent'; 'most abused Christian women are silenced, fearing church and society'; 'men should be taught about this issue as well'; 'this serious issue must be dealt with at grass-roots level not just in a Synod'; 'abuse will continue as long as boys learn they are more important than girls'; 'such violence is part of local culture but it must be opposed by the church and so *by the people who are the church*.'

This last comment leads me back to those nuns who are 'of the church' and have a salutary sense of justice and action: they are largely ignored in terms of church policy and practice.

Reacting to violence: What do nuns want to hear?

Lay church workers may more readily feel able to express a critical view of clergy attitudes and actions, although some clergy rise above that sea of silent inaction which supports abuse. Professed, committed and permanently liminal, Roman Catholic nuns can give valuable insights.

Talking to a world-respected nun in India, three things were clear. Firstly, she could speak her mind because she relied not on the local hierarchy but a worldwide order of nuns. Secondly, while her estimation of Order priests in India varied according to the Order and their attitude to women, marriage and violence, she had little regard for the bulk of Diocesan priests who 'enjoyed side-lining when not insulting resident nuns in church so the local people know who counts'. Thirdly, she had little confidence that any church would face up to marital violence because few individuals, never mind churches or seminaries, were prepared to see it as a theological rather than a social issue. The difference in attitudes between diocesan and Order priests was also made by a Mother Superior in England.

> The diocesan priests are not interested, they don't want to upset people, and most don't see it as especially important. Order priests, especially those working in mission contexts, do know about it and might talk about it in their mission field, but maybe not here.

Nuns in Tonga, working with Methodist and Anglican laywomen, lead what opposition there is to marital violence. One nun said:

> The hierarchy doesn't make a stand and say domestic violence is a sin. They approach the subject from doctrine, mainly that the woman should forgive, forgive, forgive. We stand for women making their own decisions. No church here likes that. If there's any problem, they all just call for prayer.

Asking her and two others if that means the 3Ps of perseverance, prayer and patience, they laughingly agreed, saying, 'If, in the meantime your arm is broken, just pray, and don't wonder if church doctrine and attitudes make it worse.' All working in an ecumenical Women's Centre agreed that abused women go to the police, not the priest, because, said the nun, they just say 'go home, pray and be patient and care for your children, for if you leave who will care for them'. And, continued another, 'if she told the priest her husband might kill her, he'd say, "I'll say a mass for you."' All laughed, the nun concluding with:

> In my village, few go to the priest with problems unless he is part of the family, but then you'd go to him in his kin role. You hear women saying, 'praying is okay, but if I die from him, what then?' They just say the rosary, go to Mass, and hope to live through it.

All the workers present, Roman Catholic, Methodist and Anglican, agreed that women who could speak up should, as should priests and pastors, *not individually and quietly as they thought fit to individual trusted or favoured women but speaking openly to everyone.* Two Roman Catholic Bishops *had* spoken against violence, calling it a sin, but a leading lay worker said scathingly:

> I tell people to get away as soon as he starts hitting, and to keep their passport and marriage certificate close and safe, so he cannot get it. The local nuns are best at teaching. People here say Adam was top and Eve a sinner, so women are second-class, and they don't know Adam ate the apple or that God told Adam and not Eve. Some priests here don't like our work: one said I was arousing insubordination among women and children. We need someone to talk from a biblical aspect about domestic violence, so everyone hears it: no preacher here, from any church, will do that. I say yes, you signed up for your husband in church, but if he beats you all the time, go to the police. Go to a priest, to be told 'Go home and be a better wife?' No way! People would listen if the church speaks but *because they don't speak, people assume it is okay.*

An occasional kindly word about women from the general run of church workers which contradicts their daily dose from society and church will leave no trace in the collective memory of committed lay workers, never mind those in the pew. This is an issue which came up time and again: coherent and consistent concern and action for the abused was one thing, passing kind words quite another. The speaker might feel they were 'doing their bit for the abused.' They are not.

A Kenyan nun, who needed to be careful, first gave the official version of the sanctity of marriage and the risk of excommunication for remarriage after divorce. After chatting further, she explained the unfairness for a young woman, divorced because she cannot manage the violence, who tries to stay single to remain in the church; 'men don't bother'. Her concern for divorced women was less that they avoid excommunication by staying single, but that they avoid rape by remarrying. She admitted, and this was voiced throughout the research, that 'the church does not teach about domestic violence because it will annoy the men more and they will attend even less, and too many leaders agree with hitting'. She stressed that men should be told to 'love your wife and never hit, demean or abuse her' and women should only be expected to submit to their husband in a compassionate and safe environment of mutual respect.

Pressure was even more evident in talking to a Roman Catholic church worker in Korea. While her priest-boss was present, we talked of the influence of Confucianism on modern Korean marriage. When he left, she quickly explained that the Church was only interested in expansion, not women's problems. 'It is the two nuns here who support me and without their help this work would not get done even to the extent I can help women in need. Priests are not interested in the issue. They say it is too complicated.'

She was not the only church worker with that perception. Talking to another at a church-run women's refuge in Korea, I asked whether priests ever spoke or taught about husband-wife violence. 'No' was the straight response: 'Priests are men.' 'And the nuns?' I asked. 'The sisters speak about it a little, but the priests control things.'

Asking a nun in Pakistan whether local clergy were concerned about abused women, her response was clear:

> Women religious [nuns] speak about it and do something when we can. I worked on a tribal mission, and we were strong and realised we were strong; we lived and worked without men. If a beaten woman left her husband and her family rejected her, we would take her in: usually there was no priest there so they didn't cause us a problem.

That same negative thread ran through a Malaysian sister's comments. 'My church, like others, teaches women that suffering is good and part of God's plan for you because Jesus suffered.' Priests, she said, tend to respond with an anodyne 'what a pity' if a woman reported abuse, laughing when I responded with the 'but we'll pray for you' which inevitably follows. She felt they were rather anxious talking about the Bible, especially Genesis 1.27, and Ephesians 5.21, Adam and Eve and Ephesians 5.22 being firm favourites. An utterly committed and competent nun, she summed up her views on violence thus: 'The church says forgive, forgive, forgive! Matthew is supposed to cover everything.' I responded with: 'We don't usually forgive before there is repentance: the priest doesn't give "free forgiveness" but the wife is expected to.'

> 'Yes', she said, 'The church says we are all equal before God, but eventually you just figure out that they mean you women are not equal, so don't think about that. We're supposed just to pray away. All that does is make the conscience of those who know but do nothing feel better.'

Let me end this chapter with the comment of a Chinese Assemblies of God counsellor, who once again switched from the apparent acceptance with which she had earlier begun:

> Abuse fills her, occupies her soul. He finishes her as a human. From a counselling perspective, you need to be firm and say, 'leave this man if you value your life.' Society needs a space for the abused one to go for restoration: churches should be places of refuge. It would help if the church came out strongly to say, 'We are not condemning you if you leave.' A woman needs affirmation for their faith and from their faith. My church does not give this support.

And that would be the conclusion of too many nuns and ordained leaders.

Reflection

Teaching respect and care for all to Sunday School children from four and five years old was felt by some to be the best foundation for all future teaching on marriage. However, few church workers or pew-sitters were keen to take up the challenge blaming, as we have seen, anything but their own unwillingness to risk awkward or shameful moments. Few ordained people had any idea what to say or do to support the abused, and too many who did talk to abused women put her in more danger by seeing both together, blaming her and thus increasing her despair, or gossiping. Where it is the husband as household pastor who is abusive, his wife has nowhere to go other than secular agencies, other churches and reliable discrete friends.

Talking to ordained people across the globe, including those trained in the last decade, few had been taught about abuse in Christian marriage in training, a point discussed in Chapter 7. The lay 'priesthood of all believers' was even less prepared. Clergy may hold back through anxiety or ignorance, because the abuser or church superiors may turn on them, or rich abusers leave. However, concern for family reputation may keep abuse a secret, however helpful the pastor could be. As one said: 'I only realised one parishioner was being abused when she was dying. Knowing she was not going to be hit again, she said he'd kept her in the house, hit her and then gave her poison.' Yet all, lay and ordained, should be able to rise above misogyny, name abuse as sin and proclaim a loving God. If asked, even the most uncertain can offer a degree of personal affirmation and some support.

Whatever the difficulties, *regular* preaching on the Image of God and its consequences will challenge all listening and give solace if not immediate courage to the afflicted, who must know both what counts as abuse and that it is sinful. The lack of consistency among the ordained prevents teaching against family violence becoming as obvious a part of a church as altars or hymn sheets. Churches in many countries now have information about safeguarding of the young and the vulnerable, to help keep the latter from harm and the church from being sued. It would be good were all to have similar statements about violence in marriage.

'Failure to recognise all count equally affects the health of the whole church,' one minister said, continuing: 'It is not right when many are not seen as made in the Image of God. But I'm sorry for the violent people too, because they are afraid and feel trapped, and hit out like a cornered animal,' a point touched on in the last chapter. Let me end here with a group of truly helpful male pastors in Trinidad:

> 'We in the church keep silent on behaviour which clashes with the idea that people are made in the Image of God in favour of not upsetting wife-hitters.' Another responded: 'But we collude if we don't talk about the Image of God.' 'Yes,' replied a third. 'But who do we talk to? No one wants to know if it doesn't fit what they "know to be the case."'

6

Laywomen and the church: What they think, receive and want

We have already heard much from women in this book; nuns, who are professed but still lay church workers; abused clergy wives who may do unpaid work for the church but are nevertheless lay; and female clergy. Women in each category commented on the church, whether as an institution or the people of God, on marriage, and on church and household faith leaders. While some supported the rules of various churches into which abused women must fit, or the 'Well, you know, she is difficult' exoneration- the majority were scathing, puzzled or sad, with a number determined to seek change.

This chapter homes in on women of faith who are neither professed nor ordained nor married to an ordained or appointed church worker. Rather they are women who from experience, empathy and profound dismay have views on the way in which churches talk about and to abusing Christian men and abused Christian women. Many of them know abuse directly or indirectly. They identify as Christian, may well attend services regularly, perhaps filling the many small but crucial roles which await laywomen. However, because of their present circumstances and past experience which their church enabled or otherwise ignored, they may relate to God primarily (if at all) in private. The absence of these clouds of women may radically and increasingly affect the church as the people of God and even the church as an institution, because a proportion of male lay Christians, and not just in the Euro-American world, keep their distance from church. This is not a new fashion.

Women in this chapter include the 'salt of the church', but there were times when despairing or cynical emojis best answered the question: 'What do [usually male] church leaders say about the violence of husbands to wives'?:

> 'pray for him, persevere, be patient and know that suffering brings you closer to God' … or 'that's a private issue, sort it out yourself' … or 'what were you doing to make him hit you!' … or 'don't be lazy and then he won't hit you.'

There would also be bitter emoji smiles from those who spoke of marriage in the past tense, having abandoned their partner. Those who were still hopeful, still desperate, still internalizing responsibility for another person's sin: for them multiple emojis of guilt and shame. And for those whose husband's anger, alcohol or drug dependency, underemployment, or violent masculinity makes him not the man they married, for them a two-faced emoji of sadness and irritation. Thankfully for some, the hopeful smile of a well-cared-for survivor who has found new life, whether with a new or fully reformed partner or alone.

Women as colluders in others' abuse

Not that Christian women hold the moral high ground in attitudes to marital violence, even if most marital violence is meted out to them. Indeed they are a mixed bag when it comes to responding to the violence suffered by other women, bringing to mind Albright's 2003 comment: 'There is a special place in hell for women who do not support other women.' The 'colluders' in the subheading above does not refer to those women shamefully accused of 'colluding in their own oppression' by trying to avoid violence rather than directly oppose it. It seems the height of arrogance to decree what an abused woman should do.

The issue is women who are *not* abused colluding by default or intention with abusers' excuses, validating their violence. Unbeaten women tend to give the beaten a wide berth: 'Yes,' an English Christian survivor said, 'It's as though we had measles. As soon as they knew, they almost crossed the road to avoid talking to me.' That may represent the same lack of awareness of what to say or do exhibited by clergy. Yet it may also come from that individual and collective tendency to ignore violence affecting others 'because we'd have to address it' or, like divorce, because it might be 'catching'. Men who do not abuse wives *also* commonly keep silent, becoming embarrassed or diffident if a survivor mentions the issue or, indeed, if an abuser brags.

However, it is 'rejection by their own kind' which causes most grief to abused women. This was referred to again and again, especially where 'helpful' women suggest their hurt sister should cook better or faster, lose weight or speak more sweetly. They may just want to help the survivor make the best of a bad job: but unless they also name the sin (ideally without bad-mouthing the culprit) they inadvertently support it.

A further reason (or excuse) not to speak out or offer support stems from anxiety lest it be seen as interfering in someone else's marriage. This may rebound on the supporter, especially in a small community if men object to their own wife engaging with a male friend's possession. Coming between a husband and wife could disrupt the religious and social order (Leviticus 19.17) and damage the reputation of those speaking. Similar restrictions exist in many customary law systems. Both the eighteenth-century curate and the Roman Catholic priest of Chapter 5 spoke with institutional authority even if they were not backed up by their institution. Laywomen speaking up *as Christians* against specific abuse may feel even less support. Backing off may be the pragmatic if cowardly choice, yet naming abuse as sin is surely not too risky.

However, there at least two instances where women actively collude in violence against other women. The first, already alluded to, is when a mother sends beaten daughters back to abusive husbands lest neighbours blame her 'inadequate teaching and example' for the abuse, which may hinder the marriage of her younger unmarried sisters (see Chapter 2). The view that 'only bad wives are beaten and bad wives come from bad mothers' is widespread in certain areas of the world, including eastern Kenya and South Asia. Blaming the daughter deflects attention from the mother, as in this case from Kenya, when East African Protestant and Roman Catholic members visited a survivor blinded in one eye and with broken bones. Both groups, *including* the victim's mother, said that proper submission, speaking gently to him about his mistress or waiting until a better time, would have prevented the attack. 'So,' her furious sister said, 'it was her fault?'

Another sphere in which women contribute to violence against other women is inexcusable. Men are bidden in Genesis 2.24 to forsake their family and be joined with their wife. Where parents let go of their married children, the two have a chance of making a mutually respectful marriage. But if a 'spurned' mother refuses to give up her son to his new woman, she may seek revenge, inciting her son to abuse his wife. 'She is rude to you, she does not follow your word, she cooks badly, she speaks back to you, you should discipline her, hit her' were all phrases I heard from women beaten by their husband through the machinations of his mother. Asked by a large lively group in Kenya what advice I would give, my first off-the-cuff comment was, long-term, not to bring up sons to be kings lest their sisters and wives become slaves. I then (rather unwillingly) said:

> Advise your daughters against a man who worships his mother and she him: your daughter will never do things like his mother does, and she won't let him go. But if he hates his mother, initially he'll be happy with your daughter because she isn't his mother, but later he may put her in that place. Dissuade her from

marrying a man who hit her during courtship or who insults people he reckons lesser than himself like a servant or sweeper. Later that'll be her place.

Listeners *immediately* picked out 'too-close mother', citing marriages which had broken down because the man hit the wife on his mother's instructions, or constantly went home to her. Some couples avoided this by *both* cutting the apron strings. A Kenyan lady gave the usual version:

> It happens if the mother-in-law is too close to the son. Better to move away, or you will always be under her, and she'll support him in any argument. One woman I know left her husband after a really bad beating. The church elders told her to ask her father-in-law to take her to the hospital. He didn't want to irritate his wife so pretended there was no problem.

Taking sides in favour of the son against his wife occurs widely in families. Without permission, some church leaders report a 'seriously abusive' husband to his mother: if she was the instigator, the daughter-in-law is in a worse position.

In short, women contribute to violence against other women in marriage indirectly, through ignoring or distaining the abused, and directly by rejecting a beaten daughter through shame or by inciting sons to hit daughters-in-law. However, the main sinners are husbands, a proportion of whom use local custom and half-remembered Bible fragments in 'validation', some of which were noted in Part One on church attitudes to divorce (Chapter 2), past church support for the 'disciplining' of wives and current interest in submission (Chapters 1 and 3). Let us now revisit crucial theological and biblical themes which underlie women's situation, their voices and ideally the right to live fully.

Headship and submission

As discussed in 'power over' in Chapter 2 and then Aquinas in Chapter 3, those with power over others commonly interpret actions which actually please *them* as being beneficial to the subordinate, thus: 'I [want to] hit you for your salvific benefit.' Male headship of the family does not *cause* abuse, *provided* the head consistently subordinates himself to God *and* fully respects his wife's voice as co-heir (1 Peter 3.7). However, teaching male headship without *at the same time* teaching that *any* abuse of wives is *always* sinful because it risks supporting spiritual abuse which easily validates other abuse. As an Evangelical head of a Women's Shelter said, 'The wrong understanding of male headship [by men] is the main problem,' the view already voiced by the separated wife of an abusive vicar, who also blamed the theology of headship for her husband's violence.

Moreover, there seem at least two situations where stressing male headship without qualification or caution may increase the danger for the wife. Firstly, until state law steps in, local controls over violence lessen if migration means kith and kin cease to meet regularly. This is referenced in one of the few verses in the Bible to speak bluntly against abuse of wives (Genesis 31.50), which cites the case of a son-in-law taking his two wives, Leah and Rachel, and moving away from the family to acquire land in a distant place. Laban says to Jacob: 'If you ill-treat my daughters, or take wives besides my daughters, although no man is with us, remember, God is witness between you and me.' Laban knows that such a situation was fraught with danger for an otherwise unprotected wife.

Given increased movement within and between countries, this is a worldwide problem, well-explained by a Tongan woman:

> Most of the ties which bind people loosened as extended families fell apart. In the past, everybody was involved in telling people off: no one said, 'Mind your own business.' High mobility means no one feels able to speak up. Before there was a balance between a woman's status as a sister and a wife: not now.

However, migration is not always negative, nor are extended families always positive. Even if loss of ties decreases protection for a wife, it may also give her freedom to go. A Tongan Christian social worker explained:

> Some women can be more independent and positive if there are fewer family people to pressurise her. And women learn other things from migrants who have gone to New Zealand. But the main thing is the absence of the extended family. That helps. Younger people talk more, and are less bothered about their reputation.

Secondly, stress on male headship can have particularly negative consequences amid clear role differentiation (only males provide, only females cook) if primary industry and male manufacturing jobs have gone. True, as women often said, quietly proud of their ability and often irritated with their men: 'We women are willing to earn a few cents, shillings, or rupees for tiny jobs because added up that'll buy food. Our men are too proud for that.' Female willingness to do low-paid jobs further feminizes hitherto male work, giving husbands less reason to do it.

If the man ceases to act as household head, provider and protector, either no one provides food for the children, leading to the dissolution of the family, or the wife takes that role, exacerbating the husband's resentment over her 'Christian disobedience'. This Malaysian lady sums up:

> The church teaches that in marriage the man is the head of the family. But sometimes the wife has to be dominant because the husband doesn't care. Maybe

he is jobless and she brings in the money. He stays with friends, drinks, gambles: the family is broken. She must still submit, and respect him, even if he hits her in his frustration and anger. But it is difficult.

Women insisted that ensuring food for all might need female leadership. However, people supporting male headship may use such outcomes as evidence that when women lead, the family falls apart, ignoring the sequence of events. At one meeting, a man insisted if the unemployed husband was depressed due to his inability to provide for his family, that was the *wife's* fault for failing to be loving to him: 'She should love her neighbour as herself.' Those women present disagreed, saying afterwards that slipping biblical texts in was normal. Yet again, women's job is to pick up the slack and take the blame in both domestic and spiritual spheres. But as they said: 'It's not our fault if we have to run the family. If he doesn't take responsibility because he doesn't love us, someone has to find the food, and pay school fees.' Farming wives in Pakistan said:

> We work in the fields as best we can to get money as our husbands won't work for so little. They get angry if they demand money from us and we won't give as it's for the family's food, so they beat us.

Again worldwide, women's church groups still teach single women how to be good wives but, as one irritated lady explained, 'we're not taught how to set ourselves free if he's violent, before we suicide or die'.

According to the 'headship' model, disobedience is acceptable if the head asks his wife to sin. However, an abused wife lacks the confidence calmly to point out the husband's theological and moral error. Moreover, as an informant accustomed to such treatment explained,

> It's all very well for the priest or elder to say 'This is not part of your duty' when I ask about a particular demand, but as soon as he shuts the door my husband doesn't agree and gives me a very big beating. I either do what he wants or accept a beating if I won't.

Continuing to teach what comes across as simplistic 'men's rule', without stressing that the man is responsible to God for *all* actions and decisions, too easily fuels abuse. The leader who says 'That is not part of your duty' without teaching the congregation what *is*, and *without ensuring the wife will be safe after he has left the house*, is almost as derelict in his or her duty as one who ignores an abuser's sin in stressing wifely duty. If the powder is not removed from weaponized texts, they become the propellant for spiritual abuse and hell on earth for the abused subordinate.

Submission easily merges with 'it says you must obey me'. Abused women may use such texts not only to explain (though they may do just that) but to reject and leave or place the violence in a frame wider than the intentional nastiness of their own spouse. For a Kenyan Pentecostal woman, born Roman Catholic, violence cancelled obedience:

> I should obey my husband, and divorce is not allowed. But if I marry, and he hits me, especially my eyes, I'm gone fast. And yes, I'd ask the pastor to see if he's okay for me to stay in that church, but if not, I'd go. That's how I am.

Whether she would actually leave would depend on her situation: but her intention was clear. Women's responses to the demand for obedience in Christian marriage include silent ridicule of their 'boss':

> I was 'too slow cooking?' Of course, even though cassava takes an hour to cook and we'd only been back from the farm for twenty minutes! It's always the same, but he won't let me return earlier.

Another woman said: 'He might say "It's daytime!" and I'd agree, even though I could see the moon and stars, stuff like that all the time.' Disagreeing with husbands was taken as rebellion, but rebellion is theologically grounded opposition to God, not being late with the tea.

'What does submission mean?' I asked a group of interested Methodist women in Accra. They outlined the slippery slope, as so often, from a polite and gentle start:

> I must respect him, be humble, trust him, accept what he wants. It doesn't make you less of a human to be submissive, but it does make some men feel very important, and then they control you and make all the decisions, so that sometimes we feel he is a slave master. Then they say: 'I am the head and you were just made from my rib so you are nothing,' and they hit because they want sex or money because they paid bride-wealth.

Whether disobeying the household head or answering back was a safe option for a Christian wife depends on circumstances and the specific context, criteria she must factor into any decision. His ceasing to attack the woman he had pledged to honour rarely appeared in that assessment. Church stress on wifely submission as both preventive and cure-all increased the guilt for the abused wife. 'Our pastor says, "if you submit he will not beat you, so if he does beat you that means it is your fault for not submitting."' Not all women accepted this view, seeing the vicious circle it set up. Apart from being theological and pastoral nonsense, they saw that such statements (rather like 'losing the fight against cancer due to lack of *real* faith') are both demoralizing and dangerous. Some scathingly rejected this advice and were angry if others were encouraged to remain and 'work out their sin'. They insisted that such an adviser bears responsibility if the abused woman is later killed or, as in another case, had her arm chopped off by her assailant. The sceptically received wisdom ran along the lines of: 'You are in God's care and if you *really* trust God, God will care for you,' the alternate version being: 'Trust God and get out early.'

Texts on spousal violence are replete with horror stories of women who were indeed killed because they believed their Christian husband would stop if they submitted to and obeyed him utterly. One wife explained:

> While the hierarchy of marriage can produce profound humility in some men, in others it fuels the flames of domination and even violence. Any time I objected to his behaviour, he told me I was to submit to him just as totally as if he was Jesus Christ. (Alsdurf and Alsdurf, 1990:13)

Two theologically informed and abused American women discussed submission, Susan Hagood Lee saying:

> I was a faithful churchgoer ... But where was God when one month after our wedding my husband first blackened my eyes? ... My course of action seemed clear. God's will, as the Bible instructed, was that I stay with my husband, forgiving him when he hurt me, countering his evil behaviour with my love, *cooperating with God's plan of salvation for him*. (1991:11–13, italics added)

Eventually, in silent prayer, her 'God with a magic wand on a white charger' is replaced by 'God who understood my predicament. This God did not want me to suffer: this God wanted me to be happy. But I had to save myself: God would not do it for me' (1991:15).

Some church leaders would see that last line as lacking trust in God, others that she was using her God-given sense for self-preservation and self-respect. Another abuse survivor, the theologian Ruth Tucker, had this response from her minister:

> His only concern was that we discuss the verses he had given me on wifely submission. I argued that I had already gone way too far in so-called 'submission' by not reporting [my husband's] crimes. He responded that a wife's first loyalty was not to the legal system but to Christ – and to Christ by way of submission to her husband. (2016:153)

Neither woman was saying she can do all without God: far from it. Rather, as the Methodist pastor, the Roman Catholic priest, the Salvation Army officer and many ordained (and lay) people say: 'Pray, listen, *act* and live.' That might mean that she must seek civil court help but, as Tucker says, 'How is she to do that while making sure it does not contradict the spirit of love and submission to her husband?' (2016:155). Just like women anywhere, these abused American women found the teaching on submission and headship made managing violence even more of a nightmare. However, rejecting the complementarian tenet that 'woman is a secondary creation designed to complement man as his helper' makes some feel they 'reject the Bible': 'God placed you in that awful marriage, therefore spurning God's choice is spurning God' (Schearing and Ziegler, 2013:4). Yet women in some Christian regions covered in this research who take the complementarian path may be a little better placed to find their way through abuse and faith, and for two reasons.

First, as outlined at the outset, the understanding of male and female humans as superficially varied version of the same humanity can, though need not, give a rather firmer sense of selfhood, more inwardly resilient even if physically damaged and traumatized. Second, not all Christian places (or Christian people in those places) accept Augustine's and various modern movements' stress on the ineluctable sinfulness of all. It is perfectly possible to find Roman Catholics, Lutherans, Pentecostals and others who know such views are part of their church teaching but, making neither personal nor cultural sense, set them aside for another day.

Such a bald statement may cause consternation or rebuttal, yet this seems a reasonable summary after over thirty years of research within World Christianity, talking a good deal to laypeople and to clergy. To the extent that women actually accept and internalize their 'guilt and sin', their capacity quietly to withstand the husband's use of biblical phrases demanding obedience may be that much more difficult. This is especially the case given the power of traumatic attachment (Collins, 2019:116–17) exacerbated by Christian attitudes to divorce and to female suffering.

Eve, endurance and suffering in Bible texts

One reason some clergy insisted Bible tags are *not* used as weapons or sources of self-blame is the assumption, especially among mainline church clergy in Europe, Australia and New England, that 'no one knows or uses Bible verses'. This begs the question 'if not, why not?' as well as the question 'if talk about belief is rare, why might that be?' One Australian counsellor explained: 'The women coming here are so scared from the Bible verses they've been told. They tell me: but they'd be scared to talk to the pastor in case he repeats the awful verses to them and they don't know what to say.' Being unable to give chapter and verse does not mean the content is ignored because, as has already been said, certain verses have seeped into the cultural foundations of long-Christian regions. 'Wives obey' may be the best-known validation for men hitting wives, but 'Eve as the spoiler of Eden' is the substratum on which that partial reading relies.

Eve was referred to by both men and women as the 'original cause of chaos in the world' or 'bringer of sin' which suggests, as indicated in Chapter 2, that subordinates have internalized their place in the pecking order of power or have someone else to blame beyond their own self. Added to the Adam and Eve of Genesis is the 1 Timothy 2.27 verse making only Eve guilty because 'Adam was not deceived.' From Trinidad to Tonga via Europe, Africa and Asia, the feeling, not entirely accepted, among certain Christian women (and in some contexts it seemed most) was that 'Adam was made first and Eve sinned. Most of us accept that fully: we sinned and we failed.'

Regularly I asked women, 'which creation story do you know: that we are all made in the Image of God, or Adam and Eve?' Most people in the sixteen countries covered in this research had *never* heard of the first version, just Adam and Eve, and commonly an Eve who was solely responsible for the Fall. That does not mean everyone *believed* Eve was the ultimate sinner, indeed a good many women of any and all educational levels found the idea quite silly and very irritating, although a certain negativity might stick. However, *they did not discuss it with male clergy present*, for Eve-the-Spoiler puts abused wives on the back foot, unless the church worker made the equal responsibility of both primal figures clear. The Bible easily becomes a scapegoat for the abuse of Christian wives. Yet as discussed in the first chapter, it is less the scriptural text, nor any such faith (or culture) text, which does the damage than the use of particular texts chosen for continual repetition. The more influential the person or group appropriating certain 'power' texts, the more likely they are to misuse them.

Abused women are especially likely to be told to endure, and to suffer, by both lay and ordained people, whether church or household leaders. One 'suffering' text is the already noted verse from Hebrews 12.6. Talking of hostility towards believers, it reads: 'The Lord disciplines those whom he loves and chastises every child whom he accepts.' *No woman* to whom I spoke felt encouraged by that verse, some being so burdened by it they set it (and even faith) aside. Moreover, omitted from that near-cliché is verse 4: 'In your struggle against sin you have not yet resisted to the point of shedding your blood.' Whether resisting or acquiescing, abuse survivors *have* all too often shed their own blood, making its quoting in a context of abusive violence all the more appalling.

The second, even more contentious, appears in 1 Corinthians 10.13: 'God will not let you be tested beyond your strength,' frequently rendered as 'God will not send you more [suffering] than you can manage.' This brought abused women close to tears of hopelessness and guilt if they felt they could *not* manage, as clearly lacking faith in their capacity to endure was itself a further affirmation of sin. This encouraged some to stay far longer than wise, trusting that staying would make it better. A survivor of Christian marital violence herself, Collins, after referring scathingly to Pearl's writing on violence and wifely suffering, points out:

> When someone is being subjected to abuse, telling her to suffer for Jesus mirrors the devil telling Jesus to jump off a building: it is putting God to the test. We should be partners with God in enabling people to be delivered from the evil of abuse, not insisting they have a faith that tests God. (2019:97)

Suffering through another's sin was seen more positively by Holiness and Pietist-influenced women who felt sanctified by it. Other women and church leaders might quote it to console the abused: it did not. This is hardly surprising. God does *not* send abuse on the woman: her abuser choses to sin. Suffering through the intentional sin of others is no reason to applaud the sufferer but rather to name the evil. A number of women felt 'strength through suffering' might console someone who was ill, or help the person caring for them, but not someone suffering through another's sin. Church leaders frequently said this verse was not used. Yet women in every place heard: 'Your suffering is part of God's plan for you and you will grow in faith and glory through it.' This belies the image of a loving God.

One text used to encourage women to stay with abusive husbands is 1 Peter 3.1, advising wifely submission to husbands 'so that though they do not obey the word, [they] may be won without a word by the behaviour of their wives.' Noted in Chapter 3, this view is widespread. Some abused Christian women may well stay for that reason among others but, as one Indian lady in Trinidad said: 'My husband apologises when he hits me, but he continues to do it. My witness has made no difference to him at all.' Her friend then said:

> That line is nonsense. Violence only stops if the perpetrator goes to prison, or you leave him. How long should you hold on? Till you die? If you stay long enough as a witness you will make it to heaven at his hands unless he dies first in which case you're finally OK.

Miracles apart, abused women who remain can look forward to freedom only in the death or incapacity of their abuser. Another lady, however, was sanguine about remaining in an abusive marriage (as she did) precisely for the reason given in 1 Peter:

> The woman should continue loving and obeying and being patient and doing all her duties even more thoroughly, because he might change. Even if he doesn't, and she dies because he attacks her, she will go straight to heaven and get her reward.

At one level this smacks of intentional suffering to gain a martyr's crown, rejected by the Early Church, and it elicited murmurs of opposition among her audience. Yet for Peter, as for other writers, calls for justice and mercy permeated both scripture and society. As a refuge head in Taiwan said: 'Patience is not justice if violence is there.' Some abused wives look to their own death to be released from abuse, others holding the rational if not entirely Christian hope of outliving their persecutor, allowing them to retain money, vows, children and church membership. A teacher explained:

> I do not see why you should sit in a violent marriage and wait for your death, or his. I was married. My husband was violent, but even when he wasn't hitting, he would threaten me. One day he came home, sat in silence, holding a very big piece of wood, and every so often said 'I feel like killing you.' Another day he went to the children saying, 'Where is your mother, I want to kill her.' And the church says I should stay in that and wait for my death? No!

Prayer as a support and a burden

To suggest that women enduring marital violence might not always see prayer as entirely helpful might surprise some readers, for whom sincere intercessory prayer is always the answer. But like carefully aimed Bible verses, being prayed for can oppress the object, increasing their hopelessness. As Van Leeuwen put it, 'to overcome both prejudice and abuse, praying is not enough' (1994:3). Indeed, it may be too much. A mixed group in Trinidad made clear that a combination of pressure to bear up 'because Christ suffered' in conjunction with people praying she can endure limits a survivor's decision-making:

> If an abused woman wants to bear it, OK, but if her witness, and her telling other women to stay, stops them acting and they get killed then she's part of the woman's death. And so are those women who don't say 'he's wrong, he's a sinner'

when someone says she's been hit, but just look sad, saying, 'I'll pray for you through this thing'. The woman knows they are praying and praying yet she is still hit ... *It puts pressure on her to stay with all these people praying,* making her feel worse if God doesn't even listen to others' prayers for her.

Some felt offering to pray for an abused woman was a way of avoiding real empathy or support. An angry survivor in a South Indian refuge said:

I want the church to say what happens in marriages. Very occasionally they pray in church for 'families in trouble'. I want them to say every Sunday that 'we pray for all the families in this congregation in which the woman has been spat upon and kicked and slapped and punched and threatened this week in their own house.' I want it naming.

Suggesting this strategy to a Roman Catholic deacon in Germany, he was horrified: 'Impossible in a rural community!' 'And at diocesan level?' I asked. 'No! We should only talk about joyful things in church, not like the past or like the Lutherans!' Clearly culture and brand protection counted more. Publicly naming abuse as sin is vital, yet what the above lady wanted could come across as a mixed blessing for some survivors. In the absence of pastoral and practical support and teaching, blunt but potentially unconstructive prayer may further reduce a woman's hope and her dignity when nothing improves. Occasionally asked to pray by a survivor, I would ask aloud that they see themselves as perfectly made in the Image of God, name the sin of their husband choosing to hit, insist he had no right under God, pray that the woman finds a way through the darkness and then sit in silence, my hand on her arm. To pray that someone continues to endure hell, without so naming her situation caused by another's sin, is appalling. Yet it happens.

Part of the problem is that linking 'ask and you will get' to 'with God everything is possible' topped with 'God will hear your prayer' arouses expectations that prayer will be efficacious in the terms of the request. That sets up ongoing distress. Various people talked about being prayed for, or praying, and nothing changing. A nun gave refuge clients' views:

That's why people come here: they say, 'I pray, and I pray, and this keeps happening, so I scarcely know if there is a God who hears my prayer. If there is, and God doesn't hear me, why not?' All the churches are so involved with unnecessary things, so busy with busyness, but the spirit of the people in the church? That doesn't seem to count. Unless they ask, I do not contact their priest or pastor. Because women say: 'All he does is bring us together, say prayers, exchange a kiss of peace, go home and don't do it again.'

Few examples of prayer as a weapon were as blatant as that experienced by a competent lay couple talking at a church meeting about the Image of God and mutual submission. 'The President interrupted us, praying loudly that "all must listen to ordinary people and their needs, complying fully with the Bible". He then raised his hand and cut us off. He just wants 'women obey'.

Stay or go: Weighing the scales

Some women and men advise survivors that they should stay and develop their 'gentle nurturing side even more, which makes us feel even more guilty and even more a failure as a woman and a mother'. Exclusion post-divorce in some churches and abject poverty for most apart, having children is why so many abused women stay with their abuser, especially if children must remain with their father. A departing mother takes babies, but they may have to be returned as children to the father and stepmother.

Potential stepmothers are a major object of anxiety. The worldwide pattern of really serious wife-abuse beginning or increasing just before her replacement's arrival is clearly an effort of the 'Christian' husband to get rid of the first to marry the second. The first wife will do what she can to defend herself but stays for two reasons. As a lady in Ghana explained:

> Yes, he hit me really badly, and very often, and gave no money, and sometimes locked the children out of the house. But we are in Africa, and you cannot leave, even when these things are happening. You must be there for the children, because the stepmother will not care for them. Even if wife number two is there, you stay, because 'What God has put together let no man put asunder.' You must have patience. I stayed six years till my children were old enough to be safe from the stepmother, and then she left.

Expressing my horror at what she went through in those years, the pastor sitting in on the meeting said pointedly, 'That's what *you* think!' to which the women present responded firmly: 'And that's what *we* think.' They had helped her as best as they could over those years.

Despite the step-mother risk, many said a beaten woman should leave early rather than late in the marriage, to avoid death and avoid sons following their father in violence, such imitation being clearly understood by mothers, teachers and friends who see the damage done to children. Moreover, some men and women felt that for abused women to stay gave an abuser confidence that his victim would always remain. 'Forgiving him the first time' could be the road to disaster. Yet unless the issue has been discussed before marriage or the woman expects to be hit from the beginning as 'that's what marriage is', how would many women, hit soon after marriage, be able to recognize and react to the probable outcome? Abused from the outset of her Christian marriage, Collins responded with horror when offered a place in a refuge after her violent husband had been convicted of sex offences against a girl:

> I stayed because I thought he would change if only he could choose God ... My husband wasn't abusive, he was just having a difficult time. I left the meeting incensed: why would anyone think I needed that sort of help? Soon after the meeting, he raped me. (2019:18)

Nineteen, and unaware of marital violence, she just didn't recognize it. Others lay down rules beforehand. From Tonga to Trinidad, wives spoke of warning their husband before marriage that the first hit would be the last. The explanation by a doctor is typical of this group:

> I said to my husband (I married late), 'If you hit me even once, I'll hit you and go back to my family: the first time will be the last.' I made it very clear at the beginning, and I feel that's why we had no problem. But yes, it helped that I was older and had a good job.

These were all educated (pastor, teacher, doctor), all living in countries where they could keep children on divorce, all rather older and able to earn their own living. This is not to suggest that poorer women in countries where losing children on divorce is likely will not speak firmly before marriage: but it is just that much harder.

What may unlucky women get from the ordained?

Let us now look at women's response from some to whom they go for support and help amid a violent marriage. Much has already been said, indeed this chapter started with some classic statements, but one point which has not been made is a relative lack of confidentiality. In too many places, the pastor-priest would broadcast an abused woman's experience in a sermon immediately afterwards, when all knew to whom he was referring, or pass on details of the abuse to other members of the community, including the assailant. This naturally constrained women from approaching a church leader otherwise seen as helpful. Readers might recollect the anxiety in Reformation Germany to keep such problems from the *Betfrau* (praying or pious woman) lest she tell the pastor, with a similar outcome. Indeed in modern rural Germany, and doubtless elsewhere, I heard, 'you don't want a *Betfrau* to hear if you have marriage problems, because she'll go to the priest and then everyone knows'.

A more serious risk, reported in several fieldwork sites, was for an abused and therefore vulnerable woman who asked her pastor or priest for advice to be offered the solace of his bed. As a counsellor explained,

> The pastor/priest sometimes says her, 'come to my house and stay with me'. That's the last thing a woman needs if she's been counselled. Their role must be to let the woman unload her burden by listening to her.

Several informants in different countries felt the ordained should only give counselling if they had some recognized training, and *never* if they were themselves abusers.

A weariness with what women *are* taught about marriage and duty was widely evident. The following response by women in India to my question on this could have taken place wherever subservience trumps mutuality in marriage.

> First: We got a little bit on being made in the Image of God, but much more about God cursing women and controlling them.
> Me: Does that cancel out the Image of God?
> All: Yes.
> Several: And I didn't know about the Image of God until today.
> First: Nor did I actually.
> Me: What about mutual submission in Ephesians 5.21?
> Second: That is not given any emphasis.
> All: We mean, it is never mentioned. Just 5.22.

The common pattern of women starting with a fairly neutral comment protecting their leader and moving to a more critical one is clear: 'We mean, it isn't mentioned'. A group of teachers, administrators and homeworkers in Kenya were keen to discuss the place of women in violence:

> One: It is always a wife's fault, whatever is wrong in the marriage or the day: that is the reasoning of this place and of the pastors.
> Two: Eve talked to the devil, so she was wrong, and we are Eve.
> Three: That's because she decided to disobey God.
> Two: So did Adam.

As we shall see, laypeople are perfectly able to discern bias in teaching and outline a more helpful path. What they may be less able to do is politely negotiate with their pastor or priest about what is taught or advised, which leaves departure or apparent compliance as the option. Talking to a casually assembled cluster of women in the pews after a service in India, one lady expressed irritation with stories told by pastors to 'keep us in order, make us feel suffering is in a good cause, or to get our husbands to convert'. She distrusted such tales, citing one by her pastor:

> A Hindu woman became Christian. She didn't tell her husband and sang hymns all day. Her neighbours told her husband that she was Christian, but she denied it. He heard her singing hymns and beat her, becoming so exhausted she offered him buttermilk. Her goodness so overwhelmed him that he became Christian.

She reckoned this tale was created to encourage them to suffer so that their husband would believe.

An increasingly common way of responding to marital violence, alluded to earlier, is for pastors to demonize it, removing responsibility wholly or in part from the perpetrator. One woman, beaten for fifteen years, finally went to her pastor for help and was told:

> I can't counsel you yet because you are in bondage to the devil and you must be cleansed first before I deal with your husband. You are too angry. You have to be healed before your husband is healed and you are reconciled, and your healing will help him.

If we substitute wife-husband for parent-child, Ezekiel 18.20 resonates here: 'A child shall not suffer for the iniquity of the parent nor the parent for the iniquity of the child … the wickedness of the wicked shall be his own.' The sin of the abuser counts solely to the abuser, despite the abused having cooked okra not tomato, smiled too much or not enough.

There are various points of interest here, including reconciliation and the Devil. Firstly, the Devil, who attacks the wife as the 'weaker vessel'. Commonly around 70 per cent of responsibility for the Devil's entry into a marriage was attributed by clergy to the woman and just 30 per cent to the man, but 60 per cent responsibility to the man and 40 per cent to the woman was also found. It could also be a past family member who had 'let the Devil in', which again goes against the understanding that each person is responsible for their own sin. Whichever, it goes quite some way to absolving the man of responsibility for his actions. The Devil appears across the world, in part due to Sunday morning streaming of services from key centres and on dedicated channels. Some women wanting to grasp the thinking associated with the Devil were unwilling to ask their local mainline church leader lest they be blamed for watching TV church.

Marriage is seen as a particular hunting ground for the Devil because 'Marriage is spiritual warfare. There is someone who is the enemy of your soul, who fights against the unity, understanding and love of your marriage' (Tripp, 2010:246). This seducing stirrer up of evil finds it easier to attack wives at home, as women are the weaker vessel (1 Peter 3.7). 'A wife therefore needs the spiritual protection of her husband as has been designed by God' (Kisseadoo, 2003:10). This source of marital disharmony, so often attributed to the wife's failings, may be used to 'explain' violence against wives in any church in every country. Whether epitomized as devils or spirits, too many abused women learn that 'you must have had a bad spirit or let a bad spirit into your life' to quote an exasperated Malaysian nun. The Devil has a prominent position in CBMW teaching, especially in material coming from the United States and West Africa, the latter being strongly influenced by nineteenth-century German Pietism (see Meyer in Koepping, 2011).

Secondly, reconciliation. There is *and must be* a set order to any reconciliation process: sin, reflection, repentance, forgiveness, reconciliation. However, if the survivor is expected to forgive and reconcile with her abuser despite his lack of repentance, she is re-victimized by 'not being willing to be really Christian' and forgive. Across the world, women were angry, weary or depressed by being expected by church leaders *and* other laywomen to forgive an abuser whose only intention, far from leading a new life, is to maintain power over her. Such a one-side expectation (for no one expected an abusive or difficult unrepentant woman to be forgiven by her husband) makes a nonsense of what is a psychologically and theologically sound sequence. Manzanan writes that religious counsellors, pushing for reconciliation, contribute to ongoing wife-battering (2002:210). This point, that forgiveness *must* be offered immediately in a form of 'cheap grace', whether demanded by the assailant, the counsellor or minister, rears up its ugly head again and again, and *always* to the detriment of the survivor and her faith.

Linked to this bizarre demand for forgiveness, for one can no more demand others forgive than apologize on long-dead others' behalf, is the wish for family harmony to be restored, the problem tidily swept under the carpet. Unless violence has stopped, and the abuser truly begins to treat his partner as his equal in God, or at least stops trampling on her body and her mind, neither patience nor forgiveness will create harmony, the push for which seems to take priority over justice and peace. A Christian lady in Myanmar explained her husband was uninterested in changing:

> The Church Minister talked to me but he actually wants me to forgive my husband and for us to re-unite and live in peace. My husband came back and

lived with our family then went back to his new wife. He says he will kill me if I marry again. (WCRP, 2006)

Securing 'family harmony' at the wife's expense was complained about widely, as was holding joint counselling sessions in which the wife was too cowed, or too slickly manipulated, to speak for herself even if she had retained some voice amid the abuse. This occurred across the research. Where a woman went to her pastor to talk about violence, she could not be sure he would not summon the husband for a counselling session with or without her agreement, despite such sessions not only consolidating abuse but made further abuse more likely.

Demanding *really* Christian women forgive an unrepentant abusive spouse suggests a subtext that men, not women, are the weaker vessel, already implied in wives' responsibility for their husbands' salvation. We heard it from Australia in Chapter 5, and it is implicit in the following example from India. A woman left her marriage after twenty-four years of violence. However, *leaving* was the only sin, not the violence which led to departure, her pastor advising her to return home, saying 'haven't you hurt him enough already by leaving him?' Collins reports a rather similar UK case where a church helper was only prepared to support an abused woman with children when it was clear the man would leave. Asked why, she admitted that, even knowing about the violence, she had implicitly assumed that assisting a woman to leave a marriage is wrong (2019:27).

Women in several countries spoke of being blamed not only for leaving rather than sticking to God's plan by staying with an abusive husband, but also for her husband's loss of salvation if he committed adultery, on the dubious grounds that had she remained, he would not have gone sideways. The Homily of 1563 clearly stated that if the abused partner leaves because of violence, that 'desertion' should be counted against the abuser for having deserted their vows. He chose adultery, just as he chose abuse.

Following church rules can put the abused woman at risk of serious injury. One woman, who had repeatedly asked her parish priest for advice regarding her abusive husband, found him leading a meeting at her in-laws' house, at which he publicly admonished her: 'I am God's Shepherd, and I am saying, your place is next to your husband.' She argued with him, and left the meeting feeling 'exhausted and degraded'. Reconciliation had been her hope earlier in the marriage, but not after twelve years of violence. This Lucknow lady was finally helped by a local women's NGO, which 'objected to the priest's intervention, saying the church had no authority to oppress women or precipitate a violent situation' (in Bhattacharya, 2004:173).

What women want from their faith leader

A shelter director in India had this advice for ordained and household leaders based on what her clients said:

> Stop the 'holy hush' and publicly name violence against us as a sin, as you name dowry-burning; listen more and silence us less; don't spiritualise or demonise the situation at our expense; don't tell us to forgive when he carries on: don't talk as if our life isn't valuable too. Stop hitting your own wife; stop teaching about headship but use the Image of God and other texts which oppose violence.

That sums up a good many global discussions. Let us start with the final point, as it is particularly fruitful. We saw in the last chapter that various ordained people turned, or wanted to turn, from headship to the Image of God which, *once people knew it existed*, excited book and life educated alike. The following discussion is typical:

Me:	What would the Image of God contribute to how marriages go?
First:	It puts the man and the woman equal. *But the person who claims to be the head and demands we follow doesn't want to use Genesis 1.* If they had promoted that before, equal partnership and the Image of God, it would have been much better. Now we live away from our families who might help, and men's rights run everything.
Second:	That's it, that's what they should teach. Men tell us 'We were created first' so we just say 'Yes, you were the draft, the first effort.' But that's just us trying to keep our heads up. If we can also say: 'We are both made in the Image of God and should both respect each other,' and then say from Ephesians 5, 'men should love their wife as Christ loved the Church and gave his life for it' then it would be better for us.
Me:	So the Image of God is most important for you?
Three:	If we are Christian that is the root, that is the ideal Image of God for us. But that is the one that is not taught.
Others:	Yes, that should be the way. We need the practical implications of that. But we have never heard it mentioned. Never.

This pattern, of single people or groups discussing different versions of creation and thus of what it is to be human, was an increasingly important thread in the research. Given options, women opted for the Image of God as beneficial (if demanding) for all. I asked some Indian women what the church should do in their teaching of faith and gospel.

> Start there with the Image of God because once the priest starts talking about emotion and the heart and the way we live here, the talking shifts away from

faith and gospel and we become for him just Indian women, judged by how carefully we present ourselves. *We have to keep away from the cultural pattern to talk about the faith pattern*. No one here really thinks about this, about all of us being equally human, so you must start with the young.

This is crucial, especially where 'culture' is used in the same way as a weaponized biblical verse to control and silence subordinates, the recalcitrant among whom are then 'othered'. In the discussion above, that meant being accused of lusting after so-called Western culture. These women insisted that churches should teach *firstly* that 'human beings are made in the Image of God' and *secondly* 'what that means for Christian marriage' so that church and people engage with the reality of the Image of God and not the shadow.

This exchange approaches the nub of the problem, taking us back to the start of this research: 'In my country no one bothers about domestic violence.' 'No one' or 'no one who matters' does not mean many of the women and some men contributing to this book, because they *do* bother, even if they know that marital abuse is of little interest to the church. 'No one' or 'no one who matters' seems to include abusers of wives, who tend to be absent from church and thus beyond direct teaching, even were it to be given. 'No one' seems to mean no one significant. That is surely challenged by Matthew 10.29: 'Not one sparrow shall fall to the ground unperceived by your Father.'

Why do more women not talk directly to their faith leaders? The answer, very similar to why Muslim and Buddhist women do not talk to *their* faith leaders, explored below in the Addendum, is that *really* 'listening to and taking notice of women, the poor and people from a different ethnic group', to quote from a group of honest young pastors in Myanmar I once taught, is not high on the list of pastoral duties. 'Listening' does *not* mean 'patiently waiting until the other has finished then telling them what's what' in a few slick phrases. It means *respectfully* engaging with the other person, not their social mask, in an effort to understand their words *and* their silences. As one group put it, 'Pastors must listen to the silences in what someone is saying, not just the words, and notice when the silences come.' However, there is an awareness among women firstly that listening skills are poorly developed among some pastors, priests and ministers, and secondly that there is no point going to the presbytery to be told to be an obedient slave to a husband, even if that is dressed up with being a beloved child of God.

Were there specific approaches, other than those indicated at the start of this section, which women wished their ministers would follow? One resolute woman who had been abused in her last marriage was clear:

> The church should teach ministers that if they see signs of danger, if it looks as if the man can get worse, the pastor, priest, minister should tell her to leave. Marriage is not slavery, and it is not clever to stay in a cage. You marry for happiness, not death. Church leaders should come down from the heights and face the situation as if it was their daughter. If the danger of her death is there, she should leave and not be ostracised by the church.

Women did not need or want to be told by their priest or pastor what to do, but they do want open discussion about it, 'like about adultery':

> They needn't tell you to get divorced, but to have time out. He should say, 'Come, you have faced enough, you should go, because if you don't your children will have no mother.' The danger of death was there for me: it was high time I left.

The speaker was not asking to be bossed around by the leader but, as a Christian, to be given permission to leave a life-destroying situation. Not talking about it, and not teaching about it, ensures, as an older lady said, 'the chain of imitation and memory continues'. Or, as another young woman said: 'We say stop the violence by ending the silence.' But it is not just silence by the church, or by abused women. It is the silence of the far greater number of women of faith who ignore their sisters' needs, pretending or hoping, that *they* are not vulnerable to such violence by displaying *their* housewifely prowess against the implied inadequacy of a downtrodden survivor. It is the silence by millions of men who say nothing when those peers for whom masculinity means exercising power over others brag about 'keeping the wife in order with a clout'. It is the silence which assumes violence and other forms of abuse are a result of failure in the victim, not a demonstration of raw power by the perpetrator. So much easier to blame the institution!

Reflection

This chapter has shown hurting, despairing, critical and infuriated women. It has also shown, with some exceptions, that the institutions of the church, the leaders of the churches, *and* non-abused women and men in churches do little to challenge and change the situation. Abused Christian women should be able to talk to and receive wise help from their local pastor, priest or minister, linked into relevant secular and faith-based NGOs and ideally faith-aware counsellors able to 'read' a survivor's use of scriptural verses and faith tags. They should know that all are made in the Image of God, with each person counting to

God as much as the next. Luther bid us to 'deal with our neighbours as we see God through Christ has dealt with and still deals with us.' In the same way, intimate relationships should 'model relating to partners like we relate to God, not following a narrative that Eve seduced Adam, but that all are made in God's Image, as a north Australian minister said. Christian women are calling for a coherent message, *fully part of church teaching and practice*, not just an annual 'be nice to the ladies' day.

Syrian Orthodox women in southern India belong to a group who have been Christian since the third century and thus longer than most in Western Europe. The crucial comment of one was that church leaders talking about culture do a disservice to women, miring them in a rank-ordered, highly gendered social context. That seems the case wherever (and that means everywhere) expectations about people by gender, just as rank or ethnicity, are embedded in local cultural context, so that 'our good women act thus, our worthy poor act thus, our valued elites act thus.'

Following Christ, subordinated people in various places said, should *free* them from disabling social controls and enable a full life in which they are fully acknowledged and respected as they respect their partners. Being hit, kicked, punched or knifed did not fit anyone's view of respect, whatever their rank or ethnic background, and none appreciate being subordinated by church 'culture-talk'. Christian women will continue to be abused, their families damaged and their children alienated from the church if its leaders emphasize wifely obedience even to abusive husbands or, just as unchristian, hide amid the enveloping folds of the 'holy hush of cowardice'. That it begins to be talked about on the fringes of church life is not, as a couple of male priests said at an English clergy training session on Domestic Violence, because of 'all this feminism'. It is because once again in church history, marital violence is being recognized for what it is: an elegantly massaged sin against the Body of Christ. And it is a sin the abusers share with silent observers, whatever their gender and status.

The comment by a South Indian woman priest that 'such violence must be opposed by the church and [whether lay or ordained] *by the people who are the church*' is especially relevant. If not a pastor, if not a priest, if not school chaplain, who? As the Ghanaian pastor said, '*We must act, not hope someone else will.*'

Part three

Threads to a conclusion

7

Is the glory of the church really a human being fully alive?

Drawing the threads together

If Irenaeus's statement quoted at the outset of this exploration on violence against wives in Christian marriage were lived out in church life, the response to the above question would be 'yes, of course: in every house and church, the people of God would resound with glory, supporting each human being to be alive in their fullness.'

But what if it does not? What if many leaders and followers corral God within their domain, ignoring Irenaeus and holding their own view of 'fully alive' or indeed 'human'? What if, singly and collectively, they fail to uphold the *integrity of every being* but, by word, or by deed, or by silence, assume some humans are worthy of upholding and others just worthy to uphold others? Such a church, its leaders and people, would have a major problem, compounded if texts and doctrines valuing all humans were regularly qualified with a 'yes but …,' skilfully conforming and deforming text to context. Such a church, both the people of God and perhaps especially the institution, would have turned from God in favour of worshipping culture, each in their cosy cocoon. As a Tongan ordinand explained in words of universal relevance:

> We don't help in cases of marital abuse, nor do we discipline the man because the church wants to be a safe place and safe matters. *Not 'a place of safety,'* which it must be, *but a place for safe matters, a safe place for itself.*

Irrespective of worship style or organization, churches which are 'safe places for themselves' may well be uninterested in exploring just what a human is, or how abused women freeze, how they feel or how Bible values of justice, mercy and love for all are and should be lived. Reflection may expose shameful issues, the defence of which risks churches becoming a 'refuge of lies' (Isaiah 28.16) on behalf of safe-for-us-who-count members. That is both shame and scandal.

Looking at marital abuse has certainly turned up tough issues in Christian marriage and communities across the world, marriage which for at least one participant is an exercise in sheer survival. Such marriages judged 'bad' by at least one participant illuminate what 'better' marriages are, just as in the context of feeding the world's people, 'reckless' land management clarifies 'sustainable'. Moreover, just as we reflect on the *meaning* of land to those working it when assessing land management, considering the individual in Christian marriage leads to reflection on what Christianity *is* to its followers. Evidence has been presented that persistent intentional violence within marriage which damages the body and soul of the survivor is *not* conducive to the thriving of the direct or indirect victims, *nor* of the abuser, *nor* the integrity of any church which condones marital violence through apathy or ignorance, poorly joined-up teaching or silent or voiced support.

That gets to the nub. What exactly *is* a faith which enables or ignores violence against those to whom so much love, and honour, and protection were promised? What *has* been illuminated by this careful examination of violence in the intimate relations between two humans sealed by marriage within their faith tradition? I suspect rather more cutting and twisting of texts than some churches, especially abusers and abuse-enablers therein, find comfortable. On completing this immensely challenging and spiritually fruitful cross-country research journey, which has called on a lifetime's experience in anthropology, theology and living, I conclude that, depending on who the human being is, too many churches and those in them seem not to see the 'glory of each male and female human being' as *made by God in God's Image* but rather made in our and not their image. If that is the case, what has each Christian contributed to that fact, and what can each contribute to the remedy?

Let me pause to assist those leaping to the defence of their particular faith-brand, just as doctors, teachers, police and lawyers defend their occupational territory. From long teaching and research experience, my rule of thumb is that 10 per cent of those offering for *any* profession will be superb with minimal training, and a further 20 per cent excellent with initial guidance. However, 10 per cent will never be suitable, and a further 10 per cent inadequate, making a group few would *choose* to relate to as pupil, plaintiff, patient or parishioner. The remaining 50 per cent are more, or less, competent. Those who rise to the top, however, may include a number from the inadequate base, damaging the whole enterprise.

Unless institutions (including faith communities which culpably assume faith equals virtue) accept that power over people has dangers *all the time*, not just when something goes wrong, *and* accept that a proportion of its professional workers whom they chose to accept and retain do *not* do a good job, abuse and 'collateral damage' will continue. 'Keeping things going' risks losing sight of both broad and specific aims. A number of patients, pupils, parishioners and plaintiffs will be seriously short-changed in the lifetime of those inept workers for whom advancement, or a cosy life, outweighs honourable commitment. How many will be stumbling blocks to the spiritual, physical and mental health of those they purport to serve? One is too many.

However, blaming only the institutions of the church (my position at the distant outset of this research back in 2005) is totally unreasonable. That would be like a farmer claiming *his* skill for a good harvest and *God's* will for a bad. Being 'the people of God' when things are rosy and blaming 'them up there running the Church' when inadequacy or wrong is exposed is unacceptable. That said, when the *institution* knows its leaders – anointed or appointed to whichever group – *are* committing sinful acts against wives or concubines and yet keep their eyes and ears wide shut, the church is *indeed* upholding sin by failing to clean out their own sties.

Likewise, when *followers* know what is happening and say nothing to protect their own self-image, they *who are the church* are also upholding sin, and the greater the power among the laity, the greater the culpability. Survivors may rightly blame the inadequacy and worse of pastoral support and some may see the contribution of twisted or badly taught texts to their plight. Yet they feel *doubly* betrayed by the silence of laywomen and men, by slick offers of prayer without calling out the abuse as sin, or by colluding advice to be quicker cooks or prettier ladies. As Psalm 55 points out bitterly in words appropriate both for the abusing spouse and for the silent friend:

> It is not an external enemy who is taunting me. (That I could bear.) No, you are a person of my own station, whose company I once found so delightful, with whom I used to walk about in the House of God with such feeling.

Three specific problems

Before considering four areas of concern in detail, let us look at three defined issues which have arisen thus far: Bible verses which help or hinder, the demand that wives forgive unrepentant abusers, and that they are responsible for their abusive husband's salvation.

Firstly, the contribution of certain Bible verses intentionally utilized to support the abuse of wives. Irrespective of what a Bible verse means to this or that school of biblical scholars, if 'wives obey your husbands' is linked to 'the man is the head of the household' resulting in the slapping, kicking or worse of the wife, there is a certain responsibility on those who teach the second verse to teach it carefully and safely. This appears a worldwide problem, whether linked to specific teaching or just to forgetting our capacity for self-deception to the point of self-delusion.

Given the earlier discussion about headship, and its accepted if all too often uncritical use in a good many churches, it is interesting to see that of 105 people in the survey asked which texts are used to validate violence, 85 cited Ephesians 5.22-3, 'wives obey ... for the man is the head of the house' with a further 16 (10 in Kenya, 2 in the West Indies and 4 in South India) offering Eve and the apple from Genesis or 1 Timothy 2.15 'for Adam was not deceived but the woman was'. Discussing these verses with women clergy in India, they added a number of phrases – 'your suffering mirrors the suffering of Christ' or 'it must be God's will' – saying of the lot that 'all these verses and phrases are used to justify violence and keep victims quiet'. It should be particularly concerning for churches that respondents saw violence being validated by just two ideas: that women are responsible for the Fall and that men are head of the family.

Verses which *oppose violence* were both more varied and more often given. Of the 141 verses cited, forty-two chose 'love one another as I have loved you' (John 13.34), nineteen 'love her and not be harsh' (Ephesians 5.25-9/Colossians 3.19) and twelve that a couple is one flesh (Genesis 2.24). A more theological take against violence was given by thirty-four (a figure skewed by a university class in Kenya) for whom the fact that all are made in the Image of God (Genesis 1.27) precluded violence, as did the fifteen citing Galatians 3.27 'if we live in Christ there is no difference between ... men and women', or the nineteen citing Ephesians 5.21 on mutual submission.

Were there specific biblical verses other than Genesis 1.27 or Ephesians 5.21 which women (abused or not) put forward as supporting their needs and which they wanted church leaders to use? Women in Australia, America and Taiwan mentioned Malachi 2.16: 'God hates divorce and covering one's garments with violence', the second part of which they (along with the Lutheran Study Bible) understand to forbid violence against a wife. Ephesians 5.26, 'Husbands love your wives just as Christ loved the church and gave his life for it,' was another which respondents felt should prevent violence against women if husbands took it seriously. Yet as several felt Ephesians 5:21 was of little concern to lazily colluding pastors and priests, few expect change.

Yet unless a family or church head fully submits to God rather than his human ego-centredness, he risks behaving unjustly and even abusively towards his wife and children. One abuse-aware priest nevertheless explained that he started his pre-marital counselling with Ephesians 5.22, 'about obeying, and taking care, and about love'. His image was Abraham and Sarah, with wives leading moderate lives, inwardly adorned, so that 'even if your husband does not know God, he will come to God through you'. It is a pity he did not read a little further in 1 Peter 3, as verse 6 tells wives who follow Sarah 'not to fear intimidation' (Christian Standard Bible (CSB)), 'be without fear of what your husband might do' (New Living Translation (NLT)) 'not to give way to fear' (NIV). Fear of or respect for the Lord is one thing: fear of a husband, equally imbued with the Christ whom abusive husbands hit, is quite another.

Secondly, the common expectation if not demand that a nicely behaved female Christian survivor of abuse should forgive her assailant despite him demonstrating no inclination to repent, let alone be transformed. Such a demand, too often coming from clergy *and* from family members, perverts the clear and logical progress from sin through reflection and repentance to forgiveness and reconciliation. Other women seem as quick as the ordained to demand a survivor forgive as the price of being considered faithful. As a devout Antillean woman put it succinctly: 'God's will is your story, and if you are really Christian you will stay with him and forgive him if he beats you.' Any person pressuring the survivor to forgive and reconcile without clear repentance and intention to reform on the part of the abuser is taking the abuser's side. Indeed, abusers may themselves try this line, one such in Germany demanding his estranged wife and her mother 'treat me like the prodigal son, because I came back, and in our religion, it says that if someone is regretful you must accept their apology'. Regret has many shades.

Forgiving, or reaching a state of adequate peace in one's own time, when the abuse is truly ended or the abuser abandoned, is quite another thing. It is essential for an ongoing fully human life to let past pain go, whether through knowing one is accepted by and acceptable to God, the passage of time, recognition of one's own contribution to the whole, or happier experiences. This may become forgiveness, especially if the perpetrator accepts his actions were both abusive and wrong. But being told to forgive? Repeatedly being expected to forgive an unrepentant serial abuser? We are bidden to love ourselves as well as the other: *demanding* we forgive is and contributes to further abuse.

Thirdly, and the last of these specific problems, women's apparent responsibility for their husband's salvation. Peter (2 Peter 3.1) laid the ground by encouraging wives to stay with non-believers (not violent abusers) in the hope the latter would be transformed into devout followers of Christ. Various discussants explained how pointless that had been in their abusive marriages, their husbands changing neither towards faith nor from violence. The bigger puzzle is the all too common assumption that if the woman left her husband due to violence, and he then committed adultery, *she* bore the responsibility even though he chose to act thus. The reverse was not mentioned, women apparently having control over their sexuality. Such wifely 'responsibility' was widespread. An Ethiopian church worker, for example, correctly insisted 'no one should encourage a confused abused woman to leave her husband because she may become destitute', but then warned, 'he may be put in the way of sin, because if he has no responsibilities he drinks and finds women'. He may indeed choose to do just that. Both Chrysostom and the 1563 Homily on marriage make clear that the vow-breaking abuser is the deserter when the survivor walks away.

Responsibility for hitting his wife would not accrue to the perpetrator if he was *compelled on pain of death* to do the deed. That unlikely scenario apart, deciding to abuse, just as deciding to be adulterous or to rape, is a choice. To say it is an uncontrollable urge insultingly implies that males, but not females, are wild animals. Sadly, however, the idea that 'God gave authority to men over women, and husbands over wives as family heads, and we must follow God's orders, and if that means we might need to hit our wives, so be it', as a young pastor explained, suggests hitting is of God. It is not. It is salutary to look at Jesus' words relating to men's lust after women, still as ever easily attributed to the 'intentional allure of women'. He names as sinner the one who chose to gaze and lust at the woman as object, not the woman herself (Matthew 5.29). That holds for violence against the wife.

Five areas of concern

So much for specific tensions evident in the research. Let us now turn to five areas of concern, covering the position of clergy, the training of church workers, the (ir)relevance of feminism, ministry to the abuser and the playing of the culture-card, which can easily trump all. We shall end with threads of hope in the voices of those who are the church. Some indicate steps currently being taken in various places while others outline steps which informants feel *should* be followed if churches are truly to reflect the fact that all are made in the Image of God. However, any step, just as moving beyond the following areas of concern, will only leave a footprint if those men and those women who collude in violence against wives through silence are challenged, *wherever and whoever they are.*

Area One: The position of clergy

The place of the ordained person in his or her church, their ongoing acceptance by relevant authority figures and their negotiation of church rules can be complex. Nevertheless leaders, whether ordained or household, have choices. Some in churches with fixed marriage rules, not just the retired or potential martyrs, bend or ignore them, quietly advising women to leave violent husbands while maintaining membership, or even publicly signalling that violence is wrong and leaving may be a wise and faithful option. Such 'outsider-insiders' must tread carefully, lest they are shifted to ecclesial boondocks (see Bhattacharya, 2004:175). However, if that is done quietly, or communion given to the remarried but 'not advertised', the shy or anxious may not know about and therefore cannot factor this possibility into their future planning.

Even when preachers feel they have opposed marital violence, saying it now and again is not enough, especially if the equality of both partners before God is part of neither the cultural nor the faith context. Poor irregular and culturally unchallenging teaching concerning abuse *unintegrated with Bible and doctrine* contributes to the relative failure of large-scale campaigns concerning violence in marriage in organizations such as the WCC, World Association of Reform Churches, Lutheran World Federation and the Vatican. So often, sound ideas dry up in the silent sands of small-town apathy.

One group of men who do respond to the issue are those with wife-abuse in the wider family. Whichever their church, they seemed more aware of the problem and far more generous than their church-brothers and sisters in addressing such pain among parishioners. A number offered sensitive comments about the issue and about their relative. For them, the abused person was not some 'other over there', but part of their own 'us here'. I talked to one about an Ash Wednesday liturgy which included the response, 'We deserved to be crucified' to the pastor's statement, 'Christ took the punishment that was meant for us,' and the response 'and he didn't lose his temper' to his statement 'Christ took all the abuse.' Often beaten in childhood, aware of his own shortcomings and committed to respect for all, *this* pastor *immediately* saw the impact such words may have on an abused woman.

A considerable proportion of clergy, however, were uninterested in thinking about much less addressing the issue for a variety of reasons: misogyny, inadequacy, ignorance, over-work and fear. More skirted around it, regarding it as unfortunate yet not part of their brief. Even a little imagination suggests that no normal ordained person wants to be beaten, knifed or kicked, so why should they expect that in a wife just because she and her partner vowed to live together in honour and love?

It is easy to be scathing from this quiet desk. Daily negotiations with the cliques and traditions of a congregation *are* draining, as is the weary emptiness when angry members let fly at the relatively defenceless church worker. True, the leader may have spiritual clout – if followers accept that – but is still one among many. Contradicting real or imagined 'ancestral and cultural values' and arousing fury among colleagues and congregation can be lonely. Addressing violence against women without training, or without counselling support staff to turn to for help, or against the feeling of the community that 'wives are private property' demands continual courage and conscience. And as the nun Joan Chittister says: 'Women of courage are not enough. We need men of conscience as well, if the human race is ever to be fully human' (2007).

Area Two: Inadequate training of church workers

Almost no one *anywhere*, whether old or young, received relevant teaching on this topic in seminary or ongoing education. Some, like Karen ordinands in Myanmar, laughingly recollected a mention of it in a Friday afternoon option in final semester – and lest readers think 'Oh, that's Myanmar' I assure you it could be anywhere! Those preparing for ordination were taught about marital violence in Maine from the mid-1990s (Ellison and Hewey, 1995): Nason-Clark et al. (2015:119–20) reported some sound teaching in North America. However, once again this was optional and the topic thus seen as unimportant, despite the latter's excellent Rave Project e-courses. What of Roman Catholics in Germany or India, Anglicans and Presbyterians in the UK or Kenya, Methodists in Ghana, Dominica or Tonga, whether trained five or fifty years ago? Bits and pieces at best. True, there is the odd lecture or optional hour, but given a recent ordination cohort's one lecture on ethics and domestic violence and one on Pastoral Care, dissociated from Biblical and theological studies, there is a way to go. A South Indian seminary taught about domestic violence briefly in response to student demands some twenty years ago: now nothing. It may exist here and there, but is so personnel-dependent, so dissociated from core theological teaching that, as a Kenyan Assemblies of God pastor said, 'you miss it if you blink'. As with medical training which starts with people as skeletons rather than as potential patients, adding a dose of parishioner reality towards the end would be a joke were the outcome not so serious.

Once ordained and working for a church, people may train themselves, but if pre-ordination training ignored it, hearing about much less challenging abuse seems unlikely unless the person has previous personal or familial experience of it. This poses a paradox. People are not usually accepted as church workers unless they demonstrate a willingness to follow rather than challenge church rules, whatever they are. A bishop bemoaned his priests' 'lack of fire and of passion to query, to go beyond what we see immediately, to refuse to be satisfied'. Yet are potential firebrands readily accepted by churches, or is replacing 'like for like' not more usual?

Meeting an international group of ordinands and church workers from several churches in eastern Africa gave a wonderful chance to discuss the issue. I asked if their leaders opposed marital violence. 'Not really' sums up the general view. 'On Women's Day or Mothering Sunday, they say "We are one in Christ, men and women are equal," and that's all we get.' A Sudanese said his leaders preach 'when you are saved, we are all equal and all brothers and sisters, so you cannot beat your wife'. Yet 'being saved', we agreed, removes people neither from their context nor from their personal history. An Ethiopian female evangelist insisted that churches should speak against violence and raise the status of woman, citing 'an intelligent lady whose husband cheated and then hit her when she found out, so she divorced him *because she has her own money* which was good'. An annoyed youth broke in: 'African women [clearly the last speaker!] become demanding when they are advanced.' All agreed they were taught to bring the couple together again, saying:

> 'Pray, be patient and forgive.' We can't say, 'go,' even if she's terrified of him, as she cannot remarry in church until he dies: he remarries because church is nothing for men. So how do we bring them together?

Another explained: 'If I ask the woman "Can I talk to your husband" and she says "No," I know she's the guilty one.' She may of course be afraid the violence will increase: so much easier to assume she is an adulteress or abuser. The students were keen but floundered in unknowing. Too many ordinands and people in their first decade of ministry flounder, as do old hands: few realize.

Such protection – or projection – continues in seminaries. After a very taxing talk followed by questions in that Pakistan seminary, I asked the Europe-based brother of one ordinand what the students had made of it. 'He said they were too young to hear about such things.' Those young men, aged between twenty-two and thirty, soon to be leading churches, are too young to reflect on marital violence? One is torn between laughter and horror, as indeed I was when the response from a UK seminary to my request to discuss the issue with students was: 'No, because it might awake trauma in some students.' So might any aspect of ministry.

There is no quick fix to this issue of poor preparation of church workers, hence my earlier stress on the historical dimension of the issue as well as the current situation. As I have written elsewhere, 'Placing "Man and Woman made in God's Image" as the plumb line for theological teaching and church practice will only happen if the failure of centuries to do this is brought home to us all' (Koepping, 2019:517).

Area Three: The (ir)relevance of feminism

As indicated at the outset, assuming feminism and not primarily faith underlies opposition to marital abuse is a common response. Ending violence against wives in general and those in Christian marriage in particular is a commitment to *faith*, not an interest in suddenly uplifting one sex at the expense of another. Does concern for married abused females of faith *privilege* women? If being privileged means wives are not beaten, kicked, slapped or silenced with the support of a church, then such privilege seems reasonable. But the Image of God does not talk about privilege of the one above the other: *both* are so made.

Blaming feminism for opposition to abuse by Christian husbands would make feminists of John Chrysostom, Martin Bucer, Cotton Mather and Thomas Cranmer for pursuing the logic of their faith, discussed in Chapter 3. The recent worldwide interest in human rights and women's safety enshrined not only in UN Conventions but also by new national laws demands a permanent change in or at least challenge to churches' legal obligations, teaching and pastoral support. Either churches continue to collude in the abuse of women or they will change, not to follow a cultural fad, but because the hitting of that of Christ in another person is a sin.

Would opposing wife-abuse in Christian contexts usher in rule by women and pay-back time? Would it mean that the negativity attached to women on grounds of menstruation, or childbirth, or any other marker of subordination, will suddenly end? Worldwide, and in everyone's back yard: no. Take the comment from 1300 by the French Cathar Authié, who advised his abusive son-in-law that he was 'acting against Scripture, which bids a husband be peaceful, gentle and tender'. A clear and universally valid Bible-based comment, but Authié did not therefore change his view of women, still seeing them as 'something base' (Ladurie, 1980:193–4). Nevertheless, resolutely opposing violence against Christian wives by Christian husbands should be an integral part of lived Christian faith held by all, irrespective of how one gender estimates the other and, to that end, so should challenging the all-too-common misuse of texts.

That said, there has been a tendency within some feminism simplistically and patronizingly to place women on the side of the angels. That helps no one. Women are indeed the primary victims and survivors of male violence, yet as has been demonstrated, they too collude in the abuse of other women whether unconsciously motivated by uncertainty, anxiety and fear, or consciously by gloating over other's misfortune and sheer power-over-people lust. Mary Pellauer indicated in 1995 that 'clergymen must be transformed personally and theologically, as women have been' (quoted in Ellison and Hewey, 1995:483).

Well, yes and no. Yes, *all* clergy, male and female, need training in practical safeguarding and support for abused women, and *all* should be transformed personally and theologically, but so should *all* people of God, lay and ordained, male and female, priests, ministers and household pastors. There is *no way* we can say 'women are all transformed beings'. Some people are transformed by the theological implications of the body of Christ and the body of each God-filled Child of God: many, perhaps most, are not. Talking to abused women, marital abuse was seen an obvious downside of marriage, just as useless advice from the pastor or priest is part of church life. But the patronizing words or looks from other women, their avoidance and offers to pray without naming abuse as sin, the patronizing advice which validates the assailant's action: such attitudes from other women are *truly* disempowering.

Blaming 'feminists' for disrupting peaceful church life harks back to that 'lost idyll' when the past was always warmer for sun-lovers and cooler for those who shrink from it, pleasanter for those at the top of the tree, happier for those with short memories. Realistically, that was and still is the time when a miserable marriage might be accepted as 'good' if the wife was not beaten, when intra- and inter-country migration was relatively unimportant, other than in the early stages of industrialization, and when the chance for anyone, but especially wives, to live fully to the glory of God was just that: chance. Encouraging Christian wives to accept subordination and due discipline, a growing trend in a Luddite-like effort to push back change, is more than the outcome of poorly taught faith. It puts women at risk if it recites as a mantra that women are safe if they would just follow the rules and remain submissive.

Area Four: Ministry to the abuser

The need is clear for all men as well as all women to see themselves as made in the Image of God, and to see themselves as people of worth. Just as 'loving our self' has been downplayed far too much in the self-sacrificing teaching too many Christians receive, so too have the life-affirming implications of being made in God's Image. It is helpful if all Christian men as well as women see themselves as made in the Image of God, and therefore people of worth. But just as 'loving our self' has been downplayed too much in the self-sacrificing teaching so many Christians receive, the life-affirming implications of being made in God's Image have also been largely ignored. The outcome is unhealthy both for those who are abused as part of others' 'feel-big' act or for those who do the abusing. Various groups of men are vulnerable on both counts: those whose journey through life failed to match up to what they once hoped as a child of ten, or a youth of twenty; those who work, live and (perhaps) worship in the same restricted network as their wives, yet see other resident men enjoying the freedom of external affirmation; those who saw or suffered physical and emotional abuse; and those who, because of war or its aftermath, can neither provide for their family nor enact that masculinity which is 'nothing a man simply has or is, but rather a way of being that he needs to perform and assert' (Lwambo, 2013:12 and also Sheerattan-Bisnauth and Peacock 2010). Where much is expected of men, and by men, in terms of achievement, strength, competence and leadership, the bitterness of a publicly visible shortfall is bitter indeed.

'Being a real man' so often seems to include hitting disobedient wives. That was the case in the relatively placid times of mid-sixteenth-century England, when, as the homily writer wrote, '[the common man in marriage] thinks it is a man's part to fume in anger, to fight with fist and staff', and it is the case currently in South Sudan where, as an ordinand said, 'There is violence all over, and if you marry and do not beat your wife, you are not a man.'

But, just as drink does not make every drinker into a wife-abuser, nor being born the son of an abusive father, just those sons who have already adopted the mind-set to see her as a lesser object, so too living through the violence of war, the misery of poverty, hunger and inability to provide does not make every such person an abuser. To the extent that a person has power, to that extent they have choice and to that extent abusing a partner is a sin. To suggest that violence amid misery is a natural and excusable reaction by the violator offers no way out of the downward spiral or indeed no reason not to choose violence. Moreover, this is too easily designated as the Godly way.

'I'm sorry for the violent people too, because they are afraid and feel trapped, and hit out like a cornered animal,' said one priest. True indeed, as is the fact that a number of male pastors (whether of church or household) and priests in this research linked their behaviour to having an uppity wife, not their own fear and anger. But let us pick that 'hitting out' image apart. A cornered animal is in that position when threatened by a stronger or more skilful animal: a calf by a lion or a hen by a fox, a fox by a gun-toting human, a child cowering below an angry parent. Yet neither the calf, the hen, the fox nor the child has much chance of hitting out, that being the part of the lion, the human, the parent or the husband. It is clear what the priest meant: the person who feels afraid of life, trapped in failure, may hit out in response to his evident or inner weakness, choosing a yet weaker victim. But it is not an *animal* response, but one learnt in human company and fed by poor theology and a twisted use of text.

We can see the beginnings of attempts to reach abusing men within the church context, or at least the awareness that there needs to be safe space for men in general and those with abuse issues in particular. The Malaysian nun, after role-playing domestic violence, reflected that 'I'd not realised the failure of the Church to give people an opportunity to talk about pain, violence, abuse. Church is a safe environment to talk about it for men too.' It is, but not usually in mixed church groups where men may feel the need to dominate women in whose territory they effectively are, nor can they talk openly and honestly if the pastor or priest gossips. Ideally, trained non-local facilitators meeting with groups of faith-linked men interested to explore common issues with other men can have a far-reaching impact. This is especially important where there has been or is ongoing trauma caused by natural disaster or human violence.

Lwambo describes special church groups in Congolese small towns and villages (fewer city men bothering with church) 'which communicate Christian ideals of how to be good men, such as respectful and non-violent behaviour towards others ... and allow men to communicate in a safe setting'. Such male-only meetings are already a Congolese tradition, offering 'an intimate platform for men to address conflict and problems, engage in debate and peer-to-peer education with other men they know and trust' (2013:22). As she says, *accepting* violent masculinity as a reasonable outcome of failed masculinity is wrong in social and in faith terms: making space for men to meet and talk about life and (if they wish) faith in a female-free zone, given that church is so feminized, is life-affirming. Moves across the world especially, but not only, by Evangelical, Charismatic and Pentecostal churches to run programmes for men, potentially drawing them into church life and more crucially enabling them to reflect on and learn about non-violent ways of managing intimate relationships.

Clergy abusers discussed in Chapter 4 are in a special category for they are not private people, and their sin indirectly affects many women and men. Those who know they have broken their marriage vows in this way should be able to own up and find support and help after the first such event. All those training for ministry should be made aware that there is never, ever, a valid reason for hitting or otherwise demeaning a partner, that this goes against all that Christ taught, and if they offend without immediately seeking support to be converted to a more wholesome and holy way, they should accept time out to reassess their attitudes and behaviour or find a new career. All in a pastor role, whether ordained, appointed or a household head, would do well to remember James's comment: 'Not many of you should become teachers, my brothers and sisters, for you know that we who teach will be judged with greater strictness.'

Area Five: The culture card

Another area of contention, potentially a more intractable issue than 'feminism', is 'the way we do things', the emphasis being on the usually exclusive and excluding 'we'. Christians (just as others) in some parts of the world, the richer, theologically and financially powerful parts, commonly see themselves as unaffected by their cultural context, 'culture and ethnicity' being what *other* people have, whereas *they* behave as any proper Christian (or other follower) would. A corollary of this, already noted, is that people prefer to see husband-wife violence as what *they* do over there, not what *we* do here, or rather what the *we I identify with here do*. We can 'know' that there are other ways, such as not rejecting the divorced or the battered at the church door, but yet at the same time *we* know that our way of doing precisely that, albeit in varied and subtle versions, is somehow proper or at least understandable. It is in other words a combination of cultural ownership defined by an elite which smoothly 'others' those who both experience life rather differently and refuse to follow their supposed leaders.

Working through the material gathered in this research, there were a number of ordained or professed women, and men, who were interested in this issue, angered by it and resentful of their church's lack of concern. Such 'deviants' in certain regions can be called out as disruptives with whatever label seems most damaging. It is easy in Asia and Africa, say, for beyond is to suggest those who oppose 'the right way' are influenced by Western thought and even Western theology (not that either has bothered much about wife-abuse) and they are therefore cultural traitors. Yet the woman saying her pastor or priest should 'keep away from the cultural pattern' is *not* rejecting being Indian nor wanting to be Western. She is recognizing that 'if priests refer to Indian culture, they do that to keep us in our cultural place, and that is way below men. But this faith, Christianity, offers us recognition as children of God.'

There *is* or should be interactive ongoing tension between faith and context, Christ and culture, in every place. Yet this sense of separation between clergy and people, just as between elite and subordinate in a region, is not unique to mission (not that the Syrian Orthodox speaker above is not in a 'mission field,' her forebears having been Christian for many centuries) but is also present in ministry in every place, as any subordinate knows full well. I wrote some time ago that 'Missiology – about the Other, yet not Thou – tends to be smoothly separated from Ministry – about Us, yet not I' (2007:418). Such separation obtains in *any* place, yet it is unacceptable. Too often, ministry by individuals and groups controlling a church and defining what is 'culturally appropriate' looks rather like an imperial mission, silencing the voices of those without clout. The Chinese wife of a national church leader, for example, was asked some years ago by a villager at a Kadazan Women's Mission weekend in Borneo:

> 'My husband hits me a lot: what should I do?' The questioner smiled politely when told by the visitor: 'stay with him and pray for him.' *All* the local women laughed afterwards, saying 'leave him now, possibly pray for him but probably not. She says that because she's Chinese and that's what *they* do, but *we* are Kadazan.'

No one openly gainsaid the visitor's views. She had her way, they theirs and in the institution (as in regional life) she counted, they did not. This is not, let me repeat, a mission issue only, for it recurs in every context of ministry, those on the edge keeping quiet until they sidle off.

Talking publicly about marital violence could be seen as an attack on the inner purity of the group, a stepping out of line, just as a wife complaining about an abusive husband damages the reputation for virtue of either or both families, and the abused clergy wife the self-image of the congregation. Yet that purity is an ideological statement separating the speaker from other people or ideas rather than reflecting the manifold ways of being within a aggregation of people. 'Culture' came up sporadically in discussions, but more often when clergy were less interested in theological or survivor issues than in defending their territory, wherever that was. It is not Indian, Scottish or Kenyan *tradition* which is key to useful discussion, but the *use* made of it to fill gaps, to defend one and to uphold another position even if that defeats the Word.

Onwards: Three threads of hope

Christianity talks of loving the neighbour as the self, of justice and mercy, and of behaving as we would have others behave towards ourselves, all selves being equal before God and equally made in God's Image. If the abuse of Christian wives 'is no big deal', or if it is 'a private matter' if witness and wifehood just go together with female self-sacrifice and sainthood, something rather odd has happened since loving kindness and fairness towards the frail and needy were the essential prerequisite for the baptism of male and female in the Early Church. Not that wives *are* necessarily frail and needy. But we have seen just how vulnerable abused mothers can be, how vulnerable deeply devout abused clergy and laity wives can be, how far from 'fully alive' any abused person is when treated as a punchball. And we may wonder how needy abusers are, whatever skewed theological or cultural props they hold.

'Othering' is what the theologian Cooper-White sees as the crucial process in abuse. As in war, the enemy ceases to be someone's daughter, mother, wife and lover, but a non-human. She writes: 'An abuser makes a critical shift in perspective, no longer seeing her as a human being, equally precious as himself, but only as an object to be manipulated, from a Thou to an It' (Cooper-White, 1995:19). She, just as the abusing he, is indeed precious, and the damage intentionally inflicted on her and on that which is Divine in her should scandalize and shame us all.

As has been made clear, there are men and women across the world who oppose abusers. Laity and clergy may contribute to church-linked groups on long-term teaching and support or offer practical support for abused wives, advising safety, separation and divorce even against the views of their tradition. Individual congregations may have a system of 'befriending' abused women on a non-intrusive basis or be part of regional or national churches which work to put into practice the views of faith-based organizations such as WCC, the Vatican, WARC and smaller groups as well as engage with secular systems of support.

But none of these strategies and supports are enough if adults know little beyond a list of 'don'ts': don't drink, don't swear, don't miss mass, don't whatever', but far too rarely: 'live with joy, knowing God is there for you, that you are loved just as you are, that whoever you are, you are made in God's image.' Every person has a part to play in stopping abuse, not just because abuse is destructive and mutually damaging, but because an abuser abuses that of God in the other and in himself. So how do we move onwards? Where are our guide-threads?

The first thread of hope is that some people involved in this research felt the basis for non-violence in adult life was laid in early childhood. Consequently, they advised that key texts should be used such as 'all are made in the Image of God, and "If we are in Christ, there is no difference between Jew and Gentile, Slave or free, man and woman," so that well before puberty children are better equipped to treat each other with respect'. Then, one that priest continued, 'There'd be no excuse for adults to say "we didn't know that!"' However, there are two objections to this point. One is 'Schools do that so we needn't to.' This is inadequate. Leaving such integrated teaching to schools by design or default risks a values clash, if schools say no one should hit another person, based on moral and ethical grounds, but churches are silent. Even very young children are able to take in and incorporate into their lives far more than Jesus stories or highlights of the Old Testament, important though those are. At present a *Christian* message about inter-personal relations is often not taught at all.

Secondly, keeping silent to avoid 'ending children's innocence' and by chance avoiding perpetrator's shame outweighs frightened children's need for security. Teaching the commandment to honour parents while conveying that Christian Daddies should not be beating the daylights out of Christian Mummies indeed calls for some finesse. Yet put another way, how is a child to honour parents one of whom is dead and the other in prison for her murder? As we read in Chapter 5, 'As soon as a child knows "Daddy hits Mummy," that child is alone.' That is where Christians should value faith above pride and teach children the consequences of all being made in God's Image. To counter such self-centredness, one pastor insisted that 'the pursuit of justice, equality and basic human rights should be our base-line, including the consequences, legal and spiritual, when these are not embraced.' From cradle to grave, the key thread is that this applies to us all.

A second thread of hope for thinking and acting goes back to creation. Some Christians say the first version, 'made in the image of God', is how things should be and the second, Adam and Eve, is how things are although, oddly enough, a good many prefer the real not the ideal. This is neatly brought out in this comment on Ephesians 5.21 from a Kenyan layman:

> I know males and females should submit to each other, but unless the man has that special godliness, controlling his wife is his only way. *If they are perfect,* they can live in mutual submission. That's what Paul meant. But *we are not perfect, so the wife must obey the husband.*

For this honest man, 'Both partners should be equal, men are useless at being equal so women better just accept that.' How that fits in with all being made in the Image of God and all believers having that of Christ in them is an open question.

As the last chapter made clear, 'Made in the Image of God' resonates with a good many people, not just women as women, but *especially* those women *and* men who feel insignificant, even worthless. True, the males among them might follow or adopt Adam's domination over Eve and briefly feel proud: most are not fools. They know mistreating a wife is a cheap way of feeling big, although those who truly believe it their duty to hit their wife will not see the self-serving aspect of their behaviour. *Knowing* all are wonderfully made in the Image of God: that is something to help *anyone* hold up their head.

If 'Made in the Image of God' were taught as often as 'Dominion over the world and its women' or the CBMW-inspired Trinity which 'eternally subordinates Jesus to the Father and woman to man,' faith could more surely honour every soul. Should we not, and that everywhere, first teach the Image of God before, as the Indian woman of the last chapter said, 'all that culture-talk which puts us into our place'. The key thread is that the most life-enhancing relationships, just as among the persons of the Trinity, are those of respectful mutuality.

The third thread of hope, ending abuse against wives, is a job for everyone. Some ordained hypocrites are themselves guilty of marital abuse, *totally* inexcusable under *any* circumstances. More are guilty by default, by silence, by teaching about headship so irresponsibly as to risk injury or death to women and, across the world, by implicitly utilizing cultural cues above godly ways of living in mutually respectful relationships. Every time a leader excludes a single divorced woman from Communion whom church law would accept, in order to 'strengthen the bonds of marriage', they are using, and abusing, that person, and every time they do not treat women as 'Made in the Image of God', they may be setting the stage for abuse. Even if that contributes to the abuse of one woman, that is one too many.

To that end, leaders and the pew-filling people of God have a joint task. Actually addressing abuse against Christian women by Christian husbands (just as violence in other faiths) means the 'othering' game can no longer defend apathy. Attributing marital violence to other countries, other faiths, other peoples, other castes or classes, to anyone but you, me, my neighbour: that is not the way of hope but of support for evil. Biblical and theological knowledge may well not be equally spread but *everyone* can contribute their mite.

And what must those millions who are the Church do? If they number among those who abuse their wives, they, just like abusing leaders, should stop. This is not just because they are hitting that of Christ and affecting their children's chances of growing up fully alive, but because their behaviour is a shameful refuting of their public pledge. Stopping addictive behaviour *is* tough especially, as an abused Christian friend says, as the only apology that counts is changed behaviour which eventually transforms the former abuser. It's a choice.

A choice too for those who have had little or even much to do with abused or abusive people. They may reflect on 'What does "Made in the Image of God" mean in my life and my behaviour to others?' or 'What can I contribute to church or secular-run shelters for abused women?' or 'How can my church learn theologically and reflect practically regarding abuse in our region?' What *no one* should do is pray for abused people without naming the abuse as sin, or tell abused women they must 'leave that useless rat of a man', for unless murder seems imminent, *she* must decide to 'dive headlong into the darkness' (Donovan 355), not you, and we *all* defend our otherwise indefensibles. By all means reject his criticism of her for their children's snotty noses or a tepid cup of tea, always make clear that she is wonderfully made in the Image of God and, especially relevant for colluding women, never reckon yourself tidier or more organized than her lest (apart from further reducing confidence) you support her abuser.

It is not so hard, once we all accept that no one, just no one, is less important than anyone else; that no one, or almost no sane person, really wants to behave in a way others find despicable and even weak, an issue best dealt with in a safe same-sex group discussion; and no one, no one at all, was put on the earth to shrivel and sink to the ground. We are here, all of us, to be fully alive and to relate to all who are or would be fully alive. The choice today, for all our tomorrows, is ours, each one of us, whoever we are, whatever our past and whichever tradition we abstain from, identify with or live.

Addendum
More of the same: Marital violence in Buddhism and Islam

I noted briefly in Chapter 1 that Christianity was not the only tradition with a problem of violence against women, nor the only tradition where faith texts are massaged to give the outcome an abuser wishes. Other traditions also evolved in this way, as initial openness and even equality in both text and practice revert to less challenging comfort blankets: Sikhism would be especially interesting in this regard. But let me rather pick two more widespread traditions, Islam and Buddhism, the first focusing more on scripture and the second more on ethics. Both are lived on the ground in rather varied forms. This is not just Sunni or Shi'a, Mahayana or Theravada, Tibetan or Sufi, but the way each interacts with a locality and the way of being a person in it. Uneducated rural Muslims in Borneo or educated Buddhists in New York each absorb local understanding of being a person and living in the world which inform and shape their attitude to and practice of the wider tradition, even if unconsciously. Thus the way they practise and therefore also the way they see women, men and marriage reflect local patterns. However, as with Christianity, the increasing globalization of ideas and yardsticks means that incoming so-called official version may begin to impinge on local practice in terms of, say, how marriage rituals should be performed and marriages lived.

Here, let me set out very similar arguments made by Islamic and Buddhist scholars (checked by such scholars) writing about and against such violence. Their sources are not created to oppose men, or follow a new fad. These are scholars exploring faith in relation to males and females in marriage as reflected in their particular tradition. In the process, they too, and their readers, may reflect anew on just what that tradition is.

Buddhism and violence against wives

Let us start with Buddhism, known worldwide for abjuring harm to any living thing (*ahimsa*) on the path to *nirvana*, that perfect state of liberation from greed, hatred and delusion which terminates the many cycles of re-birth through which any living thing from flea to king must go. Violence against a partner would clearly be contrary to *ahimsa*, followers of the Eightfold Path being expected, among other things, to resist evil, respect life, work for good. Yet violence against wives in Thailand and Myanmar, countries defined by Theravada Buddhism, as well as Bhutan which follows Mahayana, is among the highest in the world. How can this be?

Buddha taught men and women and insisted both could attain *nirvana* as they were. A small number of enlightened monks (*bhikkhu*) and nuns (*bhikkhuni*) were part of the monastic community around the Buddha, and indeed are shown in yellow robes being taught by the Buddha in the same room, with men on the left, in Doi Sutep Monastery in northern Thailand. However, no *bhikkhunis* were recorded as invited to the First Council held three months after the Buddha's passing. The Buddhist scholar Kabilsingh, now Venerable Dhammananda, suggests that 'unable to go against the decision of the Buddha [to accept women into the monastic order] during his lifetime, they raised the issue immediately after his Parinirvana' (1991:23). The leading monk Ananda, one of the two leading monks leading that First Council or *Sangha* of the faithful, who had supported the Buddha's acceptance of women into monastic orders, felt compelled to confess his fault in not having rejected nuns as monastics to avoid schism (1991:23).

Thereafter both the Buddhist canon and practices on which the Sangha relied were, according to Kabilsingh, 'drawn from the social and cultural background of India [and] carried with them, consciously or unconsciously, the values of that country which were oppressive to women' (1991:24). Buddha's teaching on marriage included marital love and mutual respect. However, he advised monks (and most Thai Buddhist men have been monks even for a short time) should neither look at nor talk to women, 'because nothing binds men as strongly as women' (Thai Tipitaka in Kabilsingh:26). Buddha also said the reverse applied to monastic nuns but, just as Ephesians 5.22 takes precedence over Ephesians 5.28, so too the parallel advice, 'that nothing binds women as much as men', was not referred to when teaching Buddhist women. Just for monks that may be: but such a view may leak into married men's secular life, never mind affect monks in their teaching and advising of women.

The Japanese Buddhist scholar Kajiyama noted there was no distinction made by Gautama and his close followers between men and women regarding *nirvana*, but the view that women could not reach Buddhahood as women began some four centuries after Buddha's passing, around the first century BCE. Some texts were as explicit, and as contested, as the Buddhist text 'Doctrine of Woman's Incapability of Becoming Enlightened,' which insisted 'womanhood is wholly a snare of evil', echoing Tertullian's 'Women as the Devil's gateway' or indeed Muhammed's son-in-law Ali's 'The entire woman is evil. And what is worse it is a necessary evil.' Kajiyama points out, however, that 'the *mature* philosophy of emptiness and Buddha nature in all sentient beings ... declares that a woman can be enlightened just as she is, a woman' (in Kabilsingh: emphasis added).

Despite the elements of potential misogyny within both texts and cultural context, the importance of *ahimsa* should prevent violence within Buddhist marriages. The ten wholesome deeds include 'not killing, using harsh or abusive speech, holding hatred, resentment and anger in the mind'. As Buddha said: 'All love life. See yourself in others. Then whom can you hurt? What harm can you do?' Yet he too appears inconsistent in his advice about a 'spoiled arrogant woman'.

> She who is lazy, gluttonous, and bent on doing nothing, who gossips and speaks with sharp temper, who belittles her husband's energy and effort, let her be called a shrew and a wife! If fearless of the whip and stick, even-minded, enduring in all things, calm and pure in heart, she obeys her husband's word without anger, let her be called a servant and a wife! (Clough, 2001:130)

True, there are other texts which contradict this one, such as that in the *Sigalaka Sutta*, but this view is the one which validates abusers who, as with the Christian abusers who ignore Ephesians 5.21 in favour of 5.22, cherry-pick their text. The Buddha's comment clearly presents a problem in the context of marital strife, for the one who accepts her lot and, in a sense, submits to fate is seen as good in this text. This is similar to 'Christian wives' submission' to whatever their husband commands, being praiseworthy as long as it is not directly opposed to God's word.

But there is a problem – quite apart from the frequent wish of humans to exert power over others and the equally frequent failure to control anger and eliminate hate – and it concerns suffering. For the Buddhist, unrequited cravings prevent loving kindness and tranquillity: desire itself thus leads to suffering. Our situation in this life is a consequence of our actions in a previous rebirth. Some, though increasingly not all, see efforts to oppose rather than accept a violent partner as rejecting the way of Enlightenment, *dharma*, rather than accepting one's *karma* as the ongoing outcome of past lives.

Being born female, and thus having (for most Buddhist schools) an inherently defiling and defiled nature (Jnanavira, 2006:2), is already a sign of negative karma. The abused Buddhist wife may well have been taught not only that life involves craving and therefore suffering, but also that suffering in this life results from wrongdoing in a previous life, with *karma* being

> permanent and fixed, something from the past life that people who are abused cannot do anything in the present life to change. Instead, one must be patient, accepting and forgiving'. (Khuankaew, 2007:181)

While the abuser will himself suffer in his next life, he takes little if any responsibility for his current actions, which the victim apparently merited. Khuankaew, a Buddhist teacher within the Thai tradition, explains the effect such incorrectly understood 'karmic justice' can have on a victim. When my father was violent, my desperate mother, unable to protect her children, would say, 'This is my karma.' And when my sister was in an abusive relationship, a monk told her the same thing. (2007:179). Khuankaew explained that the Buddha taught his disciples to remove the root *causes* of suffering in order to end the suffering, not to embrace it, thus giving the abused women with whom she works another perspective.

If Buddhist precepts are adhered to by both partners, there will be no violence, that being a contradiction of the core value *ahimsa*, just as love and mercy, grace and justice underlie Christian teaching. Where violence occurs, women following the values of gentleness and endurance, cited in Chapter 5 by Christian converts in Taiwan as their baseline, do not directly oppose their abuser and may follow the questionable Buddhist slant on self-blame encouraged by pastor or monk alike, an approach which recurred in Chapter 6. Khuankaew cites a monk telling a betrayed woman: 'There is nothing you can do about it, keep being nice to him, do not ever challenge your behaviour because you have done bad karma to him in your previous life' (2007:180). Enduring abuse for the sake of the next rebirth or to reach heaven maybe a choice, but it is not one which accords with either the Buddhist or the Christian demand to respect the self. Such subordination and blame can equally be discerned in Christian attitudes, whether Early Church Fathers, the sixteenth-century priest Vives or twentieth-century Pastor Pearl, just as in an incorrect Qur'anic reading of 4.34. Supine submission is neither incumbent on nor correct for a Buddhist, a Muslim or a Christian wife.

As a recent female Buddhist scholar writes:

> If one truly follows the tenets of Buddhism, then we see that being compassionate and accepting also applies to compassion for and acceptance of ourselves. That means understanding that every life is sacred, including our own, and that it is perfectly in accord with Buddhist ideals to seek safety and protection so we can continue to grow and reach enlightenment ... Karma can be viewed as a mechanism through which we learn the lessons that we failed to learn previously. (Kanukollu, 2016:348)

She notes further (Kanukollu, 2016:349) that:

> gender violence occurs within a community context that has the power to maintain or alleviate the problem, and within the Buddhist community, the *sangha* offers a network that has the opportunity to assist survivors emotionally, physically and spiritually.

Khuankaew trains women in peace building, and reports that after a three-month programme in Northern Thailand, one lady (like our English confirmand above) decided to leave her abusive relationship, saying

> I understand clearly now the real meaning of karma and the right view, and right thinking helps me realise that there is no need for me to continue to suffer in this relationship. (2007:190)

Indeed the Sangha could teach in this way, supporting women as well as men in their following of the way. However, in contexts where the position of women is socially subordinate, the sangha, rather like a Christian diocese, presbytery, or other named unit, seems to collude in violence either because they see such behaviour as appropriate or acting against it as too troublesome.

There are clear similarities with the Christian material set out thus far in this book: the deterministic use of karma to explain a woman's abuse and the directive to remain in abusive marriages as the woman's Cross have similar outcomes. Buddhist texts were reinterpreted to exclude women from full capacity to reach their faith goal by largely eliminating ordained *bhikkhuni* and the attainment of *nirvana* by females as such. As the Buddhist scholar Lekshe Tsomo notes concerning the male compliers of Buddhist and Christian scriptures:

> There is a distinct possibility that gender bias and misogyny has slipped into the scriptures ... [which] are presented as the revealed word of God or the authentic speech of the Buddha, leaving women helpless to negotiate their own status within the tradition. (1999:245)

Historically and regionally, there were changes to this, but that females could be excluded or included, given Buddha had included them, makes their vulnerability to local or changing mores clear. Secondly, and following on from that, is the manner in which suffering, almost the need to suffer, is attributed to women but not men in the marital context. Stressed is *their* suffering as punishment for their last life. Either his current abuse does not seem to be counting for his future life or he is uninterested in that, perhaps because his teachers did not recognize the gravity. Karma stresses that every action has a fruit. That may not be an immutable law of the cosmos and certainly has no fixed penalty schedule. One thing is certain: violence is never a fruit of a life lived the Buddha way.

Islam and husband-wife violence

Let us now look at processes within Islam, a more scriptural tradition yet one which shares similar gender- and regional-based exegesis, peculiarities and outcomes with Buddhism and Christianity. The Qur'an, the sacred scripture of Islam, recognizes women and men as equal in origin, Eve not being blamed more than Adam and both being forgiven. As in both books of the Bible, justice, peace and mercy run like tight threads through the Qur'an in a way which informs and even overrides verses which appear harsh at first reading. Just as with Ephesians 5:22, neither scriptures give that licence to abuse which some assume. The crucial example used by Muslim men who wish to validate hitting or beating their wife and by Christians scorning Islam for seeming to encourage violence against women is verse 34 of the fourth Sura, An-Nisa. Muslims, whether clerics or not, who support a husband's right to hit his wife can thus turn to what seems a clear text for those who support physical 'discipline':

> Men are in charge of women by [right of] what Allah has given one over the other and what they spend [for maintenance] from their wealth. So righteous women are devoutly obedient, guarding in [the husband's] absence what Allah would have them guard. But those [wives] from whom you fear arrogance – [first] advise them; [then if they persist], forsake them in bed; and [finally], strike them [*idribuhunna*]. But if they obey you [once more], seek no means against them. Indeed, Allah is ever Exalted and Grand.
>
> (Sahih International)

However, the text is more complex than at first sight, and actually *restricts* husbands' freedom to hit. Firstly, though, this verse does not apply *at all*, however translated, if the 'rebellion' is cooking goat not mutton and that badly, or having a dribbling nose, to recall the grounds on which Huguccio of Pisa felt a medieval Christian woman could be hit. Secondly, we must make the point that women should not be hit at all, for they are equally made by Allah, and equally partners within a freely entered marriage (see Barlas, 2002; El Fadl in Ammah-Koney, 2009). Prophet Muhammed's comment to women recorded in a Hadith (post-Qur'anic sayings of the Prophet) that 'many of you have turned to my family to complain about their husbands [hitting]: Verily, [such] are not among the best of men' (Ibn Kathir quoted in Roald, 2001) makes his position clear. Moreover, given the point that any verse must be read in terms of the overall intention of the text, verse 5 of that same Sura An Nisa expects husbands to 'speak to them [wives] words of kindness and justice', which is a core Islamic value.

The word often translated as strike, *idribuhunna* from the root *daraba*, has multiple meanings (Abu Sulayman, 2003), allowing a husband to *flick* her with a scarf, *hit or beat her*, or *leave her*, as the final step to bring her rebellious attitudes over specific and primarily religious issues to an end. The fact that the Prophet did not hit his wives and opposed such action gives more credence to 'stay away from or leave', although the Sahih translation above chooses another direction. The husband who swiftly hits his wife without carrying out the first two steps of verse 34 is a wrongdoer, for the mandated three-step process takes a minimum of twenty-four hours. Moreover, in doing so, they ignore alternate readings (as does the Sahih translation above) and substantiated Hadiths of the Prophet which oppose extreme violence, such as: 'None of you shall flog his wife as he flogs a slave and then have sexual intercourse with her in the last part of the day' (Sahil al-Bukhari). (This Hadith does not contradict An Nisa, 34–36, fatal flogging being of a different order than hitting.) Moreover, given even that a permissible third-step 'touch' too easily morphs into unacceptable abuse, *any* striking is unacceptable lest it leads to a wrong (Kausar, Hussain and Idriss, 2011). Incidentally, the eighth-century jurist Imam Malik (after whom the wife-supporting Maliki law school is named) notes that a husband who mistreats his wife should be admonished, then support her financially but lose the right to expect obedience from her, and if his violence continues, the sharia court should punish him (Kausar, Hussain and Idriss, 2011:110).

Irrespective of exegesis which intentionally fails to discourage violence, Muslim women, depending on area, have various means of divorcing a husband, the first being the right to divorce her husband *(khul')*, irrespective of her family's opinion or her husband's agreement, though commonly with certain constraints and the possible loss of her dower which her husband would otherwise owe to her at death or divorce. Her right to 'redeem herself' by divorce is recognized by the majority of legal schools (Hanafi, Hanbali etc.) although only the Malaki school (commoner in Africa) includes violence by the husband. *Khul'* rights have recently been formalized in state law, sometimes borrowing the Malaki school grounds. Pakistan allowed it in 1961, though with a loss of financial rights in three of four provinces, Afghanistan in 1977 and 2010 and Egypt in 2000, followed by others, Pakistan law in the Punjab being amended in 2015 to enable a partial dowry return (see Sonneveld and Styles, 2019; Yassad and Saboory, 2010). The extent to which this gives effective protection varies. The clause allowing delegated right of divorce given to the wife by her husband on marriage may be crossed out on Pakistani Muslim marriage contracts without the woman's consent. A confident and aware woman will oppose that, but the average youngster may not. Other women's capacity to secure a delegated or a *khul'* divorce will be affected, as is the case for abused women of any faith tradition, by her capacity to manage her future, to find her inner strength after it has been sapped and her capacity to withstand familial opposition. Yet it remains a beacon of strength for Muslim women.

The abusive manipulation of texts easily enabled Muslim wives, just as Christian or Buddhist, to be mistreated by apparently religious husbands. However, the common contemporary Western view that Muslim women inevitably fare badly in marriage has historically not been shared nor, given the continuous historically evidenced disabilities for Christian women, was it in principle reasonable. It was certainly not shared by abused Christian women in a country operating Islamic law. Converting to Islam gives an abused wife her freedom, whether in the Ottoman Empire (Baer, 2004), or among Coptic Orthodox women (especially wives of priests) in Egypt. In South Asia, rules on divorce for Christians place an abused Christian wife in a far worse position than her Muslim sister, unless the latter had relinquished delegated or *khul'* rights on marriage. Conversion to Islam might not produce a gentle kindly spouse: but having such a 'get out of gaol' card may give a chance of immediate safety.

Clearly in Islam, as with all other traditions, the social context speaks loudly to social action and can radically affect the way a verse such as 4:34 is understood and applied. Where Islam is settled in a relatively egalitarian context, such as rural Borneo, in which neither spouse (being ontologically equal) has the right to hit the other, there is no more violence among Muslims than among Christians. In Pakistan, on the other hand, violence against wives appears the norm based on a Qur'anic reading which ignores the first two points of verses 34–36 of An Nisa as well as verse 5 of that chapter, making men ontologically superior to women (Maududi, 1975). This, however, is not Islam, but rather the outcome of the region's view of male and female humans, an outcome which is also part of local Christian practice in Pakistan.

Currently in the UK, Muslim women have exactly the same rights as others to divorce violent husbands, although current examination of the working of Shari'a courts may seek to control those imams who (against UK law) advise an abused woman to remain with her abuser and refuse a religious divorce. 'Imams against Domestic Abuse', founded in 2011 by Imams Ad-Duha and Hasan, work hard, with support from the Muslim Council of Britain, to make clear that Islam does not condone violence against wives. Similar movements exist in a number of other Muslim-majority countries such as Malaysia. Salma Abugideiri, co-director of Peaceful Families Project in the United States, explains that in Muslim (just as in Christian) contexts, the abuser may feel remorse and seek forgiveness, with the victim often relenting. 'It's hard when you see a man crying not to believe he is genuine and sincere,' she said. 'But as soon as the woman starts to "act defiant," the abuse will start again.' Readers may recollect the wife of the Methodist minister who constantly demanded forgiveness without offering a shred of repentance, much less any inkling of transformation.

The theological problem, the cultural control and the poor teaching, typical of all three traditions explored in this book, are summed up elegantly by a Myanmar Muslim woman, Daw Molly, with a sharp turn of phrase that could apply to persons of any and no faith:

> As a leader of women, I, an Islamic woman, say that so-called Muslims have not learnt and properly processed the teaching of Islam and [have] elastically adapted Islam's code of disciplines and rules in accordance with their own desires leading their ideas to become the traditional norms that affect women's rights. (WCRP 2006:8)

Reflection

A Buddhist murdering Rohinga and other non-Buddhist ethnic minorities, a Muslim blowing up innocent bystanders, a Christian bombing women's clinics: each evil actor is just like a Buddhist, Muslim or Christian attacking the body and soul of his wife. None can lay claim to follow their tradition: each *uses* their tradition to validate violence. That is their choice. It falls to their sisters and brothers in faith, both lay and ordained, male and female, and to anyone committed to human rights for all, to reject intimate partner violence and name it for what it is, an assault on the spiritual and physical integrity of another human being perfectly made to live fully in the peaceful pursuit of their tradition. If it is time for a change, and time for people of faith to think, speak and act against faith-condoned violence in marriage, it is time for each reader, of whatever faith and none, to think: 'How do *I* think, speak and act against this evil?'

Bibliography

Adelman Howard '"A Disgrace for All Jewish Men:" Preliminary Considerations for the Study of Wife-Beating in Jewish History' *Medieval Feminist Newsletter* Vol 21 1996

Alsdurf James and Alsdurf Phyllis *Battered into Submission: The Tragedy of Wife Abuse in the Christian Home* Crowborough: Highland 1990

Alsdurf James and Alsdurf Phyllis 'A Pastoral Response' in *Abuse and Religion: When Praying Isn't Enough* A Horton and J A Williamson (eds) Lexington: Lexington Books 1988

Ammah Rabiatu 'Islamic Understanding of Creation: The Place of Woman' in *Where God Reigns: Reflections on Women in God's World* E Amoah (ed) Accra: Sam-Woode 1997

Ammah-Koney Rabiatu 'Violence against Women in the Ghanaian Muslim Community' in *The Architecture of Violence against Women in Ghana* K Cusak and T Manu (eds) Accra: Gender Studies and Human Rights Documentation Centre 2009

Ammons Linda 'What's God Got to Do with It? Church and State Collaboration in the Subordination of Women and Domestic Violence' in *Rutgers Law Review* Vol 51 1999

Anderson-Rajkumar Evangeline 'The Violence of Silence: Reviewing the Church's Stance on Domestic Violence' in *Asian Christian Review* Vol 4/1 2010

Anwar Ghazala 'Muslim Feminist Discourses' in *Feminist Theology in Different Contexts* E Schüssler Fiorenza (ed) M S Copeland London: SCM 1996

Aquinas Thomas *Summa Theologica* Chicago: Britannia 1952

Areen Judith 'Uncovering the Reformation Roots of American Marriage and Divorce Law' in *Yale Journal of Law and Feminism* Vol 26/1 2014

Aune Kristin and Barnes Rebecca *In Churches Too: Church Response to Domestic Abuse-A Case-Study of Cumbria* 2018

Baer Marc 'Islamic Conversion Narratives of Women; Social Change and Gendered Religious Hierarchy in Early Modern Ottoman Istanbul' in *Gender and History* Vol 16/2 2004

Bailey Joanne *Unquiet Lives: Marriage and Marriage Breakdown in England: 1660-1800* Cambridge: CUP 2003

Baker Lynne *Counselling Christian Women: On How to Deal with Domestic Violence* Bowen Hills: Australian Academic Press 2010

Barlas Asma *'Believing Women' in Islam: Unreading Patriarchal Interpretations of the Qur'an* Austin: University of Texas Press 2002

Bast Robert J *Honor Your Fathers: Catechisms and the Emergence of a Patriarchal Ideology in Germany 1400–1600* Leiden: Brill 1997

Bhattachaharya Rinka (ed) *Behind Closed Doors: Domestic Violence in India* Delhi: Sage 2004

Blackstone William *Commentaries on the Laws of England* Books 1–5, 1765 London ebooks: Adelaide 2014

Børresen Kari 'Image of God and Gender Models in the Christian Tradition' in *In the Image of God; Foundations and Objections within the Discourse on Human Dignity* A Melloni and R Saccenti (eds) Berlin: LIT 2010

Brasher Brenda *Godly Women: Fundamentalism and Female Power* New Brunswick: Rutgers University Press 1998

Cere Daniel 'Marriage, Subordination and the Development of Christian Doctrine' in *Does Christianity Teach Male Headship?* D Blankenhorn, D Browning and M S Van Leeuwen (eds) Grand Rapids: Eerdmans 2004

Chittister Joan 'When Violence against Women Is "Honourable," "Religious," and "Legal"' in *National Catholic Reporter* 24 May 2007

Classen Albrecht *The Power of a Woman's Voice in Mediaeval and Early Modern Literature* Berlin: de Gruyter 2007

Clough Brad 'Buddhism' in *Ethics of Family Life* J Neusner (ed) Belmont: Wadsworth 2001

Collins Natalie *Out of Control: Couples, Conflict and the Capacity for Change* London: SPCK 2019

Cooper-White Pamela *The Cry of Tamar: Violence against Women and the Church's Response* Grand Rapids: Fortress 1995

Counts D, Brown J and Campbell J (eds) *To Have and to Hit: Cultural Perspectives on Wife Beating* Urbana: University of Illinois 1992 and 1999

Cruz Gemma 'Liberating Justice: The Challenge of Wife-Battery to Christian Teaching on Justice' in *Ecclesia in Asia: Gathering the Voices of the Silenced* Evelyn Monteiro and Antoinette Gutzler (eds) Delhi: ISPCK 2005

Davies Alun 'Assemblies of God Broaden Divorce Rules' *The Religion Report* ABC Radio 2/5/07

DeConick April *Holy Misogyny* New York: Continuum 2011

Dillard Heath *Daughters of the Reconquest: Women in Castilian Town Society 1100–1300* Cambridge: Cambridge University Press 1984

Dobash Rebecca and Dobash Russell *Violence against Wives: A Case against Patriarchy* London: Open Books 1980

Dolan Frances *Marriage and Violence: The Early Modern Legacy* Philadelphia: Penn 2008

Dolphyne Florence *The Emancipation of Women* Accra: University of Ghana 1991

Dominiczak Andrzej 'In Defence of the Sacred Family; in *Law and Gender*. Polish Women's Rights Centre 2010

Donovan Jean 'Diving into Darkness: The Religion Experience of Women Survivors of Domestic Violence' in *Encountering Transcendence: Contributions to a Theology of Christian Religious Experience* L Boeve, H Geybels and S Van den Bossche (eds) Leuven: Peeters 2005

Dziewanowska M, Khomuk V and Krawczyk L 'Airing the Dirty Laundry: Exploring the Challenges of Domestic Violence in Poland' in *Law and Gender* Polish Women's Rights Centre 2010

Eilts Mitzi 'Saving the Family: When Is the Covenant Broken' in *Violence against Women and Children: A Christian Theological Sourcebook* C Adams and M Fortune (eds) New York: Continuum 1995

Elizondo Felisa 'Violence against Women: Strategies of Resistance and Sources of Healing in Christianity' in *Violence against Women* E Schüssler Fiorenza and M Shawn Copeland (eds) London: SCM 1994

Ellison M and Hewey K 'Hope Lies in the Struggle against It:' Co-teaching a Seminar Course on Domestic Violence and Theology' in *Violence against Women: A Christian Theological Source Book* C Adams and M Fortune (eds) New York: Continuum 1995

Fabricius Johann Halle Halle Archive Mission Papers 'Beispiel aus Madras' (HB 65C, 932–937) 1746, Halle

Faure Bernard *The Power of Denial: Buddhism Purity and Gender* Princeton: PUP 2003

Filemoni-Tofaeono Joan and Johnson Lydia *Reweaving the Relational Mat: A Christian Response to Violence against Women from Oceania* London: Equinox 2006

Ford David C *Women and Men in the Early Church: The Full View of St John Chrysostom* New Canaan: STS Press 1996

Fortune Marie 'The Transformation of Suffering: A Biblical and Theological Perspective' in *Violence against Women and Children: A Christian Theological Sourcebook* C Adams and M Fortune (eds) New York: Continuum 1995

Fowl Stephen and Jones Gregory *Reading in Communion* London: SPCK 1991

Foyster Elizabeth *Marital Violence: An English Family History, 1660–1857* Cambridge: Cambridge University Press 2005

Gittins Anthony 'Beyond Liturgical Inculturation: Transforming the Deep Structures of Faith' *Irish Theological Quarterly* Vol 69/1 2004

Gnadadason Aruna *No Longer a Secret: The Church and Violence against Women* Geneva: WCC 1997

Goodman Kaufman Carol *Sins of Omission: The Jewish Community's Reaction to Domestic Violence* Boulder: Westview 2003

Gottlieb Beatrice *The Family in the Western World: From the Black Death to the Industrial Age* Oxford: OUP 1993

Graetz Naomi *Silence Is Deadly: Judaism Confronts Wife-Beating* New Jersey: Aronson 1998

Griffith E Marie *God's Daughters: Evangelical Women and the Power of Submission* Berkeley: University of California Press: 1997

Groothuis Rebecca *Good News for Women: A Biblical Picture of Gender Equality* Grand Rapids: Baker 1997
Grudem Wayne 1994 *Systematic Theology* Grand Rapids: IVP 1994
Heale William *An Apologie for Women* Oxford: Barnes 1609
Henderson Jim *The Resignation of Eve* Austin: Barna 2012
Hopf G Martin *Bucer and the English Reformation* Oxford: OUP 1946
Hunter D G 'The Paradise of Patriarchy: Ambrosiaster on Women as (Not) God's Image' in *Journal of Theological Studies* Vol 43/2 1992
Hunter David G 'Augustine and the Making of Marriage in Roman North Africa' *Journal of Early Christian Studies* Vol 11/1 2003
Ingram 1987 *Church Courts, Sex and Marriage 1570–1640* Cambridge: CUP 1987
Jnanavira Dharmacari 'A Mirror for Women? Reflections on the Feminine in Japanese Buddhism' in *Western Buddhist Review* Vol 4 2004
John Paul II *Mulieris Dignitatem* Apostolic Letter August 1988 Vatican: Rome
Johnson James *A Society Ordained by God: English Puritan Marriage Doctrine in the First Half of the Seventeenth Century* Nashville: Abingdon 1970
Kabilsingh Chatsumarn *Thai Women in Buddhism* Berkeley: Parallax 1991
Kanukollu Shanta N 'Violence against Women through a Buddhist Lens' in *Religion and Men's Violence against Women* Andy J Johnson (ed) New York: Springer 2016
Karant-Nunn Susan '"Fragrant Wedding Roses": Lutheran Wedding Sermons and Gender Definition in Early Modern Germany' *German History* Vol 17/1 1999
Kausar Sadia, Hussain Sjaad and Idriss Md Mazher 'Does the Qur'an Condone Domestic Violence?' in *Honour, Violence, Women and Islam* M. M. Idriss and T Abbas (eds) Abingdon: Routledge 2011
Kelly H A 'Rule of Thumb and the Folklaw of the Husband's Stick' in *Journal of Legal Education* Vol 44/3 1994
Khuankaew Ouyporn 'Buddhism and Violence against Women' in *Violence against Women in Contemporary World Religion: Roots and Cures* Maguire D and Sheik S (eds) pp 174–91, Cleveland: Pilgrim Press, 2007
Kingdom of Tonga *National Study on Domestic Violence against Women in Tonga 2009* published 2012 Ma'a Fafine mo e Famili: Nuku'alofa
Kisseadoo Samuel *Spiritual Warfare and Family Life* Accra: Asempa 2003
Kisseadoo Samuel *Understanding the Differences between Men and Women* Accra: Asempa 2007
Koehler Lyle *A Search for Power: The 'Weaker Sex' in Seventeenth-Century New England* Urbana: University of Illinois 1980
Koepping Elizabeth 'Contested Light: Integrity and Power in Eastern Sabah Villages' in *Missiology* Vol 35/4 2007
Koepping Elizabeth *Food Friends and Funerals: On Lived Religion* Berlin: LIT 2008
Koepping Elizabeth 'A Game of Three Monkeys: Kadazan Villagers and Violence against Women' in *Sojourn Journal of Social Issues in Southeast Asia* Vol 18/2 2003
Koepping Elizabeth 'Review of Domestic Abuse in Christian Theologies by R Starr' in *The Expository Times* Vol 130/11 p 516–17 2019

Koepping Elizabeth 'Rights of Culture and Demands of Faith: Domestic Violence and the Silence of the Church' *Asian Christian Review* Vol 4/1 2010

Koepping Elizabeth 'Spousal Violence among Christians: Taiwan, South Australia and Ghana' in *Studies in World Christianity* Vol 19/3 2013

Koepping Elizabeth (ed) *World Christianity: Critical Concepts in Religious Studies* Vol III London: Routledge 2011

Kroeger Catherine Clark 'Let's Look again at the Biblical Concept of Submission' in *Violence against Women and Children: A Christian Theological Sourcebook* C Adams and M Fortune (eds) New York: Continuum 1995

Kvam K, Schearing L and Ziegler V *Eve and Adam: Jewish, Christian and Muslim Readings on Genesis and Gender* Bloomington: Indiana University Press 1999

Ladurie Emmanuel Le Roy *Montaillou: Cathars and Catholics in a French Village 1294–1324* London: Penguin 1980

Lee Susan Hagood 'Witness to Christ, Witness to Pain; One Woman's Journey through Wife-Battering' in *Sermons Seldom Heard: Women Proclaim Their Lives* A L Milhaven (ed) New York: Crossroad 1991

Lefkovitz Lori 'Not a Man: Joseph and the Character of Masculinity in Judaism and Islam' in *Gender in Judaism and Islam: Common Lives, Uncommon Heritage* in F Kashani-Sabet and B Wenger (eds) New York: New York University Press 2015

Leshke Tsomo 'Comparing Buddhist and Christian Women's Experiences' in *Buddhist Women across Cultures* K Leshke Tsomo (ed) Albany: University of New York 1999

Liu Meng 'Revictimisation: An Analysis of a Hotline Service for Battered Women in China in *AJWS* Vol 7/2 2001

Luckyj Christina A *Mouzell for Melastomus* in Context: Rereading the Swetnam-Speght Debate in *English Literary Renaissance* Vol 40/1 2010

Lukes Stephen *Power a Radical View* London: Palgrave 2004

Luther M 'The Babylonian Captivity of the Church' in *Three Treatises* Philadelphia: Fortress Press 1970

Lutheran Church of Australia: *Commission on Social and Bioethical Questions. Report on Domestic Violence* Adelaide: LCA 1993

Lwambo Desiree 'Men and Masculinities in Eastern DR Congo' in *Gender and Development* Vol 21/1 2013

Mananzan Mary John 'Feminine Socialization: Women as Victims and Collaborators' in *Violence against Women* E Schüssler Fiorenza and M Shawn Copeland (eds) London: SCM 1994

Mananzan Mary John 'Theological Reflections on Violence against Women (a Catholic Perspective) in *Gendering the Spirit* D S Ahmed (ed) London: Zed 2002

Martey Emmanuel 'Church and Marriage in African Society: A Theological Appraisal' in *Christian Perspectives on Sexuality and Gender* E Stuart and A Thatcher (eds) Leominster: Gracewing 1996

Mather Cotton *Ornaments for the Daughters of Zion* 1692 Reel Wing/1487

Matter A 'The Undebated Debate: Gender and the Image of God in Medieval Theology' in *Gender in Debate from the Early Middle Ages to the Renaissance* T Fenster and C Lees (eds) New York: Palgrave 2002

Menon N and Johnson M 'A Feminist Study of Domestic Violence in Rural India' Penn State University 2000

Maududi Abul Ala *Purdah and the Status of Women* Lahore: Islamic Publications 1975

Meyers Debra *Common Whores, Vertuous Women and Loving Wives: Free Will Christian Women in Colonial Maryland* Bloomington: Indiana University Press 2003

Miles A *Domestic Violence: What Every Pastor Needs to Know* Minneapolis: Fortress 2000

McMullin S, Nason-Clark N, Fisher-Townsend A, Holtmann C, 'When Violence Hits the Religious Home: Raising Awareness about Domestic Violence in Seminaries and among Religious Leaders' in *Journal of Pastoral Care and Counselling* Vol 69/2 2015

Mulder Anne-Claire 'Empowering Those Who Suffer' in *Fragile Dignity: Intercontextual Conversations in Scriptures, Family and Violence* J Claassens and K Spronk (eds) Atlanta: SBL 2013

Myatt Alan 'On the Compatibility of Ontological Equality, Hierarchy and Functional Distinctions' in *The Deception of Eve and the Ontology of Women* W Spencer and M Greulich (eds) Bellingham: CBE 2010

Nason-Clark Nancy *The Battered Wife: How Christians Confront Domestic Violence* Louisville: Westminster John Knox 1997

Nason-Clark Nancy 'Making the Sacred Safe: Women Abuse and Communities of Faith' *Sociology of Religion* Vol 61/4 2000

Nyabera Fred and Montgomery Taryn *Contextual Bible-Study Manual on Gender-Based Violence* Nairobi: FECCLAHA 2007

Oakley Lisa and Humphreys Justin *Escaping the Maze of Spiritual Abuse: Creating Healthy Christian Cultures* London: SPKC 2019

Oduyoye Mercy 'Catalyst, Resource or Roadblock? A Critical Examination of the Christian Religion and Violence against Women and Children in Ghana' in *The Architecture of Violence against Women in Ghana* K Cusak and T Manuh (eds) Accra: GSHRDC 2009

Oduyoye Mercy *Who Will Roll the Stone Away?* Geneva: WCC 1990

O'Faolain Julia Martines Lauro *Not in God's Image: Women in History from the Greeks to the Victorians* London: Fontana 1974

Okure Teresa 'Unwise Words in a Wise Book: Ephesians 5: 21–33' in *Women in Religion and Culture* M Oduyoye (ed) Nefer: Ibadan 2007

Paine Alastair *The First Chapters of Everything: How Genesis 1–4 Explains Our World* Tain: Christian Focus Publications 2014

Perl Debbie and Michael *Created to Be His Helpmate* Pleasantville: NGJ 2004

Phillips Roderick *Untying the Knot: A Short History of Divorce* Cambridge: CUP 1991

Piper John *Happily Ever After: Finding Grace in the Messes of Marriage* Epsom: desiringgod 2017

Pius XI *Casti Connubii* (31 December 1930) http://w2.vatican.va/content/pius-xi/connubii.htm accessed 12 October 2013

Pleck Elizabeth 'Criminal Approaches to Family Violence 1640–1980' *Crime and Justice: Family Violence* Vol 11 1989

Poos L R 'The Heavy-Handed Marriage Counsellor: Regulating Marriage in Some Later-Medieval English Local Ecclesiastical-Court Jurisdictions' in *The American Journal of Legal History* Vol 39/3 1995

Power Kim *Veiled Desires: Augustine's Writing on Women* London: Darton, Longman, Todd 1995

Potter Engel Mary 'Historical Theology and Violence against Women: Unearthing a Popular Tradition of Just Battery' in *Violence against Women and Children: A Christian Theological Sourcebook* C Adams and M Fortune (eds) New York: Continuum 1995

Procter-Smith Marjorie 'Reorganizing Victimization: The Intersection between Liturgy and Domestic Violence' in *Christian Perspectives on Sexuality and Gender* E Stuart and A Thatcher (eds) Leominster: Gracewing 1996

Ragsdale Neil *Rural Women Battering and the Justice System: An Ethnography* Thousand Oaks: Sage 1998

Roald Anne-Sophie *Women in Islam: The Western Experience* New York: Routledge 2001

Sabean David *Property, Production, and Family in Neckarhausen 1700–1870* Cambridge: CUP 1990

Salmon Marylynn 'The Legal Status of Women in Early America: A Reappraisal' in *Law and History Review* Vol 1/1 1983

Schearing Linda and Ziegler Valarie *Enticed by Eden: How Western Culture Uses, Confuses (and Sometimes Abuses) Adam and Eve* Waco: Baylor UP 2013

Schroeder Joy 'John Chrysostom's Critique of Spousal Violence' in *Journal of Early Christian Studies* Vol 12/4 2004

Scott Theological College *A Biblical Approach to Marriage and Family in Africa* Machakos: TAG 1994

Setyawan Yusak Budi '"Be Subject to You Husband as You Are to the Lord" in Ephesians 5: 21–33 Illuminated by an Indonesian (Javanese)' in *Asian Journal of Theology* Vol 21/1 2007

Shaikh Sa'diyya 'A Tafsir of Praxis: Gender, Marital Violence and Resistance in a South African Muslim Community' in *Violence against Women in Contemporary World Religion: Roots and Cures* D Maguire and S Sheik (eds) Cleveland: Pilgrim Press, 2007

Sheerattan-Bisnauth P and Peacock P V (eds) *Created in God's Image: From Hegemony to Partnership. A Church Manual on Men as Partners: Promoting Positive Masculinities* Geneva: WCRC and WCC 2010

Song Bun Korean Women's Development Institute, Personal Communication 2008

Sonneveld Nadia 'Divorce Reform in Egypt and Morocco: Men and Women Navigating Rights and Duties' in *Islamic Law and Society* Vol 20/1 2019

Stair Lord *The Last of the Law of Scotland Deduced from Its Original* 1675 quod.lib. umich.edu/e/eebo

Starr Rachel *Reimagining Theologies of Marriage in Contexts of Domestic Violence: When Salvation Is Survival* Abingdon: Routledge 2018

Strickland Angela January 2020, personal letter

Strom Kay M *In the Name of Submission: A Painful Look at Wife-Battering* Portland: Multnomah 1986

Sulayman Abu *Recapturing the Full Islamic Spirit of Human Dignity* London: International Institute of Islamic Thought 2003

Taves Ann *Religion and Domestic Violence in Early New England: The Memoirs of Abigail Abbot Bailey* Bloomington: Indiana University Press 1989

The Journal.ie 27 December 2012 accessed 21 March 2019

Thistlethwaite Susan 'Every Two Minutes: Battered Women and Feminist Interpretation' in *Interpretations of the Bible* L Russell Feminist (ed) Oxford: Blackwell 1985

Tripp Paul *What Did You Expect? Redeeming the Realities of Marriage* Nottingham: Intervarsity Press 2010

Tucker Ruth *Black and White Bible, Black and Blue* Wife Grand Rapids: Zondervan 2016

Van Leeuwen Mary 'When Praying Isn't Enough: Religion, Prejudice and Abuse' in *Priscilla Papers* Vol 8/3 Summer 1994

WCRP: Women and Child Rights Project (Southern *Who Will Roll the Stone*) 'The Plight of Women and Children in Burma' Issue 3/2006 June 2006: Bangkok

Websdale Neil *Rural Woman Battering and the Justice System: An Ethnography* Thousand Oaks: Sage 1998

Wendt Sarah 'Christianity and Domestic Violence: Feminist Poststructuralist Perspectives' in *Affilia May* 2008

Whately William *Bride-Bush: A Wedding Sermon Describing the Duties of Married Persons* London: Bourne 1617

Whately William *Bride-Bush: A Direction for Married Persons* London: Man 1619

Wieben Corinne 'As Men Do with Their Wives: Domestic Violence in Fourteenth-Century Lucca' *California Italian Studies* Vol 1/2 2010

Williams Rowan *Why Study the Past* Grand Rapids: Eerdmans 2005

Willmott Michael and Young Peter *Family and Kinship in East London* London: Penguin 1957

Wink Walter *When the Powers Fall* Minneapolis: Fortress 1998

Witte J 'Church State and Family in John Calvin's Geneva: Domestic Disputes and Sex Crimes' in *Law and Disputing in the Middle Ages* P Andersen, K Salonen H M Sigh and H Vogt (eds) DJØF 2013

Yassad Hajma and Md Hamid Saboory 'Sharia and National Law in Afghanistan' in *Sharia Incorporated: A Comparative Overview of the Legal System of Twelve Muslim Countries in Past and Present* J M Otto (ed) Leiden: Leiden University Press 2010

Index

Abugideiri, Salma 165
abuse. *See also* wife-abuse
 levels and methods of 14–16
 physical/emotional/psychological 3–5, 23, 40, 44, 63, 65, 69, 76, 82, 114, 116, 119, 148, 166
 as sin 108, 113, 123
 spiritual 3, 63, 65, 73, 76, 82, 85, 114, 116, 161, 166
 women as colluders 3, 22, 60, 72, 112–14, 143, 147, 155
adult baptism 91–4
advice 9, 14, 27–8, 35, 39, 51, 78, 86–7, 94, 101, 113–14, 126, 129
 by Lutheran pastors 53
 for ordained and household leaders 130
 patronizing 147
 teaching and church 60
Africa 10, 21, 49, 72, 150. *See also specific African countries*
 Christian marriage 35, 91
 electronic preaching 54
 marital disharmony 128
 meeting, international 145
 Roman Catholicism 23
 short-term marriage contracts 32
African Initiated Churches 10
ahimsa 158–60
Allah 162–3
Alsdurf, James 24, 64
Alsdurf, Phyllis 24, 64
Ambrosiaster 44, 47
androcentrism 5
Anglican 10, 15, 27, 52, 57, 99, 105, 144
 confirmation 92
 freehold title in England 71
 universities 14, 81–2
 weddings 90
anxiety 9, 55, 71, 76–7, 103, 124, 126
Aquinas, Thomas 41, 45–6, 114
Asia 3, 10, 21, 49, 72, 150. *See also specific Asian countries*

confirmation 92
dalit 19
electronic preaching 54
rules on divorce 164
Assemblies of God 10, 17, 70, 79, 98–9, 107, 144
Augustine 26, 41–4, 48, 54, 58, 119
Australasia (Australia and Tonga) 3, 10, 17, 26, 33, 40, 140, 144
 clerical abuse 67
 marital disharmony 128
 marriage and power 39
 nuns 105
 pastors opposing church rules 99
 pre-marital weekends 89
 seminary 68
 teaching texts in 54
 universal relevance 137
Antilles. *See* the Caribbean (Trinidad and the Antilles)
Authie, Cathar 146–7

Bailey, Abigail 33, 47, 53
Baptist 10, 20, 57, 68, 75, 79, 81, 89, 100
Basil of Caesarea 43
Battered into Submission (Alsdurf & Alsdurf) 24, 64
Baxter, Richard 52
Beijing Conference on Women 26, 85
Bible 5, 7–8, 14, 25, 30, 33, 50, 55, 63, 107, 114–15, 137, 162
 Eve, endurance and suffering 119–22
 pastor-husbands, abuse and 64–6
 teaching with 94–8
 wife-abuse, support 139–41
Bible references
 1 Corinthians 12, 43, 121
 1 Peter 6, 38, 50, 56–7, 66, 114, 121–2, 128, 141
 1 Timothy 38, 65, 95, 120, 140

Colossians 52, 56, 140
Ephesians 5–6, 38, 44, 55–7, 59, 65, 77, 89, 95, 98, 107, 140–1, 154, 158, 162
Galatians 21, 96, 140
Genesis 5–6, 12, 21, 24, 38, 59, 89, 93, 95–7, 107, 113, 120, 140
Malachi 65, 140
Matthew 12, 17, 50, 107, 131
Philippians 95
Biblical contextualization 38, 40, 56–7, 60, 97, 114, 116, 119, 131, 140
blame 7, 9, 11, 18–20, 30, 44, 52, 76, 97, 114, 116, 132, 160, 162
    for divorce 99
    feminism 146–7
    inadequate teaching 113, 139
Borneo 18, 20–1, 55, 151, 157, 164
Brasher, Brenda 58
Bucer, Martin 48–9, 54, 146
Buddha/Buddhism 5, 54, 56, 157, 162
    disciples to remove suffering 160
    mature philosophy 159
    teaching on marriage 158
    and violence against wives 158–62
Buddhists 4, 10, 157–8, 160–1, 165
    Sangha 158, 161
    text 159, 161
    unrequited cravings 159
    violence 13
    women, abuse 5

Calvin, John 33, 48–9
Canada 17
Canon Law 46, 86
Canori Mora, Elisabetta 59
the Caribbean (Trinidad and the Antilles) 3, 10, 13, 26, 87, 90, 98, 109, 120–2, 125
    pre-service training 92
    Presbyterian tradition 35
    violence by minister 79
Casti Conubii (Pius XI) 28
catechisms 47, 92
The Centre for Violence against Women 24
Chan, Frances 57
Cherobino, Friar 47, 54
Children 115, 122
    in abusive households 92–3, 149

    baptism and confirmation 91
    on divorce 125
    impact of violence 8–9, 124, 133, 141
    innocence 72, 93, 153
    prayer 105
    short-term and long-term, effect on 3, 8–9, 15, 26, 28, 65, 72, 89, 92, 97, 155
    teaching and disciplining 47
    violence, forms 3
China 21, 31
Christian marriage, violence 58, 125, 137–8, 154–5
    divorce 100
    faith 146
    human propensity 18
    obedience, demand for 117
    pre-marriage counselling and marriage homilies 88–91
    surveys 13–14
    in training 108
Christian women 5, 132–3
    advice 87
    Eve 5–6
    forgiveness 128–9
    silence 19, 104
    as victims and survivors 7, 141
Christians (Christianity) 4, 6, 10, 18, 23, 29, 31–2, 37, 49, 157, 161
    American 19, 38
    clergy violence (*see* clerical abuse/abuser)
    disobedience 115
    European 19, 49
    Evangelical 26, 55, 57–8, 67, 76, 89, 100, 149
    Eve (*see* Eve)
    faith 91, 147, 151–3
    forgiveness 77, 128–9
    matrilineal Meghalaya 30
    thought and teaching 42–8, 54–60
    use of texts 6, 161
Chrysostom, John 41–2, 44–5, 48, 50, 54, 142, 146
church(es) 10, 14, 22, 24, 27, 34–5, 40, 57, 91, 94, 99, 108, 149
    CBE 55, 57
    collusion 9, 24, 146
    early and medieval (*see* early and

medieval church)
  as institution 13, 22, 28, 38, 40, 67, 111, 132, 137, 139
  leaders 7–8, 12, 19, 54, 56, 60, 95, 98, 100, 114, 118, 120–1, 132 (*see also* clerical abuse/abuser)
  modern world (*see* modern world church)
  as people of God 22, 111, 137, 139
  silence of 11, 20, 132
Church Law Reform (*Reformatio Legum Ecclesiasticarum*) 49–50
Church of England 52, 69, 75
Church of England Inquiry (2018) 75
Church of South India (CSI) 14, 81, 90, 92
church workers 4, 10, 12, 33, 58, 60, 92, 94, 99, 106, 142
  and abused women 102
  marriage etiquette 86–8
  oppose church rules 99
  professed/ordained/lay 20, 83, 85–6, 104–6, 111
  training of 8, 133, 142, 144–7
Churches Say NO to Domestic Violence (Lutheran World Federation) 24
clergy, position of 143–4
clerical abuse/abuser 63, 150
  churches and violent clergy 68–71
  clergy wives, silence 72–4
  congregation-wide implications 78–80
  congregational collusion 66–7
  faith and forgiveness 76–7
  favoring their own 74–6
  role and the Bible 64–6
  survey responses 80–2
Collins, Natalie 121, 125, 129
collusion 20, 54, 66–7, 94, 140
  by churches 9, 24, 146
  by institutions 23
  by other women 3, 22, 60, 72, 112–14, 143, 147, 155, 161
Common Tenure Church of England 2008 71
complementarian 55, 59–60, 89, 119
complicity/complicit 3–4, 11, 20, 60, 83
confirmation 91–4
Confucian 21, 27
Confucianism 34, 106
Congo 25, 36, 68

pre-/early post-marriage meetings 89
Congregational church 54
Convention on the Elimination of Discrimination against Women (CEDAW) 25, 27
conversion 15, 90, 127, 150, 160, 164
Cooper-White, Pamela 152
Council for Biblical Equality (CBE) 55, 57–9
  on marriage and family life 58
  mission statement 57
Council for Biblical Manhood and Womanhood and Women (CBMW) 55–9, 89, 128, 154
Council of Trent (1587) 41
Cranmer, Thomas 49–51, 146
Created to Be His Help Meet (Pearl) 56
creation 43, 119, 130
  sin 11
  thinking and acting 153
culture 8, 10, 20, 22–3, 29, 40, 57, 81, 88, 94, 98, 123, 131, 133
  accommodating to 55
  card 150–2
  marriage and 36–7
  worshipping 137
'culture-free true-faith zone' 36
The Danvers statement (1988) 55

death 15, 26, 53, 98–9, 122, 142, 164
decision-making (survivors) 17, 32, 98, 103–4, 122–3
Desiring God (Piper) 57
Devil 54, 56, 127–8
diocese/presbytery 10, 14–15, 17, 27, 32–6, 47, 70–1, 75, 78, 81, 85, 90–1, 98, 101, 103, 105, 123, 131, 161
divorce 23, 28–31, 34–5, 44, 50, 53, 67, 94, 98–100, 102, 119, 152
  banning of 73
  19th century Connecticut 52–3
  clergy violence 69–70
  for cruelty 52
  khul' divorce 163–4
  losing children 125
  rate in India 30
  reasons 46, 48
  and remarriage 31, 48, 52, 85, 99–100, 106

Dolan, Frances 52
domestic violence 3, 10–11, 22, 25, 28, 31, 44, 50, 58, 65, 75, 77, 93–4, 133, 138, 144, 149, 151, 166. *See also* wife-abuse
  church-linked movements 24
  criminalizing 27
  incidence 15–17, 19
  legal changes 23, 26
  modern world church 54–60
  opposition 4, 8, 12, 14, 40, 49, 54, 68, 95–6, 105, 143, 145–6
  pre-service training 92, 144–6
  predilection 19
  reject 6, 41
drunkenness/drink/alcohol 17–19, 27, 51, 112, 116, 142, 148

early and medieval church
  beaten woman, response 43
  husband's right to chastise wife 46
  Image of God, woman as 44
  law of marriage 44–5
  Rules of Marriage (Cherobino) 47
  subordination of women 43
  wifely suffering, benefits 47–8
egalitarian 22, 57–8, 60, 164
Elizonda, Felisa 59
England 6–7, 10, 17, 45, 47, 49, 86, 100, 103, 105, 148
ethnicity 29, 36, 133, 150
Europe (England, Scotland and Germany) 10, 19, 21, 23, 30, 36, 41, 47, 54, 72, 92, 119–20. *See also specific European countries*
evangelicals 58–9
Eve 5–6, 8, 83, 95–6, 107, 133, 140, 153
  as Adam's helper 44
  endurance and suffering 119–22
  failings of 97
  as prime sinner 97
  sin 8, 89
  as symbol of woman 45
  women subordination 95, 97
extended family 28, 115

Fabricius, Johann 53
faith 7, 19–20, 23, 26, 40, 92, 138, 142–3, 146–7, 149, 151–2, 166
  and forgiveness 76–7
  law and 28
  obedience 91
  teaching and practice 41, 130, 153
  text 120, 157
  themes 5
  traditions 4–5, 8–9, 37, 81, 164
family 10, 19, 23, 35, 52, 64
  Christian values 27
  disruption 4
  extended 28, 115
  harmony, securing 128–9
  head 42, 83, 114–15, 140–2
  honour 27, 30
  husbands, responsibility 29
  husbands as pastor 44, 56, 58, 60, 108
  integrity of 28
  pastor as head 89, 141
  patrilineal, inheritance 31
  post-marriage ties 30–1
  prayers 66, 77
  privacy of the 8
  rights and benefits 28
  violence 3, 24, 26, 29, 53, 65–7, 108
Fellowship of Christian Councils and Churches in the Great Lakes and Horn of Africa (*FECCLAHA*) 25
feminism 59
  (ir)relevance of 142, 146–8
  militancy 6
  and modernity 23
  simplistic blaming of 146–7
fieldwork 21, 126
forgiveness 76–7, 91, 101, 107, 128, 141, 165
Fortune, Marie 24
Fowl, Stephen 5

Gataker, Thomas 52
gender violence 24–5, 161
Geneva Catechism (1542) 33, 48
Germany (German) 10, 53, 67, 101–3, 141, 144
  Betfrau (praying/pious woman) 126
  Roman Catholic women 4
  silence 77
Ghana 10, 14, 26, 81, 101, 124, 144
  clerical violence 65, 67, 70, 79
  confirmation classes 92

incidence 16
patrilineal inheritance 31
suffering 37
universities 81
wife-beating pastors 78–9
Gnanadason, Aruna 24
Good News for Women (Groothuis) 58
Goodman, Kaufman Carol 6, 51
Gramsci, Antonio 38
Gratian 41, 46, 54
Groothuis, Rebecca 58
Gruden, Wayne 57
guilt 43–4, 48, 50, 95, 112, 117, 119–21, 124, 145, 154

Haddad, Mimi 58
Happily Ever After: Finding Grace in the Messes of Marriage (Piper) 57
headship 5, 22, 55–6, 58–9, 95–6, 100, 114, 130, 140, 154
  disobedience 116–17
  local controls over violence 115
  role differentiation 115–16
  and submission 91, 117–19
heathens 51
hegemonic power 38–9
Hindu 4, 10, 33, 127
honour 27, 30, 50, 64, 66, 72, 77, 82–3, 90, 117, 138, 153–4
hope 50, 86, 122
  creation, thinking and acting 153
  non-violence 153
  wife-abuse, ending 154–5
household 6, 26, 46, 65, 77, 87, 143, 149
  children in abusive 92–3
  head 13, 27, 30, 42, 87, 91, 93, 115, 117, 140, 150
  leaders 130, 140
  male tyranny 6
  in the sixteenth century 47
Hugucio of Pisa 41, 46, 48, 54, 163
human anger 18, 98, 112
human rights 4–5, 22, 34, 94, 146, 153, 166
humanity 21–2, 96, 119
husband's abuse. *See* wife-abuse
husband's salvation, women's responsibility 141–2
husbands as household pastors 44, 56, 58, 60, 64, 108. *See also* clerical abuse/abuser
hypocrite/hypocrisy 5, 20, 64, 154

Image of God 6, 22, 31, 43–5, 54, 83, 124, 130, 146
  made in the 11, 36, 49, 82–3, 91, 93, 95–7, 108–9, 120, 123, 126, 131, 133, 140, 142, 146, 148, 152–5
  preaching on 108
  teaching 96, 154
Imams against Domestic Abuse 165
inculturation 40, 49
India 10, 26, 86, 93, 96, 98, 140, 144, 158
  advice 130
  clerical divorce, forbidding 73
  confirmation/adult baptism 92
  continual violence 70
  divorce rate in 30
  leaving as sin 129
  nuns 105
  Orthodoxy 23
  prayer 123
  response, women 126
  seminary 144
  survey responses (clerical abuser) 81
  wife-beater 68
  women as colluders 113
  women in matrilineal Meghalaya 16, 30
institutions 4, 13, 22, 28, 40, 65, 67–8, 72, 74, 81–2, 111, 132, 137–9, 151
'Instructions to Christian Women' of 1523 (Vives) 47–8
internalize 7, 38, 119–20
international conventions and secular approaches 23, 25
  CEDAW 25, 27
  criminalized domestic violence 27
  DAVAW 25, 27
  Declaration of Human Rights 26
  Istanbul Convention on Domestic Violence 28
  Women's Conference, Beijing 26
Irenaeus 3, 137
Islam (Muslims) 4–6, 10, 19, 26, 54, 98, 131, 157, 160
  abused woman's experience 31
  and husband-wife violence 162–5
  sexual obligation 37
  text 162
Istanbul Convention on Domestic Violence (2011) 28
Italy, wife-abuse deaths 26

180　　　　　　　　　　　　　　　　*Index*

Jesus Christ Victory Church 39
Jewish (Jews) 4, 6, 19, 26, 153
John Paul II, Pope 24, 59

Kabilsingh, Chatsumarn 158–9
Kajiyama 159
Kanyoro, Musimbi 24
karma 5, 160–2
karmic justice 160
Kentucky, violence 4
Kenya 4, 10, 26, 65, 86, 126, 144, 154
　advice 113–14
　Anglicans 14, 89, 99
　CEDAW (1984) 27
　clergy violence 71, 79
　criminalized domestic violence 27
　levels of violence 14–15
　nuns 106
　Pentecostal 99, 117
　universities 81, 140
　women as colluders 113
Khuankaew, Ouyporn 5, 160–1
Knight, George 57
Korea (South) 10, 13–14, 22, 26, 65, 107
　Anglican University 81
　CEDAW (1983) 27
　Confucianism on modern marriage 106
　covenant-contract basis, marriage 34–5
　criminalized domestic violence 27
　culture-free true-faith zone 36
　hypocrites 64
　opposing divorce 98
　Presbyterian University 81
　teaching texts 54
Kroeger, Catherine Clark 24, 58

Laurence Hispanus 41, 46, 48, 54
law/legal 4, 12, 21–4, 26–30, 33, 39, 49, 54, 65, 94, 113, 115, 118, 146, 153, 162, 164
　canon 46, 86
　and faith 28
　of marriage 44–5, 50–2
laywomen 11, 20, 34, 60, 105, 111–33
　forgiveness 128
　silence of 139
Lee, Susan Hagood 118
Lekshe Tsomo 161
levels and methods of abuse 14–16

listening 11, 82, 102, 108, 131
Luther, M. 49, 95, 133
Lutheran 10, 24, 39, 53, 57, 65–6, 90, 95, 97, 119, 143
Lutheran Church of Australia 24
Lutheran Synodal Declaration (1993) 24
Lutheran World Federation 24, 143
Lwambo, Desiree 149

Malaysia 10, 26, 55, 165
　nuns 93, 128, 149
　proactive and reactive 93–4
Maliki law school 163–4
Manzanan, Mary John 24, 42, 128
Mar Thoma 10, 98
marital disharmony 128
marital violence. *See* domestic violence
marriage 12, 29, 41, 49, 55, 114, 124–32, 138, 147–8
　1563 Anglican Homily on 50–1
　anxiety 9, 112
　being a person 29–31
　CBE's statement on 58
　contract or covenant 31–6, 42, 164
　and culture 36–7
　enrichment, meeting 78
　etiquette 86–8
　as exercise in mutual submission 58
　faith-condoned violence 166
　female submission 54, 57
　homilies and sermons 53, 90–1
　interference 23, 112
　khul' rights on 164
　law of 44–5, 50–2
　male headship 58, 96, 100, 114–16
　monogamous 23
　pictures of 46
　and power 37–9
　pre-marriage counselling 88–91
　rights and responsibilities 25–6
　sanctity of 52, 106
　suffering 48, 56, 93
　teaching on 108, 158–9
　texts on 59, 95
　ties to family after 31, 115
Maryland 53
Mather, Cotton 51, 146
Methodist and Methodist Zion 10, 15, 33, 57, 77, 88, 92, 105, 117–18, 144, 165
Meyers, Debra 53

migration 115, 147
ministry to abuser 142, 148–50
Missiology 151
modern world church
    CBMW and CBE 55–9
    electronic preaching 54
    position of woman as wives 54
    theological feminism 59
modernity and feminism 23
St Monica 42, 91
Monteiro, Evelyn 24
Muhammed, Prophet 163
Muslim Council of Britain 165
Muslims. *See* Islam (Muslims)
Myanmar 4, 10, 100, 128, 131, 165
    clergy violence 68
    training of church workers 144
    wife-abuse 158

Nason-Clark, Nancy 17, 24, 144
national laws 23, 26, 146
nirvana 158–9, 161
No Longer a Secret (Gnanadason) 24
non-violence 153
North America (United States) 10, 19, 26, 30, 36, 52, 144

Oakley, Lisa 3
obedience 5, 33, 43, 76, 91, 97–8, 100, 117, 119, 133, 163
Odoye, Mercy 24
Orthodoxy 23, 85, 91, 133, 164

Paine, Alastair 6
Pakistan 4, 10, 26, 93
    abused woman's experience 31
    Christian practice in 165
    congregation-wide implications 80
    farming wives 116
    khul' divorce 164
    nuns 34, 107
    seminary 12, 145
parental violence. *See* domestic violence
pastoral care 78, 94, 100, 144
    what women get 130–2
    what women want 125–9
pastoral problem 8
patrilineal systems, marriage 30–1
Paynims 51

Pearl, Debbie 56–7
Pearl, Michael 56, 76
Pellauer, Mary 147
Pentecostal 10, 15, 22, 24, 67, 71, 85, 87–8, 91, 95, 98–100, 119, 149
perseverance, prayer and patience (3Ps) 102, 105
Phillips, Roderick 48
Phiri, Isabel 24
Piper, John 57
Pius IX 58
Poland
    CEDAW (1980) 27–8
    law and faith, example 28–9
police-support, preference for using 11, 102, 104–6
poor anger management 18, 19
power 22–3, 29, 34, 45, 54, 57–8, 69, 85, 120, 128, 132, 159
    marriage and 37–9
    modes of 39
    over person 18, 37–8, 40, 60, 83, 103, 114, 138, 147, 159
pray/prayer 6, 9–11, 14, 60, 64, 66, 77, 85, 93–4, 101, 103, 105, 119, 145, 151
    silent 118
    as support and burden 122–4
    without naming abuse as sin 139, 147, 155
Presbyterian 10, 13–15, 17, 32, 70, 74, 78, 86, 90–1, 96, 98, 144
    covenant-contract basis, marriage 33–5
    opposing divorce 98
    University 81
The Presbyterian Church of Taiwan 17
privacy 8, 29, 70
proactive approaches/teaching
    long-term 86
    pre-marriage counselling and marriage homilies 88–91
    short-term 86
    teaching opportunities 91–4
Protestantism 23
Protestants 14, 22, 24, 35, 45, 48, 97, 99–100, 113

Qur'an 5, 160, 162–4

reacting to violence
  clergy, utterance 100–4
  core problem 94
  divorce 98–100
  nuns 104–7
  teaching with Bible verses 94–8
reconciliation 34, 128–9, 141
religion 4, 10, 26, 37, 141. *See also specific religion*
remarriage
  divorce and 31, 48, 85, 99–100
  excommunication, risk 106
reputation of church/family 17, 67, 108, 151
research process 10–14, 23
'Responding Well to Domestic Violence' 75
Roman Catholicism 23, 30
Roman Catholics 4–5, 10, 15, 22, 24, 27, 32, 49, 85, 97, 99, 105–6, 119, 144
  catechisms 47
  inequality in marriage 88
  leadership 55, 57
  nuns 58, 104
  opposing divorce 98
  practice 35
  schools 93

sacrament, marriage as 35, 85
Salvation Army 10, 54, 63, 96, 118
Sangha 158, 161
schools, teaching 10, 93–4, 108, 153
Schüssler Fiorenza, Elisabeth 24
Scotland 4, 7, 10, 22, 49, 63, 81, 92
Scots law 33
Scottish Episcopal Church 10, 32, 81
Scripture, critical reading of 5
seminary(ies) 6, 10, 12, 14, 30, 68, 86, 95, 105, 144–5, 144–6
separation 12, 26, 44, 48, 52, 67, 69, 98, 102, 151–2
shame 3, 6, 13, 17, 31, 45, 51, 67, 72, 76, 78–9, 101, 108, 112, 114, 137, 149, 152–3, 155
Sigalaka Sutta 159
Sikhism 157
silence/silent 3–4, 7, 29, 34, 64, 66, 83, 90, 117, 131–2, 137, 143, 151, 154
  about marital violence 36

Christian women, abused 104
  of churches 11, 20, 68, 97, 153
  clergy wives 72–4
  complicity 20
  on issue 87
  of laywomen 139
  legal changes 23
  privacy of the family 8
  suffering 19, 77
sin 7–8, 11, 30, 43, 47, 55, 60, 63, 66, 68, 72, 79, 104, 112, 119, 128, 139, 141–2
  abuse as 108, 113, 123, 152
  of abuser 63, 116, 127, 133
  avoidance of 48
  against Body of Christ 133
  bringer of 120
  of conscious choice 12
  Eve 8, 89
  intentional 63, 121
  leaving 129
  of necessity 12
  suffering 121
  of violence 20, 79, 93–5, 98, 105–6, 130, 146, 148
sine manu marriages 42
social disruption 4
Spain 18, 47, 49
Stair, Lord 33
Sudley, Agnes 24
suffering 3, 8, 15, 19, 25, 37, 59, 95, 102, 107, 111–12, 119, 127, 140, 148, 159
  benefits of wifely 47–8
  in Bible texts 119–22
  in Buddhism 160
  intentional 122
  marriage 48, 56, 93
  as punishment 162
  in silence 19, 77
survivor (of abuse) 3, 7–8, 11, 20, 38, 63–4, 76–7, 85, 87, 95, 100–2, 112–13, 118, 121, 147, 151, 161
  blame 18, 139
  decision-making 17, 32, 98, 103–4, 122–3
  prayer 123
  reconciliation 128, 141
  scriptural verses, use of 132
Syrian Orthodox 10, 133, 151

Taiwan 10, 39, 57, 72, 122, 140, 160
   human rights movement 34
   marital disharmony 128
   nuns 85, 88
Tate, Kim 57
texts 5, 24, 33, 56, 59, 76, 95, 118, 121, 153
   manipulation or massaging of 37, 40, 77, 138–9, 149, 157, 164
   oppose violence 130, 140
   Reformation 48, 50
   use of 5–6, 20, 147, 149
   validating violence 38, 140
   written/cultural/oral/scriptural 4–5, 20, 29, 54, 116, 120, 159, 161–3
Thailand
   wife-abuse 158
   women in peace building (training) 161
theology/theological 7, 12, 22, 41, 44, 49, 57, 65, 76–7, 80, 82–3, 85–6, 91–2, 94, 105, 117, 128, 138, 140, 150–2, 155, 165
   feminism 59
   of headship 63, 114
   of humanity 21, 96
   of marriage 31, 35, 58, 89–90
   power 38
   teaching/training 5, 8, 25, 63, 96, 101, 144, 146–7
Theravada Buddhism 158
'Thursdays in Black' movement 24
Toma Holladay (Saddleback Church) 26
Tonga. See Australasia (Australia and Tonga)
tradition 6, 10, 19, 22, 26, 32, 37, 40, 77, 90, 97, 144, 149, 152, 157, 160–2, 166
   faith 4–5, 8–9, 37, 81, 157, 164
   Kadazan 20
   Presbyterian tradition (Korea and Trinidad) 35
   Scots marriage 33
   to validate violence 165
training of church workers 8, 133, 142, 144–7
transformation 82, 103, 141–2, 147, 155, 165
Trinidad. See the Caribbean (Trinidad and the Antilles)

Trinity 41, 43, 57, 154
True Jesus 10, 34
Tucker, Ruth 118–19

UN Declaration against Violence against Women (DAVAW) 25, 27
United Church of Australia 25, 87
United Kingdom (UK) 6, 11, 26, 49, 129, 144, 146, 165
United Nations (UN) 16, 25–6
United Nations Convention 4, 25–9, 146
United Nations Declaration on Human Rights (1948) 4, 26
United States 10, 26, 30, 36, 49, 52, 54, 65, 86–7, 140, 144
   CBE 55, 57
   CBMW 55, 128
   Peaceful Families Project 165
   pre-service training 92
universal human rights 5

Van Leeuwen, Mary 122
the Vatican 26, 59, 75, 143, 152
violence. See also domestic violence
   avoidance 68, 73, 106, 112
   Buddhism and 158–62
   as choice/choose 8, 27, 30, 35, 56, 119, 138, 142–3, 155, 160
   defined 25
   forms of 3, 38, 132
   impact of violence 8, 64
   Islam and 162–5
   othering as avoidance strategy 18–21, 98, 152, 155
   reacting to (see reacting to violence)
   reality of 14–18, 60, 82
Vives, Juan 47–8

wedding homily 90–1
Western culture 131
wife-abuse 27, 33, 46, 53, 58, 72, 74, 78, 81, 102, 115, 120, 122, 124, 152
   advice 103, 152
   befriending, system of 152
   Bible supporting 139–41
   Buddhism and 158–62
   Chinese value 20–1
   Christian woman (Pakistan) 18
   deaths 26

ending 154–5
  by faith traditions 5
  family headship 5, 22, 83, 114–15, 119
  Islam and 162–5
  pastor-husbands 64–6
  physical attacks 3, 23, 67–9, 71, 80, 120, 128
  stay or go 124–5
  and suffering 121
  teaching 114
  wifely obedience 5, 98
wife-beater 48, 68
Witte, J. 48
women 11, 59, 87, 111, 120, 147, 154. *See also* Christian women; wife-abuse
  as colluders 3, 22, 60, 72, 112–14, 143, 147, 155
  in congregations 78
  God's Image 36, 43, 49, 96, 155
  in matrilineal Meghalaya 16, 30
  in peace building (training) 161
  subordination to men 43, 95, 97
  suffering 25, 59, 107
women's collusion 3, 22, 60, 72, 112–14, 143, 147, 155
Women's Movement (1970) 24, 57
World Association of Reform Churches (WARC) 143, 152
World Council of Churches (WCC) 24, 59, 143, 152
  'Decade of Solidarity with Women' 24
  'Thursdays in Black' movement 24
worshipping culture 36, 137

Zwingli, Ulrich 48–9

www.ingramcontent.com/pod-product-compliance
Lightning Source LLC
Chambersburg PA
CBHW070640300426
44111CB00013B/2185